Hiking
Wyoming

Bill Hunger

FALCON®

GUILFORD, CONNECTICUT
HELENA, MONTANA

AN IMPRINT OF THE GLOBE PEQUOT PRESS

ᴀFALCONGUIDE®

All photos by the author unless otherwise noted.
Cover photo by Fred Pflughoft.

Library of Congress Cataloging-in-Publication Data

Hunger, Bill.
    Hiking Wyoming / by Bill Hunger
      p. cm.
    "A Falcon Guide" —T.p. verso.
    Includes index.
    ISBN 1-56044-672-2
    1. Hiking—Wyoming—Guidebooks. 2. Trails—Wyoming—Guidebooks.
    3. Wyoming—Guidebooks. I. Title
    GV199.42.W8H87 1998
    917.8704'33—dc21   98-13923
                                                                          CIP

Printed in the United States of America
Second Edition/Third Printing

CAUTION

Contents

Wyoming Range

WESTERN WYOMING
Gros Ventre Range

Mount Leidy Highlands

Gannett Hills

Snake River Range

NORTHWESTERN WYOMING
The Washakie Range

Absaroka Range

Washakie Wilderness

North Absaroka Wilderness

Beartooth Mountains

Acknowledgments

Many people helped this book into being and helped expand it into the current revision; unfortunately, I don't even know the names of most of these folks. The numerous Forest Service, Bureau of Land Management, National Park, and Wyoming State Parks personnel who answered my questions; the many folks met along the way who freely gave advice or offered directions or clued me onto a new and exciting adventure; the special persons who helped extricate me from the seeming disasters that happened throughout the journey: I can only send a lump *thank you* to you all, hoping it expresses the gratitude I feel.

Special thanks go to the friends who contributed to this book, people whose names you'll discover when you read their hike descriptions.

As before and still so true now, the most thanks—and the book's dedication—go to you, Jill. Without your multilevel support and love, nothing could have happened.

Map Legend

Interstate	(00)		Campground	▲
US Highway	(00)		Cabins/Buildings	▪
State or Other Principal Road	(00) (000)		Peak	9,782 ft.
National Park Route	(00)		Hill	
Interstate Highway	⟹		Elevation	9,782 ft.
Paved Road	⟹		Gate	•—•
Gravel Road	⟹		Mine Site	⚒
Unimproved Road	======⟹		Overlook/Point of Interest	◙
Trailhead	◯			
Main Trail(s) /Route(s)	•••••••••		National Forest/Park Boundary	⌐ ¬
Alternate/Secondary Trail(s)/Route(s)	–•–•–•–			
Parking Area	(P)		Map Orientation	N
River/Creek	∿		Scale	0 0.5 1
Spring	⌐			Miles
Pass	)(			
Waterfall	∥			
One Way Road	One Way ←			

Location of Hikes

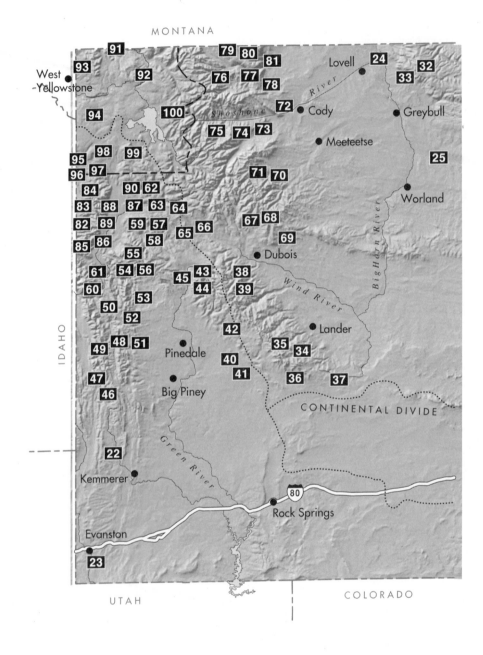

MONTANA

West Yellowstone

IDAHO

91
93
92
79 80 81
76 77 78
Lovell
24 32
33

River
Shoshone
72 Cody
Greybull
94
100
75 74 73
Meeteetse
95 98 99
96 97
84 90 62
83 88 87 63 64
82 89 59 57
85 86 58
55
61 54 56
60
50
52
53
49 48 51
47
46
71 70
67 68
69
Dubois
65 66
45 43
44
38
39
Wind River
42
35 34
Lander
40
41
36 37

25
Worland

Big Horn River

CONTINENTAL DIVIDE

Pinedale
Big Piney

22
Kemmerer

Green River

80
Rock Springs

Evanston
23

UTAH
COLORADO

SAFETY

If you've ever sat on a 12,000-foot Wyoming mountain pass on the Fourth of July, huddled and shivering in a collapsed tent with a soggy sleeping bag around you, watching the landscape and your summer trip die under 6 inches of raging white blizzard, you know that the high country does not play gently with the unprepared.

Every Forest Service handout and hiker's guide supplies a safety checklist, and it certainly is a good idea to review something so beneficial before venturing into the backcountry. But I've noticed that hikers who read standard checklists often are ignorant of the importance of why certain items are included in these lists. This particular safety list is presented from an EMT-trained wilderness ranger's perspective, and it offers you some of the more common emergencies and blunders that a minimal amount of preparedness would have eliminated or at least mitigated.

In simple terms, there are several principles—all equally important—that should be an automatic part of every hiker's internal repertoire.

- Be trained in, and be able to execute in the field, advanced first aid techniques and cardiopulmonary resuscitation (CPR). In drownings, traumatic and lightning-shock situations, as well as heart attacks and other such emergencies, CPR saves lives. Being able to stop bleeding, splint fractures, and dress burns properly is critical. When no one in a group of 6 hikers knows first aid, that leaves 5 people capable of running out to get help and no one able to help the accident victim. And if only one person in such a group knows first aid, the same situation may result if that one person gets hurt.
- Know, and again be able to execute in the field, survival techniques and tricks. A little knowledge in this field can go a long way in unexpected circumstances. An important part of this preparation is to carry proper emergency gear. We can't all be Tom Brown, Jr., world-renowned survivalist and tracker who apprenticed under an old Apache Indian. But there *are* steps we can take to better our own survival chances in the wilderness. An emergency shelter and dry matches, a flashlight, a whistle and signal mirror, some first aid supplies, and high-energy food rations, all carried constantly in a small survival pack, may make a big difference the day things don't go as planned. In one of the descriptions in this book, I relate how I—with 25 years of hiking experience—became totally lost on a simple 3-mile day hike. A couple of times I've found backpacks at the bottoms of cliffs, which must have taken an unforeseen roll from some distance high above, after which they were unrecoverable. I can only hope that these suddenly packless individuals were well versed in survival techniques.
- All the emergency and survival training in the world won't help you if panic claims the mind. In a minor rock slide, the panicked person freezes and gets pelted with flying rocks while the calm person anticipates the stones' pathways and dodges the missiles. A lost hiker who

panics usually travels a wayward path that further displaces him (making rescue all the more difficult), while someone in the same predicament who calms his mind and thinks through the situation can often backtrack or rationalize his way to safety—or at least remember to stay in one spot until searchers find him. If panic isn't hindering or blocking it, the rational or intuitive mind can usually create or remember a solution to a bad situation.

•Actually, there is an equally important principle that has yet to be mentioned—competent map-reading skills. In fact, much of the wilderness country of Wyoming demands that you be astute in the art of map and compass orientation. Included in an appendix to this book is a short course on the subject. But as the treatise author says, be certain you've practiced this necessary skill thoroughly BEFORE you venture into the wilds.

Being prepared for wilderness emergencies is an important consideration. But many situations that require emergency action wouldn't have happened if folks had been more aware of certain dangers and taken action to prevent the problem before it began. The following represent some of the more common ticklish situations I've seen (for both others and myself) that simply beg for an ounce of prevention.

ALTITUDE SICKNESS

Few guidebook safety lists mention this one, but it's a fairly common problem. It's amazing how many people journey into the Wind Rivers from sea level, planning an ascent of Gannett Peak, Wyoming's highest, without realizing that altitude could become a factor. The unacclimatized brain and body, deprived of oxygen at higher altitudes, can experience symptoms ranging from vomiting to total disorientation and confusion. I have practically carried babbling, seemingly mindless persons off peaks and had them not remember a moment of the ordeal when they reached a lower altitude and reclaimed their senses. If you're not acclimated to high elevations, go slow. Take several days to inure yourself before bounding to a peak summit. If you feel woozy, sit down and rest and relax your pace. If you start to get lightheaded and sick, have your friends help you to a lower elevation. DON'T be left alone, and DON'T leave someone alone if altitude sickness is a potential problem.

A less serious occurrence is when once-a-year hikers overuse an underdeveloped body. Hiking 15 miles with a full backpack on your first day out can so tie up the muscles in your body that the rest of the trip—if you can stand to hike at all—becomes agonizing. Remember also that boots wear differently when you start hiking through mountainous terrain than they do in your living room. Blisters take about a week to heal. The point of this paragraph is that distance isn't as important as preserving your body and enjoying the beautiful surroundings. If you do feel a "hot spot" beginning to develop on one of your feet, covering it immediately with a small bit of duct tape or moleskin can make a big difference.

HYPOTHERMIA AND DEHYDRATION

Most safety treatises stress the first condition and ignore the second. The truth is that one of the factors that contribute to hypothermia *is* dehydration. The other more obvious factors are cold, wind, and wet. Hypothermia can catch even the most experienced hiker unaware, and surprisingly, most cases develop when the air temperature is above freezing in the 30 to 50 degrees Farenheit range. Prevention is the easiest cure. Stay dry. Keep your energy up with lots of snacks and drinks. Continually adjust how many layers of clothes you wear so that you neither sweat too much when exerting nor get chilled when resting. A hypothermic person experiences shivering fits, fumbles things, slurs his speech, stumbles, appears exhausted, and is exceptionally slow to get started after a rest. A hypothermic person will also deny that he or she is hypothermic. There is virtually no way a hypothermic body can warm itself; outside heat sources are required. Warm drinks, warm and dry clothes, and a fire can help a mildly impaired person. But you can wrap a severely hypothermic person in a dozen sleeping bags and his core body temperature will continue to decline. Your nearly bare body next to his nearly bare body, both inside the bags, is the key to rewarming and survival.

Another note on dehydration: when the body is thirsty, it's already slightly dehydrated. Prevention calls for frequent drinks, even when not thirsty, and "tanking up"—drinking a very large amount of water in one sitting—if the distance to the next drink is far.

WEATHER

Be especially aware of the possibility of lightning. Lightning striking humans rarely happens in the wilderness, but getting caught in a violent and scary electrical storm in the Wyoming high country offers a better-than-average probability. Common sense says don't climb the peak that day if storm clouds are rapidly forming in the morning. But more often than not, a day begins perfectly and then a sudden cluster of nasty-looking clouds comes out of nowhere when you're a far distance from timberline and shelter. Don't panic. Instead, take this opportunity to witness one of the most spectacular and powerful displays of nature's might while you crouch on the leeward side of a boulder or rock overhang. And do crouch. Don't sit or lie on the ground. While lightning almost never strikes a person, when it strikes the earth it creates erratic electrical currents that travel through the ground. Squatting on your rubber-soled boots better insulates you from the charges. Also, it's wisest to seek separate shelters and not cluster your entire group in one area. If a mishap does result from the storm, not everyone will be hurt, and there will be someone capable of rendering aid.

Winds, violent and erratic, can rise at any moment, day or night. Be sure that you've visually checked the trees around your campsite to ascertain that none lean precariously toward your tent.

Are you prepared (footgear included) for 3 solid days of rain? For a hard freeze during the night? If it snows and freezes during the day? Can your face and nose and ears handle 8 days of intense, high-altitude sun beaming on them? Is your protective gear capable of handling all sorts of challenging elements? Count on one double negative when it comes to backcountry weather: it will not NOT surprise you.

STREAM CROSSINGS

Wyoming's paths and trails were originally designed for horse travel. We who propel ourselves with our own legs for our own enjoyment are a more recent evolutionary species, and many of the state's backcountry trails haven't adapted to the reality of our foot travel. Bridges over streams and rivers in many areas are nonexistent. These waterways, even the smaller ones, are swift and ice cold with slippery, unstable rocks and deep potholes. More than half of the possible emergencies described above can suddenly become a reality with one flubbed stream crossing. A long, solid walking stick and a pair of lightweight tennis shoes on the feet greatly aid the wading process. Have your pack waist strap unbuckled so if you slip and go under the water you can extract yourself from your pack and not be pulled down by it. NOTE: Many mountain streams are easily crossable in the cool morning, and then due to snow melt they become raging torrents by evening. Many day hikes have been transformed into impromptu overnighters because of this factor. Ultimately, don't chance crossing a waterway if it looks or feels too treacherous.

GIARDIASIS ET AL.

The moment you decide that the mountain water gods must like you because you've never gotten sick from the water, you may discover that the mountain water gods have a morbid sense of humor. Even Wyoming hiking guidebook authors occasionally have to relearn this lesson—there's nothing quite like the serious trots 20 miles deep inside the Gros Ventre Wilderness, all because the stream water looked so pure. Giardiasis is to be considered a potential threat in every drop of water everywhere in this country. The affliction is absolutely preventable only by boiling water (at least 5 minutes) or by purifying it with a filter designed for the purpose. Chlorine and iodine will not affect the giardia cyst. If you find yourself experiencing sudden fits of diarrhea, fatigue, and severe cramping, it's time to leave and seek medical help. If infected, remember to drink large quantities of liquids to combat the dehydrating effects of this invisible protozoan.

CRITTERS

Little ones, that is. (Bears, etcetera, are discussed in another section.) Wyoming's horseflies can seem bigger than sea gulls and more persistent than Montana winters. Bites from deer flies are the epitome of a painful experience. The number of mosquitoes in certain areas at certain times of the year will give you a vivid definition for the word "infinite." Long-sleeved and long-legged clothing, and adequate bug dope are the sanest preventions. Also know if you're allergic to bee stings and tick bites. Snakes are out there, too—most of the Wyoming high plains country rings with that heart-stimulating, don't-tread-on-me buzz, the rattlesnake's warning.

Common sense is the simple prescription for hiking and camping safety. If she hadn't camped right on the trail, she wouldn't have been run over by a herd of horses galloping toward the trailhead at night. If he hadn't stepped so close to the cornice's end, he wouldn't have slipped on the ice and slid out of control down several hundred feet of steep snow to ricochet into the boulder field below. If I had positively identified that mushroom, my friend and I wouldn't have spent the night vomiting and being too weak to raise a finger to do anything about it. If a certain person hadn't decided that 20 feet closer to the buffalo would afford a better picture. . . well, you get the point. Planning, preparation, and common sense are the keys to backcountry safety. Make them constant and automatic, and you can enjoy Mother Nature and your backcountry experience to the fullest.

Backcountry Ethics

As a wilderness ranger I was often asked, "What is the worst situation hikers might encounter on their long trips into the backcountry? Bears? Getting caught in a ferocious lightning storm or rainstorm and the resulting flooding creeks? Breaking a bone far from the nearest trailhead?"

Actually, the answer is "people." Not you and I, the people searching for beauty and adventure by hiking wildland trails. If people themselves were a trauma to me, I never would have become a wilderness ranger whose job was to contact and communicate with people, and I surely would not be writing a hiker's guide that exposes some of my favorite areas to other persons. But I do admit to pain and resentment when I witness the disagreeable results of the actions of unthinking or uncaring people in the backcountry.

Managing agencies began promoting no-trace camping and pack-it-in, pack-it-out ethics about 25 years ago. They had no choice; 25 years ago it was already becoming obvious that multiple campfire rings, stomped-to-death campsites, firewood shortages, and ubiquitous human waste and toilet paper piles were destroying the fragile resource called wilderness. Trails are like rivers. They funnel large groups of people into singular and specific, often fragile, areas. Thousands of pristine acres can surround the hiker and yet he or she will discover that the immediate setting around a campsite is an absolute mess, because that is where everyone visiting has to hike, camp, and defecate.

What follows is a brief list of the dos and don'ts of backcountry ethics. These principles are a simple mixture of common sense, courtesy for others, and respect for the land. They can be found in every Forest and Park Service handout and in every hiking book. But as we enter the twenty-first century, there's an added factor. Today, the "pack-it-in, pack-it-out" guidelines need to be amended to, "pack out more than you pack in" and "leave the country in better shape than you found it." This often translates into cleaning up somebody else's mess. If you feel like showing appreciation to the wild country that gives you so much, it's easy to acquire and practice this caring attitude.

SANITATION

The Forest Service recommends that you do your "duty" at least 100 feet from any water source, trail, or campsite, but that's not far enough in my opinion. After 30 years of this advice, popular campsites are now surrounded by septic rings of little troweled pits and displaced rocks—and you know what's under them. This is all a mere 100 or so feet away from where you sleep and eat. In this situation, think not in terms of feet, but in terms of yards: 200 yards, or even more, should be the norm. By traveling that far you'll see views and microenvironments no one else witnesses, and you won't be unearthing someone else's sewage while disposing of your own.

A hole dug 6 to 8 inches deep is the recommended waste burying procedure. A bit shallower, if you can still camouflage the action, is better. More bacteria reside in the soil closer to the surface, and through their action the waste will decompose faster. Burning toilet paper is a good practice, but if your shallow hole is surrounded by dry organic matter, it's safer to pack out the TP in a plastic bag.

TRASH

The only thing more certain than the fact that aluminum does not burn is the fact that a surprisingly large number of people believe it does. An outfitter guide and I spent an entire night sitting around a blazing campfire, telling Forest Service jokes and kindling a hot fire fueled on the challenge of a bet. He wagered that aluminum did disappear if the fire was hot enough; I maintained that the stuff was elemental and couldn't vanish. The result? Probing the campfire ashes the next morning revealed thousands of tiny aluminum blobs sitting beneath the burn pile. From that night on I never saw a trace of aluminum or anything else left in this man's campsites. Such must be the case with all trash, including the ubiquitous candy wrapper. The practice of packing out what others leave behind goes a long way in helping wilderness remain wild.

NUMBERS OF PEOPLE

The days of 40 people in a single survival class all camping by a lake and fishing it out in 3 days are mostly gone. It's both illegal in the administrating agency's eyes and undesirable to the school's program. But everyone hiking still encounters large groups. The resulting noise and impact on meadows and lakes is inevitable, no matter how conscientious the people. If your group is large—8 or more—consider splitting into smaller parties.

On the other hand, most books and experts warn against hiking alone. If a backcountry emergency or accident arises and no one is there to help, you can imagine the situation's seriousness. It is important, whenever you are heading out on a hike, to let someone know where you'll be and when you expect to return. This rule is especially important for anyone going out alone. Also, extended periods of wilderness solitude are not for everyone and especially unwise for beginning hikers.

But wait! When I wrote the first edition of this book, I tried to include a 3-page thesis on the spiritual joys of being alone in the wilderness. The editor at the time cut it down to a single paragraph; it's still included here, however, because as the pace of the world winds its mainspring ever tighter, the kind of reality checks that solitary journeys into wilderness offer are ever-more needed. That paragraph: "At the same time many of the higher ideals we now express as a civilization have been given to us by sage philosophers who spent time alone in the wilderness: Emerson, Thoreau, Muir. To those who are experienced backpackers and at home in the remote wilds without conveniences, many parts of Wyoming still offer the opportunity to get away from the crowds, be alone and renew the spirit."

FIRES AND CAMPSITES

Rarely is anyone going to hike a trail and find a place where many people before have not already camped. Please camp on that same spot. If you build a fire, use a fire ring that's already there. Then, if it's obvious that this is a popular camping spot and that many more people are likely to follow you, leave the site clean and the fire ring intact. That particular spot is receiving use beyond any immediate recovery, and the more that camp on it the better. There's no sense in beginning the use cycle on another pristine site. Also, we've all seen campsites that contain three or four or more fire rings. Be willing to dismantle and scatter most of these extra blackheads on the landscape

On the other hand, if you're off the trail on a cross-country adventure and camping in a virgin or near-virgin location, make sure that no one who comes by a few hours after you leave will have an inkling someone camped there. Fires built in a shallow pit or on a rock that has been coated with an inch of soil, fires kindled with small squaw wood and allowed to burn down to fine white ashes—these fires can be covered or scattered and made to vanish without a trace. And remember: ALWAYS extinguish your fire completely. And watch the edges; many times I've extinguished smoldering peat 5 or more feet from a camper's water-drowned fire.

Apply the same no-trace philosophy to your campsites in these virgin areas. You don't need to dig rain trenches around the tent, and you can scatter pine needles or grass over the flattened area to return to it a natural, undisturbed look.

BATHING

Take it from a ranger who spent weeks at a time in the woods and still had to appear presentable when talking to visitors. You can enjoy all the amenities of cleanliness and never get a drop of soap in a waterway. Jump in, swim in, or play in the stream or lake. Soap up away from the water and rinse by pouring pots and/or canteens of water over yourself. The same is true when cleaning eating utensils: wash and rinse them well away from the stream or lake.

OTHER CONSIDERATIONS

If a trail will get you to where you're going, stay on it. Just a few people cutting a switchback or blazing a shortcut will soon leave ribbons of trails across the landscape. This holds especially true in alpine high country, where just a few footprints can begin a scarring process on the land.

The only reason a hiker needs a hatchet or an ax on a camping trip is to remove trees that may have fallen across the road leading to the trailhead. Once there, lighten the pack and leave these tools behind. If the country doesn't supply enough downed squaw wood for a fire, better carry a stove.

Avoid the overly popular areas, especially during peak season. Many recreational foresters have let me know that I and this guidebook wouldn't be doing them or the land any favors by telling more people about already overcrowded areas. Wyoming is, so far, big enough to allow hikers to seek the qualities and solitudes of scenery that isn't overrun and consequently restricted.

Hiking Wyoming is the most comprehensive and up-to-date hiking guide for the entire state. But a few words of warning need to be voiced concerning the essential nature of trails in many areas. In several of the state's mountain ranges, the soil is friable, trail maintenance is non-existent, and the sheep/cattle/horses are numerous. I can hike a trail in the spring and issue an accurate description of it, and then that fall a flock of 500 sheep can traverse the area and completely change the trail system. A horse pack train can rototill out a new trail in a day's time, and it often looks more traveled than the original and official path. And more often than not these days the overseeing land agency, facing massive and disproportionate recreational budget cuts, has no ability to send maintenance crews into every area. Many trails are now "maintained" by horse packers and other volunteer groups. The overseeing agency may not even have the manpower to know what is currently happening on sections of their more unpopulated trails. Still, they do a great job of caring for their areas with what they're given. Checking with the local land management agencies for further information and updates, and for restrictions and warnings, can save you from starting down a trail no longer passable because of a fire, or alert you to an area where wild animals have been a problem.

Another feature in the continually changing landscape of hiking opportunities that needs to be mentioned is user fees. The same recreational budget cuts that leave trail crews thinned and wilderness enforcement personnel nonexistent also prompts a supposed need to begin charging hikers for their use of the land they visit and the trails they hike. There has always been an entrance fee in the case of national parks and monuments. But recently the idea is spreading to wilderness and other recreational trailheads. Most of Wyoming, as of 1998, remains unaffected by this concept, but also, most of the overseeing agencies I've talked to are actively considering initiating some form of user fee in the future. A few of the trailheads have donation boxes; a few more have self-payment stations set up near the trailhead. Perhaps it is more than fair that hikers pay a few bucks to keep some maintenance and repair on the trails they use. But considering the decades of subsidized logging, mining, and grazing, it'll take quite a while before these fees don't feel like another unnecessary tax.

Hiking in Bear Country

When promised some anecdotes on the uniqueness of Wyoming trails, you can bet that bears will be involved in several of them. All Wyoming mountains and forests harbor bears, and northwest Wyoming is one of the last refuges for the threatened grizzly bear. Grizzly habitat includes the Yellowstone and Grand Teton National Parks areas, the Targhee, Bridger-Teton and Shoshone National Forests, and all private, BLM and Indian reservation land immediately surrounding these areas. Admittedly, in 30 years of hiking, my most common view of a wild bear has been of its rear end in full retreat from me. I propose to keep things that way, and here are some precautions that will make it possible. But do remember that there is no generalizing when it comes to bear behavior. Avoiding an encounter is the primary rule.

- •Watching for signs of bear on and near the trail is the first-step safeguard. Tracks (believe me, if it's an adult grizzly's track, you will immediately know what it is), fresh scat, bushes that look like a whirlwind has disheveled them, torn-up stumps, and displaced rocks are indications that a bear is in the area. Fresh bear signs, especially if some of those signs come from a mother with cubs, are sufficient reason to change direction and trail plans.
- •Many people drape themselves with bells or other noisemakers while

Much of the Wyoming backcountry is in bear country. CHRIS CAUBLE PHOTO

hiking. The idea is valid. Noise gives the bear notice that you are coming, and since most tooth and claw encounters happen when the bear is surprised by a hiker, lots of noise offers no chance of surprise. There is a side effect to this technique, however. Some popular trails now echo in a continual jingling cadence. Veteran hikers, who miss the silence of the woods, jokingly wonder what would happen if bears ever began associating bell sounds with "lunch." When brush and undergrowth is thick, and bear images form in your mind, clapping hands, singing, or whistling for a few moments will also serve the purpose.

•We love our pets, but leave your dog at home. I once took the neighbor's shepherd for a walk. The dog woofed and ran after something in the woods. Something in the woods woofed back and the dog yipped; the dog ran back to me for protection from the boar black bear on his tail. That particular bear was human shy, luckily, and retreated upon seeing me. Don't believe that will always happen.

•There are always stories of a bear attack that happened during a woman's menstruation period or after a couple's lovemaking. There's no scientific proof beyond coincidence to confirm a link between an attack and these two events, but they are situations to keep in mind.

•Camping etiquette in bear country can be summed up in one word: cleanliness. Leave no fish guts and scatter no leftover dinner scraps around the campsite. Taking this idea a step further and avoiding aromatic foods is also a wise idea. If I was a grub-and-berry-satiated bear, and the delicious scent of frying bacon or spicy sardines was filling my exceptionally sensitive nose, I might be tempted to investigate.

•Many folks hang their packs, food, and cooking clothes from a tree or from a rope suspended between 2 trees. I've seen grizzly bear claw-sharpening marks 10 feet up an aspen tree, so this gives you some idea of how high you need to hang this gear and how large the bear can be. Also, black bears are both smart and adaptable. Some are learning that all they have to do to invoke manna from the sky is to chew through this rope from which your gear is suspended. Many Forest Service districts are now renting lightweight, bear-proof containers to hikers and packers for very reasonable rates.

•If a bear is interested in your camp, not only give him all the room (and gear) he desires, but also realize his interest might be spurred by a previous camper who left garbage behind and allowed the bear to begin an association of food with human camps. For the sake of the person after you, leave a clean camp. Report bear-robber incidents to authorities, for perhaps a minor problem bear can be captured and moved before it becomes a major problem bear and has to be killed.

•These next two pieces of advice offered in most bear-safety raps are those that sound good on paper but in reality are difficult to follow. They are: "If you do confront a bear, don't panic and don't run," and, "If the bear looks aggressive (example: stands up on its hind legs), look for a tree to climb." Excellent advice, but attempt a spontaneous trial run sometime (when there's no bear around). Drop everything and try to climb a nearby forest tree in 15 to 30 seconds. Most people attempting this exercise realize that climbing conifer trees—especially pines—takes practice and skills they don't have. It also takes experience and training not to first be overcome by fear when a bear suddenly looms ahead.

You cannot outrun a bear. Some have been clocked at 30 mph in short bursts. But if running is a viable or only option, a bear's leg structure does not let them run as quickly downhill. People have avoided bear attacks by slowly backing away from the encountered bear, by talking in a soothing voice, and by removing their pack and leaving it for the bear to investigate. Doug Peacock—the man after whom Edward Abbey modeled his "Hayduke" character for his novel, *The Monkey-Wrench Gang*, and a lifetime aficionado of grizzly bears—notes in his lectures that a person should never, never look directly into the eyes of a bear. Such a look, in bear language, means challenge and confrontation, whereas looking off to the side means submission and retreat.

•Most bear maulings usually involve a charging bear and offer little time for anything except curling the body into a position that protects head and stomach, and playing dead. This nonresistant tactic has yielded many bear attack survivors. As with the Borg (of *Star Trek* fame), "resistance is futile." Often, resistance only provokes further attack. The most common denominator in bear maulings is a sow bear with cubs. If you see bear cubs or fresh signs of bear cubs, skedaddle. Mother is nearby.

•Recently, an effective and benign protection aid has emerged on the camping scene, and I think it should be primary gear when traveling in bear country. Stories from hunters and park rangers and hikers and other recreationists continually filter in on the effectiveness of pepper spray against harassing or charging bears. A formula of 10 to 20 percent cayenne pepper in a canister that discharges a 20-foot mist of spray is forming a new approach that prevents maulings by teaching bears that humans have a "sting." This technology cannot be considered the end-all for bear encounter prevention, and again, one can't effectively use this stuff when panicking. I know a person who, upon rounding a corner and meeting a grizzly, whipped the pepper spray can out and blasted himself in the chest and face (the bear, even though his meat was now seasoned, walked away uninterested). You also need to be aware of wind direction and speed when using this stuff.

NOTE: The last several years have seen an unprecedented number of mountain lion attacks and maulings in Colorado, Idaho, Montana, and Wyoming. Young cats who haven't learned an instinctive fear of humans while being forced out on their own by their mothers, coupled with an increase in lion population and an increase in humans occupying lion habitat, has created this situation. Advice on actions to take if confronted by a mountain lion rings almost opposite of that of bear confrontations.

•Face the mountain lion. Most attacks occur from the rear. Make lots of noise. Yell and throw things at them. A cat will generally not attack something larger (especially taller) than itself, so enlarge your image. Hold something over your head to give yourself a bigger profile. If you're with a child, stand up tall and hold the child high in the air or place him/her on your shoulders.
•If attacked, DO NOT play dead. If knocked down, stand up. Cats are not used to prey that fights back.
•Dogs are not a deterrent. In fact, evidence suggests they may be an attraction.

There's a final addition to all this advice: feel and listen. If you see signs of bear, especially cub tracks; if you hear of cat or bear sightings from other hikers and your spine tingles and your hair stands on end; if every radar siren inside you is sounding warnings of potential danger; then listen to these warnings. Get out of the area and avoid an encounter.

Encounters with bears and mountain lions are rare, and attacks are even rarer. Fearing their possibility is not enough reason to cancel a backcountry trip. But there's definitely enough potential to warrant extra caution and preparedness.

Northeastern Wyoming

The broken prairies of the northeastern corner of Wyoming include a small portion of the Black Hills known as the Bear Lodge Mountains. Bear Lodge is a name derived from an Indian description that refers to the vertical furrows creasing the area's most prominent landmark, the Devils Tower volcanic plug (Hike 1). Most of the geological remnants from this area's billion-year-old Precambrian schists and granites were pushed and fragmented into mountains in South Dakota's Black Hills. Wyoming's Bear Lodge section of this event was formed more as a side effect of these neighboring activities than as an individual geological undertaking.

The Black Hills name comes from two Sioux words that mean "hills that are black." When seen from a distance, the pine-covered hills rising above the surrounding prairie appear dark colored. The mountains have long been used by plains Indian tribes as a place to purify themselves and seek visions. The 1897 Black Hills Forest Reserve became the Black Hills National Forest in 1905.

For the hiker, these mountains and their surrounding areas offer early season adventures in a state where high elevations keep many trails snowbound until July. It's a unique landscape, with open grassland parks and gently forested hills that are often pleated by variegated gulches and small canyons. To hike this country also requires some singular planning and preparation. Public land in the Wyoming section of the Black Hills National Forest is scattered and minimal. Most of the forest land is heavily logged and densely roaded, while recreational trails are just beginning to find a few footholds in the area. Hiking opportunities will often originate on or cross private land. (See Appendix I.)

While not offering hikers the chance for week-long mega-hikes, the Bear Lodge Mountains area of Wyoming is a wonderful arena for the person who discovers a small mountain or an unknown creek canyon and blazes his own cross-country day hike into the more open terrain. A wonderous potpourri of unique prairie buttes and winding creek bottomlands surround the forested hills. Permission is usually required to explore these areas on private lands. The Bearlodge District of the Black Hills Forest has recently completed its second official hiking/biking trail system (Hike 4), and it's a beauty. As always, voicing your opinion about converting a bit more of their timber and grazing lands into areas for nonmotorized recreation to the Black Hills National Forest—and to any government overseer agency—can prove to be valuable for future hiking trails.

1 Devils Tower National Monument

General description:	3 separate hiking trails around a towering volcanic formation.
Distance:	7 total miles of trail.
Difficulty:	Easy to moderate.
Elevation gain and loss:	Less than 200 feet.
General location:	On the western fringe of the Bear Lodge Mountains, 55 miles northeast of Gillette.
Special attractions:	A unique example of a volcanic/monolithic formation in the middle of the Wyoming prairie.
Applicable fees:	$8 per vehicle (seven day pass); $3 per person (walk in, motorcycle, or bicycle); $20 annual park pass (one year, Devils Tower only); $50 Golden Eagle pass (one year, any national park); $10 Golden Age (U.S. citizen over 62 years, lifetime). It also costs $12 to camp in the monument's campground. **Maps:** USGS: Devils Tower; Black Hills National Forest visitor map; Devils Tower National Monument trails pamphlet distributed by the National Park Service.
Manager:	Devils Tower National Monument.

Devils Tower from the Joyner Ridge Trail.

Finding the trailhead: Exit Interstate 90 about 27 miles east of Gillette. Drive 26 miles north on U.S. Highway 14 to the Devils Tower Junction (Charlie Junction on older maps), turn north on Wyoming 24, and drive 6 miles. Follow Wyoming 110 west for 0.5 mile to the entrance station.

The hike: Three completely different trails offer hikers a chance to explore the many aspects of the looming "Mateo Tepee" or "Bear Lodge," the volcanic plug called Devils Tower. Spend the day in the area and hike all 3 trails. America's first national monument has many faces, and the quick drive to the visitor center and jog around the shorter Tower Trail that most tourists opt for do not reveal the moods of this sacred landmark. This creviced rock giant gently tapers to a 275-foot flat summit that sits 1,262 feet above the Belle Fourche River. The fluted face of Devils Tower measures 865 feet from base to top, the tallest such formation in the U.S.

SOUTH SIDE, VALLEY VIEW, AND RED BEDS TRAILS

Beginning at the south end of the visitor center parking lot, the nearly 4 miles of this well-marked and easy-to-follow trail will take you on a grand tour through the many different worlds that immediately surround Devils Tower. Ponderosa forests, open meadows, cactused badlands, and river-carved sedimentary layers make appearances. All the while, the awesome faces of Devils Tower loom over the various landscapes.

After hiking 0.8 mile along this trail, the signed Valley View Trail intersects and journeys downhill toward the Belle Fourche (pronounced "bell foosh") River. A swing along this loop introduces you to the peaceful meadows and cottonwoods that surround the prairie river, and it offers remarkable views of the tower from a flatland perspective. An active prairie dog town thrives within this trail's boundaries. Looping back across the road to rejoin the Red Beds Trail, the path continues into many astounding vistas. It also reveals a perspective of what Wyoming countryside looked like before cattle and grazing claimed the state.

The trail is rated moderately difficult due to the quite noticeable elevation loss and gain. Incredible views of the river and the reddish, friable sedimentary layers it has cut through are an added attraction to this hike. The trail circles around Devils Tower and ends at the north end of the visitor parking lot. There is no water along the trail.

THE TOWER TRAIL

Although it always feels unnatural to have pavement instead of pine needles beneath the hiking boots, the 1.3-mile paved Tower Trail that surrounds the base of Devils Tower is well worth the hour it takes to hike. Neck-craning views of the 800-foot rock columns that rise directly above you engender amazement and respect. Viewing some of the rock climbing parties inching their way up shear walls and little cracks adds a sense of proportion to the scene. (NOTE: Anyone planning to climb is required to

DEVILS TOWER NATIONAL MONUMENT

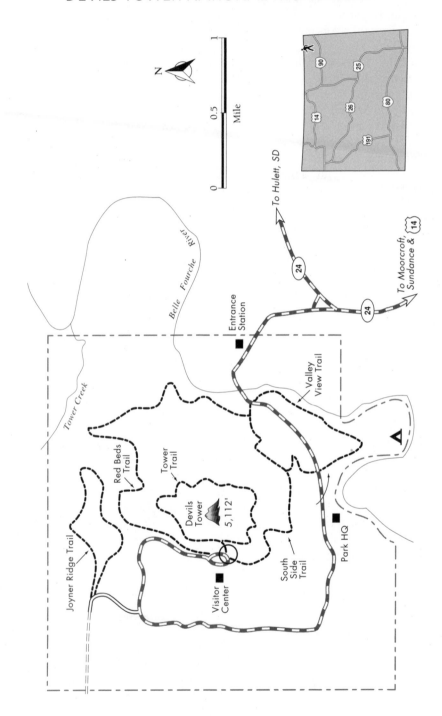

register before and check in after a climb. Also, out of deference to the sacred beliefs of Northern Plains Indians, there is a voluntary closure to climbing during the month of June.) Wayside exhibits along the trail explain the Tower's natural processes.

The trail is well marked and begins at the east end of the visitor center parking lot. Rattlesnakes have been seen along these trails, and interestingly, they also live on the rocky football field top of the Tower.

JOYNER RIDGE TRAIL

Devils Tower can become quite crowded with visitors during the peak tourist season. At 0.6 mile on the road before the visitor center, an unmarked, hard-surface road leaves the main thoroughfare and journeys north for 0.3 mile to the Joyner Ridge Trailhead. This unpopulated section of the monument offers the most glorious views of the Tower imaginable, the best in the park.

The 1.5-mile trail is as sweet and serene a hike as one could wish for. It first traces the lands where meadow and forest merge. Then it drops past sandstone cliffs, cuts through secluded meadows, and wanders into ravines with groves of deciduous trees and shrubs. The trail loops back through the open prairie and ends where it began. Photographic opportunities exist every step of the way. The trail contains minimal signing and a few waysides.

Spring, early summer, and fall are optimal times to visit this monument. Its margins are small, but some wonderful opportunities for cross-country wandering exist, especially along the northern and western boundaries of the park.

2 Keyhole State Park

General description:	A day hike beneath and atop the sandstone cliffs that help create the Keyhole Reservoir on the Belle Fourche River.
Distance:	6 miles, round trip.
Difficulty:	Easy.
Elevation gain and loss:	Less than 100 feet.
General location:	12 miles east and 8 miles north of Moorcroft, on the western fringe of the Bear Lodge Mountains.
Special attractions:	Unique sandstone butte formations, water sport activities including fishing and swimming, and the best, most diverse, and abundant bird watching in the state of Wyoming.
Maps:	USGS: Carlile and Grasshopper Butte quads, and the park map distributed by Keyhole State Park.
Fees:	Wyoming resident entrance: $3 per vehicle; nonresident entrance: $4 per vehicle; camping: $4 per night.
Manager:	Keyhole State Park.

Keyhole State Park

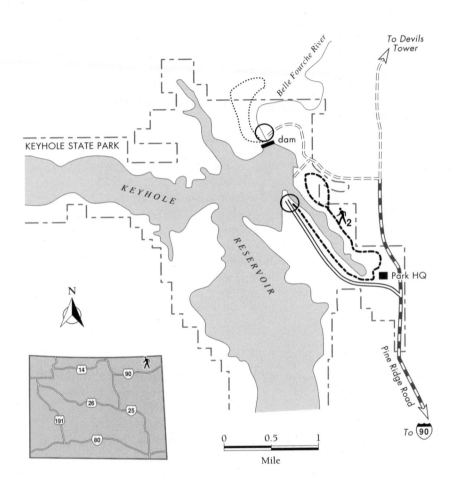

Finding the trailhead: To reach Keyhole State Park, leave Interstate 90 13 miles east of Moorcroft at exit 165, the Pine Ridge Road exit. Follow this aptly named road to the north for 7 miles and into Keyhole State Park—named after a keyhole-shaped brand used by some local ranchers. Turn left or west at the information booth, drive past the park headquarters for 1.7 miles toward the marina, and park near the trailer court, where the trailhead begins on the southern shores of the mouth of Cottonwood Bay.

The hike: Note on Volksmarch walks: the Wyoming State Parks and Historic Sites organization deserves a collective handshake and thanks from everyone who feels hiking forms a special part of his or her life. They've implemented a program called "Volksmarch" in 10 of their state parks. Volksmarch is an international walking group that helps create 10-kilometer (6-mile) excursions designed to help people discover the beauty, uniqueness and diversity of an area through the wonderful means of walking. The term "Volksmarch" literally means "a walk of the people." Information is available from the Department of Commerce, State Parks, and Historical Sites, 16101 Yellowstone Road, Cheyenne, WY, 82002, 307-777-7695, and from the American Volkssport Association, 1001 Pat Booker Road, Suite 101, Universal City, TX, 78148, 210-659-2112.

The path follows the waterline of Cottonwood Bay. It passes below trailers and a campground before gaining some solitude by circling the bay and traversing a series of wooded sandstone buttes. The park has recently upgraded the first mile of this trail leading from the parking lot to Archrock Campground by paving it to make it wheelchair accessible. The complete walk traces the northern Cottonwood Bay shoreline, makes a large loop among the buttes, and then follows the original shoreline pathway back to the trailhead. Brown and yellow IVV signs mark the trail's pathway.

The park is also completing a half-mile trail from the Marina parking lot to Pats Point Boat Ramp. This short wander often affords shorebird, beaver, and deer sightings.

The many years of drought that left Keyhole a half reservoir are over and the lake is once again almost full. Also, the rolling country around the water is quite intriguing. Exploration did lead to an alluring section of land that offered an excellent two-hour to half-day hiking adventure amid a splendid and secretive setting.

Instead of turning left at the park information sign, continue northward for another 1.5 miles to the end of the pavement. Here a gravel road jogs to the left or west and leads to the reservoir's dam structure. About 0.5 mile later this road forks; turn right or north and follow a windy narrow road 1.2 miles to the parking lot beside and below the reservoir dam. Across the Belle Fourche River, and directing its course, a crescent of sandstone buttes and cliffs sweep to the north. This escarpment offers a wonderland of hiking and exploration excitement.

The most exceptional quality of the Keyhole area is its feathered life. More than 220 different species of birds have been sighted at or near the lake. By spending the morning in this second area, hiking up the dam and then following the game trails that travel near the edges of these butte tops, I must have spotted a third of these birds. By descending the cliffs via various ravines and tracking other game trails back along the western shores of the river, I probably saw another third. The final third remained hidden, but they were singing a chorus of songs that was almost deafening. This cross-country wandering along the rather tiny Belle Fourche River offers privacy, silence and peace, glorious scenery, great wildlife, escape from the commercial development that usually accompanies such reservoirs, and a small chance to touch a tiny section of pristine Wyoming.

NOTE: Private lands do surround the butte just described, and permission is needed to explore the woodlands and prairies they contain.

3 Cliff Swallow Loop Trail/Cook Lake Trail

General description:	Diverse hiking and mountain biking trails beginning and ending near the only natural lake found in the Bear Lodge Mountains.
Distance:	1 to 3.5 miles.
Difficulty:	Easy to moderate.
Elevation gain and loss:	Less than 400 feet.
General location:	14 miles (as the raven flies) north of Sundance, in the heart of the Bear Lodge Mountains.
Special attractions:	Deciduous riparian habitat complete with beaver workings.
Maps:	Black Hills National Forest visitor map; USGS: Black Hills quad, Alva quad is optional; Bearlodge Ranger District pamphlet with map.
Fees:	$10 camping at the Cook Lake Recreation Area.
Manager:	Bearlodge Ranger District.

Finding the trailhead: You might envy the raven who can cover the long and winding road to Cook Lake in 14 easy air miles. Forest Road 838, the Warren Peak Lookout Road, allows you a wonderful chance to seek out the nontrailed and cross-country exploration opportunities available in the Bear Lodge Mountains. This north-south "thoroughfare" travels through wooded canyons and ravines, beside lower-elevation peaks, over divides, across flats and along streams, and offers many chances for one to park the car and wander to an unnamed summit or into a remnant wild creek beginning. Drive 2 miles west of Sundance on U.S. Highway 14 and turn right where the brown Forest Service sign directs you north to the Cook Lake Recreation Area via Forest Road 838. The pavement survives for 7.5 miles where another Cook Lake sign directs you to turn right onto a gravel road. Approximately 5.6 miles of this graded gravel road passes you over splendid divides and through thick aspen forests to a stop-signed intersection with Forest Road 843. Turn right here, following the Cook Lake sign. Turn left at another intersection 1.7 miles later, where the sign says you're 5 miles from Cook Lake. Almost 4 miles later, Forest Road 842 cuts to the left and leads you the last mile to the Cook Lake Recreation Area. If a major rainstorm pummels the area, the last 4 miles of this route will need some drying time before a low-clearance vehicle can navigate it. Drive along the east and around the north shores of the lake, and 0.2 mile farther west to the day use parking lot. The trailhead begins at the northern boundary of this lot.

The hike: I can't imagine a sweeter or more diverse day hiking experience than this easy 1-mile loop around a peaceful forest lake followed by a 3.5-mile loop trail through creek and forest settings. For over a mile the Cliff Swallow Trail traces a vibrant and quite "alive-with-beaver-activity" creek bottom. Some excellent campsites exist in the various riparian settings for those who wish to escape the tumult of a developed recreation area. Please notice that little sign of camping activity exists along Beaver Creek, and do your part to keep that no-use look healthy. After about 1.2 miles, the trail crosses a barbed wire fence (a good fence, one that keeps cattle out of the watershed environment) and begins a long wind up the north side of a pine-covered mountain. Easy to follow, the trail tops out and skims a high ridge for the next 1.5 miles. This section climaxes at an impressive overview of

The Black Hills. Beaver Creek during high runoff.

Cliff Swallow Loop Trail/Cook Lake Trail

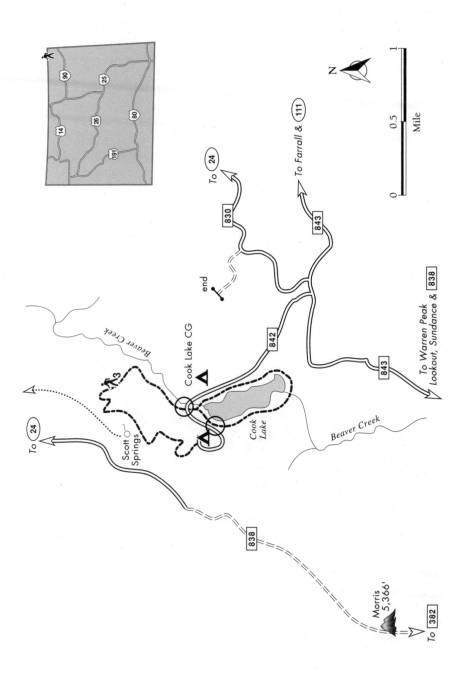

the Beaver Creek valley. After gently switchbacking back down the mountain, the trail ends at the day use parking area. This excellent hiking trail is moderate due to the 400 feet of elevation gained and then lost again, but proper switchbacking greatly eases that difficulty.

These trails and the Sundance Trail System (Hike 4) represent the Bearlodge Ranger District's active energy toward creating viable hiking and biking routes in their section of the Black Hills National Forest. I hope readers will write the district and compliment them on their expansion of this needed resource.

4 Sundance Trail System

General description:	A fascinating series of loops covering everything from low creek drainages to high ridges. Several day and/or overnight routes can be planned in this area.
Distance:	1 to 56 miles, depending on hike chosen.
Difficulty:	Easy to difficult, depending on hike chosen.
Elevation gain and loss:	100 feet to 1,600 feet, depending on hike.
General location:	5 to 8 miles north of Sundance, in the southern section of the Wyoming part of the Black Hills Forest.
Special attractions:	An opportunity to explore the unknown canyons and ridgetops of the Black Hills of Wyoming.
Maps:	*Bearlodge Trails, Sundance Trail System and Carson Draw Trails*, map and guide available from the Bearlodge Ranger District. USGS: Sundance West and Sundance East.
Fees:	Reuter Campground and Sundance Campground have an $8 per night camping fees (and believe me, the ranger is up and checking compliance mighty early.
Manager:	Bearlodge Ranger District.

Finding the trailheads: You really need to get the *Bearlodge Trails* handout from the ranger district for an accurate location of all the road/trail intersections. For trailheads on the west side of the Sundance Trails area, Interstate 90's exit 185 at Sundance leads to U.S. Highway 14. One mile west along this road places you at the Cook Lake Recreation area sign and paved Forest Road 838 journeying 2.5 miles north to the Reuter Campground. There are about 5 trail/road intersections in the next 4 miles, but signs are rather scarce; look for the brown, narrow fiberglass rods with a bear paw print near the top. Some of the trails are derived from usable roads and from old roads being converted into trails. Some of these roads are still driveable, but gates are gradually being placed along their routes.

The other major trailhead area is at the Sundance Campground. Take exit 185 off Interstate 90 to U.S. Highway 14, but this time go east on U.S.

Sundance Trail System

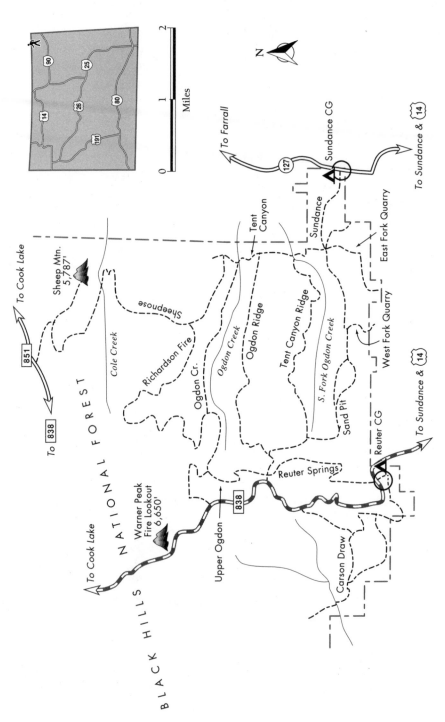

Highway 14, past the outskirts of Sundance until you connect with Crook County 123. Take this road north 3.5 miles to the trailhead.

The hike: The recreational forester at the Bearlodge Ranger District in Sundance deserves many compliments. In a time of crucifying recreational budget cutbacks, he has managed to put together a fabulous 56-mile trail loop system that affords hikers, mountain bikers, and horse riders a chance to explore the gentle Wyoming Black Hills. This partly non-motorized trail system weaves through densely forested canyons and winding open ridges. Any number of loop hikes are possible, and treks can encompass everything from low-elevation walks along the eastern flanks of the National Forest to the eastern slopes of Warren Peak and its sweeping views of the Bear Lodge Mountains, Devils Tower, and the surrounding Wyoming prairies.

The Black Hills have become an over-roaded, overgrazed arena of managed development, and converting a chunk of territory back to non-mechanized recreation is going to take some time. Many of the trails are roads being reclaimed through disuse. All in all, more than 56 miles of trail create quite a system of exploration possibilities. Added to this, several bicycle cut-acrosses—not shown on this book's map but illustrated on the *Bearlodge Trails* handout—and many closed-to-motorized-vehicle roads intersecting the established trails greatly increase the hiking possibilities.

The Carson Draw trails on the western side of this system are mainly cross-country ski trails (groomed during the winter) and never really afford the variety and views of the other Sundance trails. The trails along the eastern side of this area (Tent Canyon, Sundance, East Fork Quarry, and Sheepnose) offer incredible views of the eastern Wyoming prairies. The trails to the north (Richardson Fire, Sheepnose, Sheep Mountain, and Upper Ogdon) reach the highest elevations. In between all of this, great ridge and creek hiking prevails.

Be sure and check with the Forest Service district for updated information, as the trail system is continuously being expanded and improved. Drinking water is available at both campgrounds/trailheads, and several springs and creeks exist along the trails. As usual, purification is necessary due to livestock.

Southeastern Wyoming

THE LARAMIE RANGE

Wyoming's geological connection to Colorado's impressive Front Range mountains is a long and erratic cluster of granite named the Laramie Range. Extending from south of Casper to north and west of Laramie, these rugged mountains have a unique drainage system. Many of the creeks flow west to east across and through the entire range. These waterways originate in the high valleys west of the mountains and refuse to allow the granite-cored peaks to hinder their eastward trek.

Streams and peaks survive as best they can amidst a hodgepodge of land ownership designation. Roads (many, many roads in this country) and routes cross and recross so many boundaries that one could not guess how many private property permissions one must acquire to hike an area. Checking with the Forest Service districts or the BLM offices in Casper and Rawlins may help in your information search.

Medicine Bow National Forest recently updated its visitor map, greatly improving the accuracy of the forest overview. Be sure and ask for the revised edition. Also, the forest now has 2 separate maps, 1 for the Snowy Range and the Hayden/Encampment areas, and 1 for the Laramie Peak/ Douglas Ranger District areas. Also, land swaps and right-of-way acquisitions have occurred in the Douglas Ranger District and the district now lists 4 hiking trails in the Laramie Mountains. These trails are open to motorized vehicles. But beginning in 1997, and contingent on funds, Douglas Ranger District will be re-opening old forest trails in the 5,000-acre Ashenfelder Basin area north of Laramie Peak for non-motorized use.

This entire range is exceptional in its ruggedness and beauty, but you do need to know where you are if you venture cross-country (see Appendix I).

5 Laramie Peak

General description:	A fairly steep day hike to the highest summit in the Laramie Range.
Distance:	10.5 miles round trip.
Difficulty:	Moderate.
Elevation gain:	2,372 feet.
Key elevation points:	Friend Park trailhead: 7,900 feet; Laramie Peak summit: 10,272 feet.
General location:	45 miles directly south of Douglas.
Special attractions:	Rugged lands that are a bold cross between mountains and high prairie.
Maps:	Medicine Bow National Forest Laramie Peak Unit Map; USGS: Laramie Peak.
Manager:	Douglas Ranger District.

Finding the trailhead: Two roads carry you to Esterbrook, which is not really a town but a Forest Service work station. The most scenic route leaves Interstate 25 at Glendo (exit 111) and wanders westward for 22 miles on Platte County 59, then to Forest Road 614 (also called the Esterbrook Road). A second route, Wyoming 94, leaves the interstate directly south of Douglas. About 17 miles of it is paved before it becomes graded Converse County 5. Eleven more miles places you in Esterbrook. Parts of these roads have the potential to be difficult to negotiate with a two-wheel-drive vehicle during or just after a rainstorm. From Esterbrook a signed intersection guides you west along Converse County Road 5 and along the 18 miles to the Friend Park Campground and Laramie Peak trailhead.

The hike: The scattered mountains of the Laramie Range are generally forested all the way up to their summits, and are quite rugged due to the rocky landscape of the granite-cored anticlinal uplift that formed them. The trail follows beautiful Friend Creek for a mile before crossing the water (via a bridge) and beginning a steep ascent that never relaxes its grade for the next 4 miles. This is, a wide and well-maintained trail, but also one on which you know you're hiking uphill. The mountainside that it traverses is a never-ending slope of behemoth granite boulders. Lodgepole pines poke through the rock where they can, creating a thick and sterile forest.

A trail sign at 2 miles notes Friend Creek Falls, which looks more like a steep cascade than a waterfall. This will be the last water available along the trail in later summer. Be aware that into June, although the lower countryside appears long past winter, some intense snow stomping may still be the mode of hiking near the peak's summit.

Glorious panoramas from the summit spread in every direction of the Laramie Range forms a fascinating rock hodgepodge below. Be prepared for unpredictable weather, and give yourself an entire day to hike this trail.

Laramie Peak

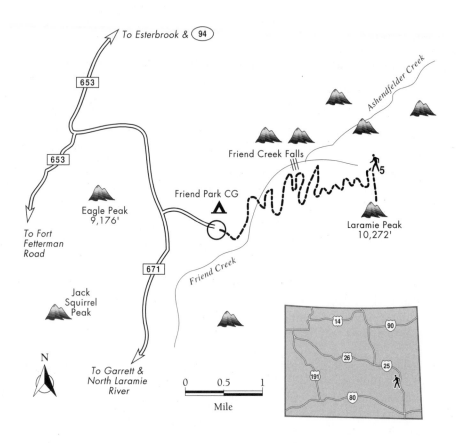

To Esterbrook & (94)

653

653

To Fort
Fetterman
Road

Eagle Peak
9,176'

Friend Park CG

Friend Creek Falls

Ashendfelder Creek

5

Laramie Peak
10,272'

671

Jack
Squirrel
Peak

Friend Creek

N

To Garrett &
North Laramie
River

0   0.5   1

Mile

14   90

26
191   25

80

6 LaBonte Canyon

General description:	A fun and especially beautiful day hike that follows a major creek drainage into a deep mountain canyon.
Distance:	6 miles round trip.
Difficulty:	Easy.
Elevation loss and gain:	600 feet.
Key elevation points:	Trailhead: 6,800 feet; end of trail: 6,200 feet.
General location:	35 miles southwest of Douglas, in the Medicine Bow National Forest.
Special attractions:	Some of the best wildlife habitat in this section of Wyoming.
Maps:	Medicine Bow National Forest Laramie Peak Unit map; USGS: Saddleback Mountain.
Manager:	Douglas Ranger District.

Finding the trailhead: Leave Interstate 25 at exit 146 and drive southeast on Wyoming 96 for 3.2 miles to the intersection of Wyoming 91. After 12.8 miles of southward driving, the pavement ends, state maintenance ends, and Converse County 24 comes into being. Three miles farther the road forks. Turn left onto Converse County 16, the Fort Fetterman Road, and drive approximately 15 miles until you intersect the well-signed La Bonte Canyon/Curtis Gulch Campground Road. This dirt road journeys eastward and parallels La Bonte Creek for 5 miles and ends at Curtis Gulch Campground, where the trail begins.

The hike: The LaBonte drainage is a prime example of a creek that begins west of the Laramie Range yet travels uninterrupted east through the mountains. This area contains a large proportion of contiguous Forest Service land. The hiker can freely explore adjacent creek drainages and surrounding hills. And exploration is what the LaBonte area is all about. La Bonte, by the way, was a French trader and trapper who frequented the region in the 1830s. Here he should have remained. The Ute Indians killed him in Utah in 1840.

The trail crisscrosses the creek several times for the first 2 miles, but the canyon is easily hikable by simply skirting the north side of the creek. This is a south-facing slope and therefore quite open. Game trails usually follow the untrailed side of the creek, and where rocky structures do descend onto the stream's side, it's not difficult to switchback a short way up the mountainside and pick a route around them.

By the time you follow both the regular trail and the impromptu trails 3 miles to the end, you will have been amazed by this spectacular and generally undiscovered hiking paradise. Be prepared for lush meadows, gallant cottonwoods and pine forests, picturesque rock cliffs, flowers beyond description (especially in May and June), and wildlife everywhere. The creek bottom is classified as the La Bonte Big Game Range, so livestock grazing is

LaBonte Canyon

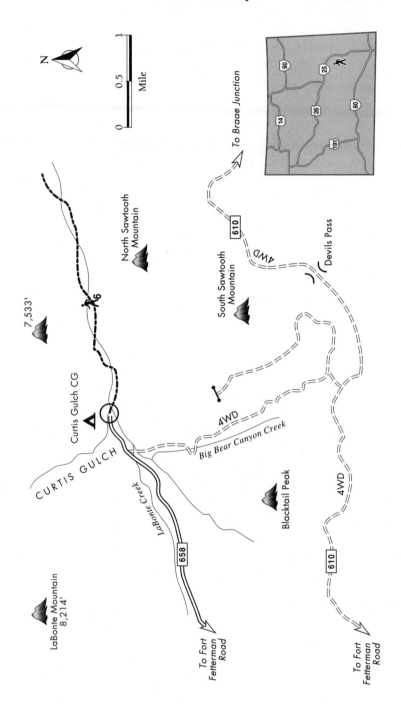

N

0   0.5   1
Mile

To Braae Junction

90   25   🧍

14   26   80

191

610

4WD

Devils Pass

North Sawtooth Mountain

South Sawtooth Mountain

7,533'

6

Curtis Gulch CG

CURTIS GULCH

LaBonte Creek

Big Bear Canyon Creek

4WD

Blacktail Peak

4WD

610

658

LaBonte Mountain 8,214'

To Fort Fetterman Road

To Fort Fetterman Road

not allowed here. Beyond the trail's end, the canyon becomes especially rugged and narrow, and private land soon claims the area. Note that the trail is signed as open to motorcycles, ATVs, horse, mountainbike and foot travel.

7 Twin Peaks

General description:	A day hike into some of the incredibly variegated landscapes of the Laramie Mountain area.
Distance:	6 miles round trip.
Difficulty:	Moderate.
Elevation gain and loss:	1,610 feet.
Key elevation points:	Trailhead: 7,600 feet; trail leaves Roaring Fork Creek drainage: 8,200 feet; South Twin Peak: 9,210 feet.
General location:	30 miles southwest of Douglas, in the western portion of the Medicine Bow National Forest.
Maps:	This is a newly constructed trail, and maps do not show its location. The Medicine Bow National Forest, Laramie Peak Unit shows the road and land layout; USGS: Warbonnet Peak.
Special attractions:	Untrammeled country and some exciting views. Nearby LaPrele Creek offers good stream fishing.
Manager:	Douglas Ranger District.

Finding the trailhead: Directions out of Douglas are the same as for Hike 6, until you come to the intersection of Converse County Roads 24 and 16. For this hike, stay on Converse County 24 to the right, and follow this road for 12 miles after the pavement ends. This can become a pretty greasy stretch of country road if it's wet. 0.5 mile beyond where Roaring Fork Creek crosses the road, a well-marked trailhead and parking area sit to the west side.

The hike: Half of the excitement in exploring this trail is the last 12 miles of driving to the trailhead. The awesomely rugged country one travels through looks like a vast and unknown, super-extended Vedauwoo-type landscape (see Hike 10), with towering granite pinnacles bouncing off and over woodland prairie settings. The land ownership is a mixture of private, state, and federal, so a property location map will be needed if a side canyon or rocky embankment calls to be explored.

The first few hundred yards of the trail cross state land, then it winds across obvious access-granted private land for another half mile. The owner has been doing lots of clearing, and roads jot off every which way. Stick to the main-looking track that travels south of the creek. This heads directly west and up the canyon and will take you into another square-mile section of state land. Day use is allowed but overnight camping is prohibited on this section.

Twin Peaks

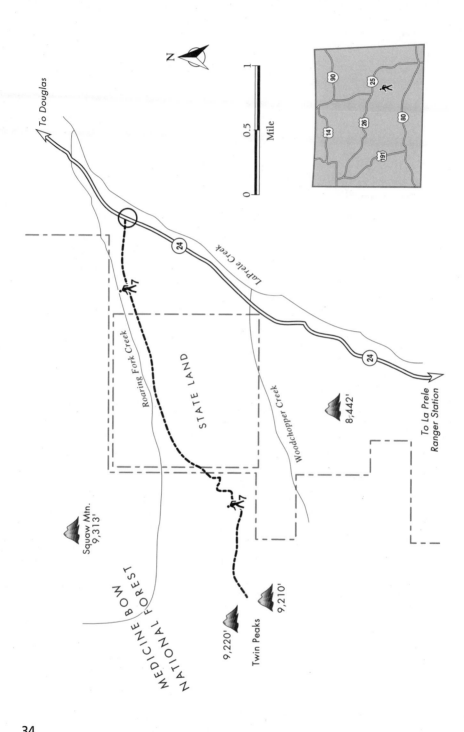

This is a wide and easy-to-follow trail, and for the next 0.7 mile it parallels gentle Roaring Fork Creek. At 1.3 miles the trail leaves the creek bottom and begins a steep ascent to the south. The next 1.2 miles find the hiker traveling through a mixed lodgepole/aspen/spruce forest. Sometimes the trees are thick, sometimes they thin out; sometimes the trail cuts steeply uphill, and sometimes it climbs gently. At 2.5 miles you leave the thicker forest and begin 0.5 mile of pretty and peaceful ridgetop hiking.

At 3.0 miles the trail tops a small crest where it ends completely. There never really has been, up to and including this point, a sweeping overview of the countryside. North Twin Peak and its obvious jutting rocky summit lie to the northwest. Ascending this rock pile requires a harsh, cross-country trek through downfall and then a rough, fourth-class scramble. There is a first set of boulders just northwest of where the trail ends that offers a nice lunch spot and view of the valley to the east, yet doesn't require rock climbing skills to reach.

South Twin Peak, to the southwest, simply requires a gentler, longer hike through thinner forest to reach an open meadow atop the mountain. The views from this summit are not as encompassing but still open the heart.

There is no water once the trail exits the canyon bottom. And even Roaring Fork Creek is exceptionally suspect, due to livestock.

8 Guernsey State Park

General Description:	A day hike amid the animated canyons, prairies and buttes that surround the North Platte River.
Distance:	Loop one: 4 miles; loop two: 2.2 miles.
Difficulty:	Easy to moderate.
Elevation gain and loss:	Less than 500 feet.
Key elevation points:	Guernsey Reservoir: 4,380 feet; museum hilltop: 4,580 feet; prairie high point: 4,700 feet.
General location:	13 miles north and 15 miles east of Wheatland, along the North Platte River.
Maps:	USGS: Guernsey Reservoir, Guernsey; Guernsey State Park Volksmarch map handout.
Special attractions:	Fascinating Civilian Conservation Corps (CCC) historic buildings and artifacts from the 1930s. Great views, good birding, and some interesting prairie hiking.
Fees:	$4 park entrance fee; $5 per night camping fee.
Manager:	Guernsey State Park.

Finding the trailhead: Taking exit 92 off Interstate 25 sends you eastward on U.S. Highway 26 toward the small river town of Guernsey. About 15 miles from the interstate and just west of the town, a sign directs you northward to Guernsey State Park. After passing the fee collection building, follow the main paved road 1.5 miles. Shortly after you cross the dam, a gravel road turns right and winds its way uphill to the park's museum. Here the hiking begins.

The hike: A small and geologically unimportant thrust named the Hartville Uplift, aided by the cutting powers of the North Platte River, has created some very scenic country in the southeastern area of Wyoming. In 1927, after Charles A. Guernsey kidnapped a group of Denver-bound U.S. senators by detouring their train to Hartville so he could show them his proposed dam site, the Bureau of Reclamation completed a 105-foot earthen dam, changing river canyons to lake shorelines. Guernsey State Park was created when the CCC established itself in the area from 1933 to 1936. If you enjoy adding historical fact-finding to your hiking adventure, the Guernsey State Park museum and other remnants of CCC activities in Guernsey Park are worth seeking.

The park's 6.2 mile Volksmarch trail (see Hike 2) consists of 2 separate loops. The trick to following these sometimes confusing trails, besides acquiring a free copy of the Volksmarch trail map, is to look for the International Volksmarch trail sign. These brown and yellow beacons consist of an "I" sitting atop a "V" sitting atop another "V."

Loop 1 leaves the museum parking lot and retraces 0.5 mile of the gravel road which brought you to the museum. IVV signs will first direct you westward for a short jaunt to a small butte and back, and then send you northeast through eastern Wyoming prairie and open forestland. The walk

Guernsey State Park.

Guernsey State Park

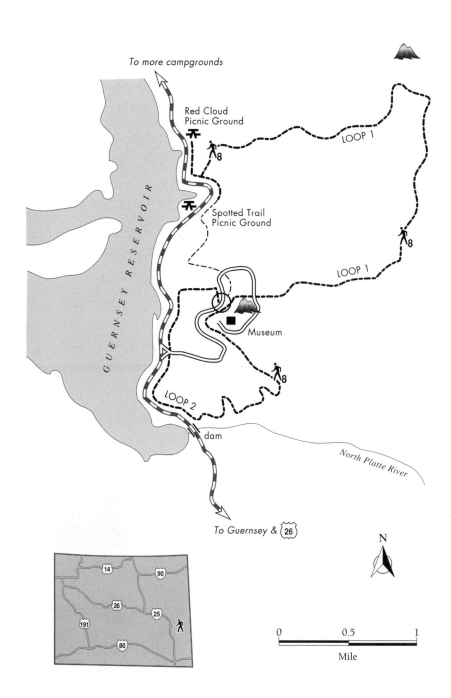

To more campgrounds

Red Cloud
Picnic Ground

LOOP 1

Spotted Trail
Picnic Ground

LOOP 1

GUERNSEY RESERVOIR

Museum

LOOP 2

dam

North Platte River

To Guernsey & 26

N

14

90

26

25

191

80

0   0.5   1

Mile

wanders northward to the foot of some high sandstone escarpments and then traces a way westward, down and along a dry ravine and to the lake. Here it follows a main paved road for 0.5 mile before again going cross-country through the juniper and ponderosa hills and back to the museum. This first loop is about 4 miles in length. There is also some fine cross-country hiking along prairie hilltops if you leave the northern most point of the trail.

The second loop of this walk, about 2 miles in length, begins at the north-western side of the museum, again marked well by IVV signs. It winds quickly down to the paved road where it follows the highway south for nearly a mile. At the dam, the trail then cuts eastward along the cliffs over-looking the North Platte River. Quite spectacular views and old CCC structures add to the trail's story. The last 0.5 mile of the trail climbs some old and new roadbeds back to the museum.

Some other old and exciting CCC trails do exist on the west side of the reservoir, and future park plans do include reconstructing them. It should also be noted that every year in late summer the reservoir is completely drained, so nearby irrigation ditches will be lined with the lake's accumulated silt and become more waterproof. That may or may not be an exciting time to visit the park.

9 Glendo State Park

General description:	Two half-day journeys into Wyoming high prairie wetland.
Distance:	First trail: 4 miles round trip; second trail: 1.5 mile loop.
Difficulty:	Easy.
Elevation gain and loss:	Almost none.
Key elevation points:	Glendo Reservoir: 4,635 feet.
General location:	75 miles southeast of Casper and 35 miles north of Wheatland, along the North Platte River in eastern Wyoming.
Special attractions:	Lots of fauna and flora associated with riparian habitats. Incredible cottonwood forests and prairie hiking.
Maps:	Glendo State Park handout map; USGS: Sibley Peak, Cassa, Jewel Springs, Glendo.
Fees:	$4 park entrance fee; $5 per night camping.
Manager:	Glendo State Park.

Finding the trailhead: Leaving Interstate 25 at exit 111, a well-signed road shortly leads you eastward to the tiny town of Glendo. Turn south on Glendo's main street, Wyoming 319, at the Glendo Dam Recreation Area sign. One block and another sign directs you left or eastward onto Lincoln Avenue,

Glendo State Park

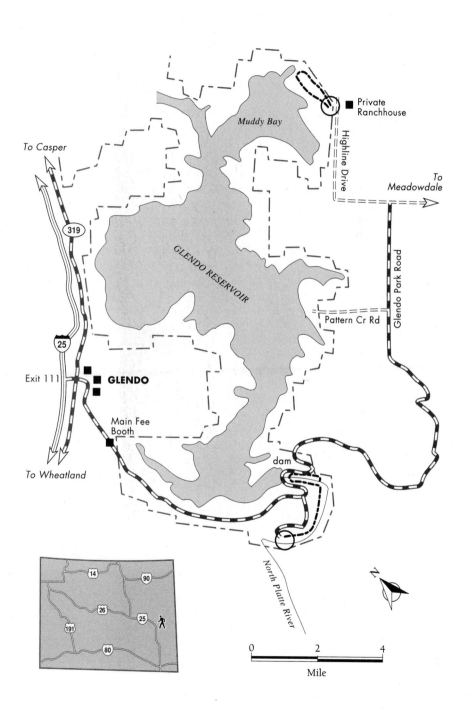

where, after a half-block's distance, yet a third sign points you right onto Glendo Park Road. From here it's 1.5 miles to the entrance station.

The hike: Glendo's first trail explores a wetland surrounding the North Platte River below the spillway of the dam. Four miles from the park entrance station, a sign saying "Glendo Power Plant" marks a paved road leading to the south and traveling 1 mile down a steep hill. Before the power plant, turn left onto a gravel road and drive 0.2 mile to an obvious day use area. Here begins the Glendo Dam Wetlands Interpretive Trail.

More than half (1.1 miles) of this almost 2-mile-long level trail follows an old roadbed along the north side of the river. Here the trail splits, one side crossing the river and leading to the dam itself, the other side (west side) heading northward for 0.5 mile to end below the dam's spillway. There is no way to cross the dam's bottom to turn this into a loop.

Although this hike is simple and short, a lot of unique habitat can be observed. River and swamp riparian settings housing fish, frogs, and waterfowl nestle between dry canyon slopes proclaiming (via pines, sage and larks) their totally different biotic makeup.

Glendo's second trail requires a slightly more adventurous drive to reach. 9.5 miles from where paved Glendo Park Road crosses the dam (and outside of the park boundaries), the asphalt ends at a graded road T with Highline Drive. Turn left or west onto this road and follow it, first west and then north, for 3 miles. Across from a small and very isolated ranch house, a "Muddy Bay" sign points you west to a parking lot. Here begins the "Muddy Bay Wetland Interpretive Trail."

The park notes that this leisurely, level trail is wheelchair accessible, but a loose gravel base and an unmaintained appearance make that statement questionable. If a person were to just hike the loop trail, the 1.5 mile distance would hardly make the long drive worth the effort. But this is interesting country to be in. High prairie wetlands interspersed with solid cottonwood forests reveal a totally unique landscape. The bird watching, especially in spring, is incomparable. In places the prairie is reclaiming old farmland; in other places original grasslands reveal what the Wyoming landscape was like before grazing.

The opportunities to wander cross-country across both the above area and the park lands surrounding the rest of the reservoir are endless (note that the northern end of the trail loop is pretty swampy). This book's map only details the southern half of the reservoir and park. An incredible amount of public land surrounds this manmade body of water. Approximately 8 miles upstream the river forms the alluringly named Platte River Canyon. A boat traveling up reservoir, or private property access permission, may be needed to be able to explore that land.

THE SHERMAN MOUNTAINS

Nearly 40 million years ago, about a dozen miles east of where the city of Laramie would one day rise, nature flipped a few handfuls of leftover Rocky Mountain granite onto the Laramie Plains. These rocks eventually formed the Sherman Mountains, a limited group of small hills skirted by Interstate 80 on the south and west sides. Time weathered many of the prominent, massive boulder formations into fascinating glens of piled and balanced rock structures.

A small section of this boulder-mountain country is owned by the Medicine Bow National Forest. Although hiking opportunities are limited in this tiny, over-roaded section of forest, a couple of unique walking experiences do exist.

10 Vedauwoo

General description:	Interesting explorations through unique blocks and towers of weathered Sherman granite.
Distance:	0.75 to 5 miles.
Difficulty:	Easy.
Elevation gain and loss:	Less than 100 feet.
Key elevation points:	Parking lot: 8,540 feet.
General location:	17 miles east of Laramie, just north of Interstate 80, in the southern section of the Sherman Mountains.
Maps:	Medicine Bow National Forest Laramie/Hayden visitor map; USGS: Sherman Mountains West.
Fees:	$8 per night camping.
Manager:	Medicine Bow National Forest, Laramie Ranger District.

Finding the trailhead: Leaving Interstate 80 at exit 329, 17 miles east of Laramie, and following Forest Road 700 east for 1 mile, you'll intersect a lightly paved road—Forest Road 720—and a sign directing you north to the Vedauwoo Campground. Continue along this road as far as it goes to the north end of the parking lot.

The hike: The Vedauwoo area (pronounced VAY-da-voo), an Arapaho Indian word meaning "earth born," has been used through the ages by Indians as a site of ancient religious rites. In more modern times it grew into an area recognized for its challenging rock climbs. Now a picnic area and campground have transformed it into a popular day and overnight recreation site.

Just past the wooden parking barriers and to the left, a nature trail begins ascending up and through the amazing green and pink, lichen-covered rock

Vedauwoo

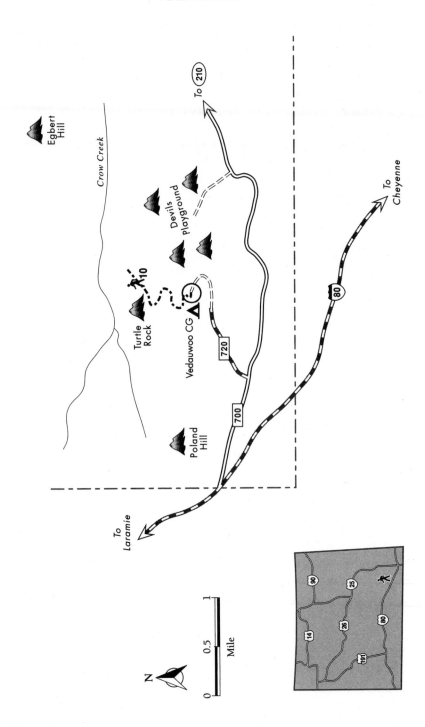

Fascinating Vedauwoo rock formations.

mountains. Smooth granite boulders display a gamut of shapes and sizes. The trail zigs and zags for about 0.75 mile, ending way too soon at a lofty and picturesque overview of the Crow Creek valley and the jagged Sherman Mountains to the north.

Although a short trail, the opportunity for play and exploration in this area is unlimited. A person can easily log 5 or more miles by simply exploring around the rock bases and by scrambling up any alluring ravines that pleat the rock structures. Such exploration opportunities become especially true if you continue eastward along Forest Road 700. For 6 miles past the campground area there are endless places to park the car and wander into unique and exciting rocky, high mountain prairie and woodland settings. In fact, the popular campground area can be quite crowded while the Devils Playground to the east of it is empty. As is so often the case, isolation and unappreciated beauty await but a mile away from the crowds. The land is gentle, open, and conducive to cross-country hiking.

Water should be carried in this country, as most of the streams dry up as summer progresses. Also remember that climbing up the rocks is much easier than climbing down, and rescues of stuck hikers are not uncommon.

11 Headquarters National Recreation Trail

General description:	A fun day hike through an amazing variety of mountain habitat.
Distance:	4 to 8 miles.
Difficulty:	Easy to moderate.
Elevation gain and loss:	+600 feet, -200 feet.
Key elevation points:	Summit Rest Area Trailhead: 8,420 feet.
General location:	13 miles east of Laramie in the Sherman Mountains.
Maps:	Medicine Bow National Forest Laramie/Hayden visitor map; USGS: Sherman Mountains West.
Manager:	Medicine Bow National Forest, Laramie Ranger District.

Finding the trailhead: Turning south after leaving Interstate 80 via exit 323—the Happy Jack Road exit—takes you to the Summit Rest Area. Instead of turning into the rest area, continue south on Forest Road 705. There is a trailhead 0.5 mile down this road, where the pavement ends. Being next to the rest area, it was fairly crowded, and I opted to seek out the "other side of the mountain." The views were well worth it; drive 4.3 miles along Forest Road 705 to a well-signed intersection where Forest Road 707 jogs to the north. Another 2.2 miles along this gravel road brought me to a sign announcing the Headquarters Trail. No other cars were at this trailhead.

The hike: The Sherman Mountains, viewed from Interstate 80, appear to be bland little blips of rock sitting atop an uninteresting prairie. The Headquarters Trail again proves that books should not be judged by their covers, especially when read at 70 miles per hour. The mountains are named for Civil War General W.T. Sherman by a surveyor, Grenville Dodge, who discovered them when he was chased this way by Indians in 1855. Sherman Pass, at 8,235 feet elevation, was the highest point on the Union Pacific's turn-of-the-century railroad.

This well-maintained and easy-to-follow National Recreation Trail can be hiked as a 4 mile round trip to a scenic overlook, an 8 mile round trip to the Summit rest area and back, or a 4 mile one-way (2-car exchange or thumb back) jaunt to the rest area. Whatever you choose, it's the kind of trail that urges you to take your time and enjoy the scenery. It passes through a gamut of environments, from sage and grassland meadows to aspen, ponderosa, lodgepole, and limber pine forests; from moist north-sloping climates to south-sloping dry and rocky biotas. At any point one can leave the trail and climb the pinkish granite rock outcroppings for exceptional views of the endless prairies below. The first 1.5 miles sport a fair uphill grade. The last half mile of the trail, before it reaches the rest area, crosses a high and treeless plateau. In between, the country and plant life constantly change.

Headquarters National Recreation Trail

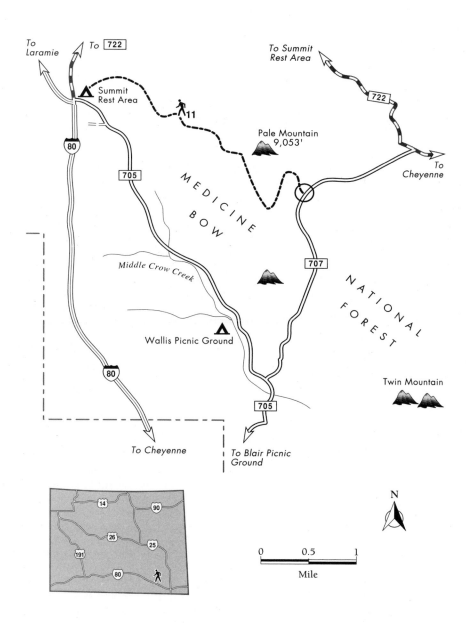

A surprising feeling of wildness holds the entire area.

Water will probably be nonexistent both on the trail and in the forest should you decide to camp in the country. Both Vedauwoo (Hike 10) and these mountains, with all the exposed rock, really cook in July and August. Spring and fall are ideal times to hike here.

South-Central Wyoming

THE SIERRA MADRE RANGE

Wyomingites have created a poignant economic history of cyclic booms and busts that center around natural resources, especially minerals. An exceptional, lower-altitude Continental Divide range named the Sierra Madres has been the site of this oft-repeated history. When a simple sheepherder's red clay turned out to be 70 percent pure copper in 1896, the path was paved for the (then) world's largest copper mine to spring into being. A dozen years passed before the owners went bankrupt. The Encampment area's glorious precursor to the state's future uranium and oil booms and busts slipped into ghost town ruins and forsaken human ambitions.

Today the mining is a memory, but the friendly town of Encampment survives as a take-off point for excellent hiking. Approximately 45 miles of the Continental Divide National Scenic Trail cross through the Brush Creek/Hayden Ranger District of the Medicine Bow National Forest. Four smaller wilderness areas thrive in these mountains, offering the hiker everything from rugged and narrow river canyons to high-elevation grandeur to secluded forest paths. If history is a hobby you pursue, nowhere is it more vividly presented than at the Grand Encampment Museum located in the town of Encampment. A few hours spent touring this no-cost and incredible re-creation of historic buildings and settings will add much depth to the sights (or sites) you might discover when hiking this area. Call or write the Grand Encampment Museum, P.O. Box 395, Encampment, WY, 82325, 307-327-5308.

12 Encampment River and Wilderness Area

General description:	A 2- to 3-day hike beside the rushing rapids and calm, smooth stretches of a unique wilderness river.
Distance:	16 miles, one way to shuttle.
Difficulty:	Moderate.
Elevation gain:	1,300 feet.
Key elevation points:	Encampment BLM Trailhead: 7,500 feet; Commissary Park Trailhead: 8,800 feet.
General location:	6 miles south of the town of Encampment, on BLM lands and in the Medicine Bow National Forest.
Special attractions:	Rugged and uncrowded canyon; brook and brown trout fishing in the Encampment River.
Maps:	Hayden section of the Medicine Bow National Forest visitor map; USGS: Encampment, Dudley Creek.
Manager:	Brush Creek/Hayden Ranger District, Medicine Bow National Forest.

Finding the trailhead: To reach the Encampment trailhead, take Wyoming 70 west through the town of Encampment. Just 0.2 mile west of the town, a BLM sign points left or south to the Encampment River Trail and Campground. This gravel/dirt road is easy to follow for its 2 mile length. A second road skirts a wooden fence surrounding the campground and leads to an obvious parking lot. Walk through a gate and a short distance upriver, across a bridge, and you're at the trailhead.

To reach the Commissary Park trailhead, drive west from Encampment on Wyoming 70 to the forest boundary. Turn south on well-signed Forest Road 550 and follow it for 15.5 miles. Turn left or southeast onto Forest Road 496 (Rim Road) and drive 3 miles to the parking lot.

The hike: Local history—not to be confused with official history—tells the story of how Thomas Edison once went fishing in the Encampment area. He shattered his bamboo pole beyond repair and, that night, he threw the splintered rod into the campfire. The stringy bamboo filaments glowed in the heat and supposedly inspired Edison to try a filament for the lighting elements in his bulbs. If Edison ever actually did fish in the area, I'm surprised he ever left to return to his laboratory.

The Encampment River is a surprisingly large and swift-moving stream. Hiking its shores in May and June can place you beside powerful cascades of whitewater. The first 4 miles of the trail are a BLM production. The surrounding hills are sage covered and rather bald, while the river is lined with cottonwoods. Scenery-wise, the country is awesome. It's a real treat to watch the conifer trees slowly invade, then predominate the habitat as you walk up the river. If you plan this trip as a day hike, a delightful view of the

Encampment River and Wilderness Area

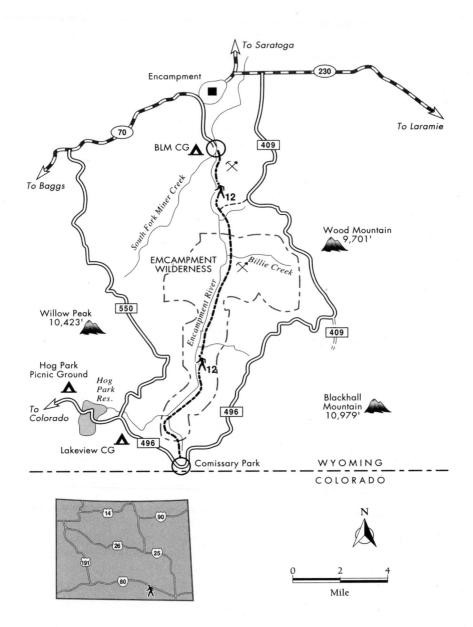

river canyon setting can be found in the first mile beyond the Forest Service boundary (4 miles up the trail). Here the trail climbs a hillside and cuts back into Purgatory Gulch. This aspen-lined creek marks the wilderness boundary.

For the first few miles after entering the wilderness, the trail meanders peacefully through various woodland settings. Several campsites are found here, and the river seems to sing a mostly mellow song. Go 7 miles up canyon and the trail again climbs high onto the hillside. The water now carves its way through a narrow and rocky gorge, and the river churns powerfully. A few miles later the trail does return to the river bottom, but the forest is now thick lodgepole and spruce and campsites are scarce to find in the rocky and narrow channel.

This 16-mile trail ends at a trailhead named Commissary Park. A great one-way, two-vehicle trip could be had by parking one car at the BLM campground and the other at Commissary Park. The Encampment River is a blue-ribbon fishing area. Be advised that the first mile of the river from the BLM campground has no public access. Other than 1 private holding near the Forest Service boundary, the rest of the river is open to fishing. The lower trail loses snow and is hikable early, but you should plan on conducting a thorough tick inspection afterwards. Of the several side streams that cross the trail, I only had to wade Billie Creek, and it was no more than knee deep and a short distance.

13 Platte River Wilderness/ Northgate Canyon

General description:	A long and rugged day hike or enjoyable overnighter beside the shores of a wild and scenic river.
Distance:	14 miles round trip.
Difficulty:	Moderate.
Elevation gain or loss:	Less than 500 feet.
Key elevation points:	Sixmile Gap Trailhead: 7,800 feet; Platte River Trailhead: 7,420 feet.
General location:	25 miles southeast of Encampment, in the southwestern corner of the Medicine Bow Range.
Special attractions:	Blue-ribbon trout fishing, abundant and varied wildlife and waterfowl, a powerful river.
Maps:	Hayden section of the Medicine Bow National Forest visitor map; USGS: Elkhorn Point, Overlook Hill, Horatio Rock, Keystone.
Manager:	For the land west of the Platte River: Brush Creek/ Hayden Ranger District, Medicine Bow National Forest. For the land east of the Platte River: Laramie Ranger District.

Finding the trailhead: Wyoming 230 begins its roundabout journey to Laramie 1 mile north of Encampment. On this most scenic route look for a green road sign 24 miles east of Encampment pointing east to what's called the Sixmile Road. This is also Forest Road 492 and leads to the Sixmile Gap Campground. Forest Road 492's 2-mile distance is graveled and quite narrow, and deadends just east of the campground at the trailhead. Here an information sign explains the Platte River Wilderness and introduces Platte River Trail Number 473.

The hike: The Encampment River (Hike 12), despite its large size, radiates the lively spirit of a swift mountain stream and feels like an instrument playing a high alto string. The neighboring North Platte River vibrates in solid bass tones. Its water moves more surely and with a deeper, more powerful rhythm.

I hiked this canyon in late May, and the water volume and hydraulics were awesome to behold. Some feel that fall is the best time to experience this canyon, when peaceful waters offer more fishing, swimming, and bald eagle observation opportunities. They may be right in one sense. Traveling this trail in the spring yielded more ticks per mile than any other trail I've hiked.

This is a fairly rugged trail that traverses equally rugged country. The first several miles are not thickly forested but do contain many great and towering conifer trees. Every half mile or so, flat land benches overlook the

The Platte River Wilderness Area.

Platte River Wilderness/Northgate Canyon

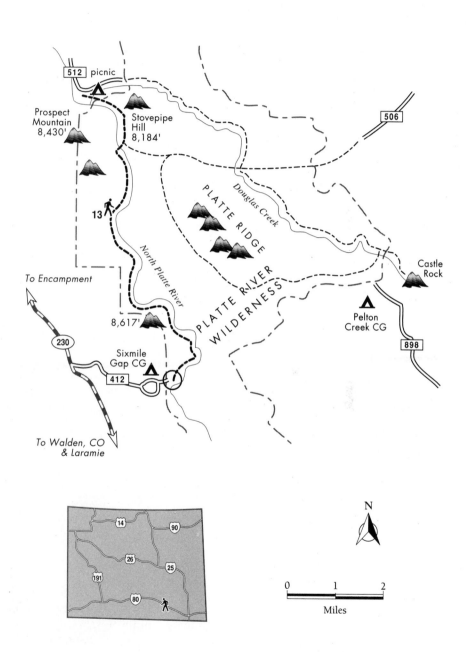

river and afford good camping spots. After 3.5 miles, the canyon narrows while the trail climbs to high and rocky overviews of the area. It's another 1.5 miles before the trail rejoins the river bottom. These last miles, beyond North Gate Canyon, offer an entirely different face: an easy-going river and cottonwood/aspen-covered land benches that gently slope toward the water. Here, open slopes afford great cross-country journeying. After 6 miles of hiking, the trail grows dim, and 1 mile later it ceases to exist. The district ranger notes that during late August and September it is sometimes possible to ford the river and follow a trail along the eastern shore 2 miles north to Pickaroon Campground and the northwest boundary of the wilderness.

If you are a bird watcher, waterfowl and raptors are ubiquitous and abundant in this area. Be aware that the only source of water on this particular trail is the river; there are no real side canyon streams along the trail. The North Gate Canyon is a river runner's paradise. Often the trailhead parking lot will appear crowded, but most of the vehicles belong to water buffs. Most of the anglers who frequent the trail never travel more than the first few miles.

Three other trails now exist in the Platte River Wilderness area (see map).

14 Savage Run Wilderness

General Description:	A day or overnight journey into an unknown, tiny, 23-square mile wilderness.
Distance:	18 miles roundtrip.
Difficulty:	Easy to moderate.
Elevation loss:	1,880 feet.
Key elevation points:	Trailhead: 9,650 feet; trail end: 7,770 feet.
General location:	40 miles east of Laramie, on the southwestern flanks of the Medicine Bow Mountains.
Special attractions:	A great little place of forest preservation amid a very over-roaded mountain range. Unique forest and meadow habitat.
Maps:	The Medicine Bow National Forest visitor map; USGS: Keystone, Overlook Hill.
Manager:	Laramie Ranger District.

Finding the trailhead: From Laramie, follow Wyoming 130 west for 24 miles. Here, 6 miles before Centennial, Wyoming 11 veers southwest toward Albany. Continue through Albany and you automatically find yourself on well-maintained, gravel Forest Road 500. Several roads will intersect this main route, but all are signed. If in doubt, always opt for the fork indicating French Creek Campground or Forest Road 500. Almost 14 miles from Albany, a sign will point south or left to a four-wheel-drive-only road and the Savage Run Wilderness. Take this rough road 2 miles to a large sign announcing the Savage Run Wilderness trailhead.

Savage Run Wilderness

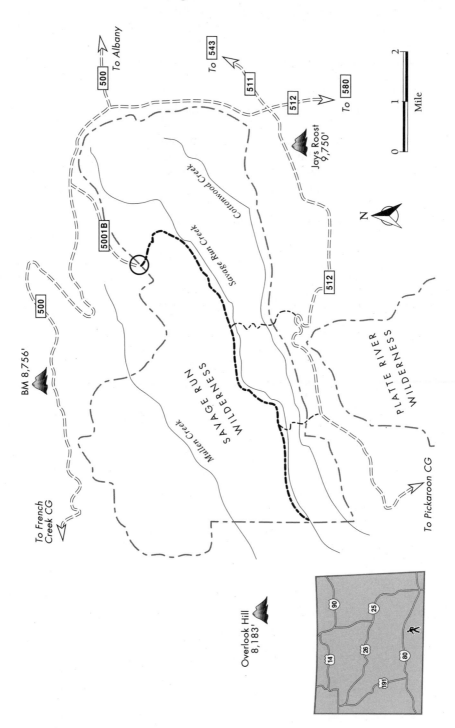

The hike: Unusual in this mountainous country, the Savage Run Trail is a gentle downhill hike. Just a short distance through a recent clearcut puts you inside the wilderness boundary and provides a living example of why wilderness protection is so badly needed. The trees in this lodgepole forest are huge, yet unlike most similar forests, the floor of the woods looks almost manicured. As the trek downhill continues, the woods do get thicker and more jumbled as a blend of spruce trees infiltrate the lodgepole domain.

At 1 mile a large meadow appears to the left, and at 1.5 miles the trail crosses a boggy part of that meadow. If the trail becomes hard to follow, just continue south, staying along the west side of the meadow. At 2 miles the bog turns into a little creek, and this pretty and polite Savage Run creek will be your companion for the next 7 miles as the trail wanders along its northern banks through ever-changing forest settings. You won't be treated to any sweeping views, but if you're into listening to forests speak, this is the place.

Two short and steep exit-to-the-south trails exist along this run, one about 4 miles along and another a bit over 7 miles. They are neither marked nor easy to find.

Camping is wonderful all along the creek, and the water is good. The trail has to be hiked as an out-and-back deal, as it deadends about 9 miles downstream at some private property. Remember, it's easy to get trucking downhill and forget that the last half of the journey—the exit—will be moderately but continuously uphill.

15 Baby Lake Trail

General description:	A generally secluded trail through forests and mountain meadows.
Distance:	9 miles one way to shuttle.
Difficulty:	Strenuous.
Elevation gain or loss:	-400 feet, +1,250 feet, -100 feet.
Key elevation points:	Trailhead: 9,150 feet; Continental Divide: 10,000 feet.
Special attractions:	Offers a chance to tie into the Continental Divide National Scenic Trail.
General location:	20 miles west of Encampment, in the northern section of the Huston Park Wilderness Area.
Maps:	Medicine Bow National Forest visitor map; USGS: Bridger Peak, Red Mountain.
Fees:	$6 to $9 per night at area campgrounds.
Manager:	Brush Creek/Hayden Ranger District, Medicine Bow National Forest.

Finding the trailhead: Drive west from Encampment on Wyoming 70 for 20 miles. On the way, you'll cross the Continental Divide at Battle Pass (9,916 feet). This spot, and a location 1 mile south at the Huston Park Trailhead, are good places to park 1 vehicle if you want to make a 9 mile, one-way hike on the Baby Lake Trail. Approximately 6 miles farther, a few hundred feet before the Lost Creek Campground, turn left (south) onto Forest Road 811. After 300 feet make another left turn onto a more primitive road and travel 0.75 mile south to the trailhead. If you're driving a low-clearance vehicle, you should park along the gravel just off the highway.

The hike: The Baby Lake Trail is a scenic hike through lodgepole pine forests and high mountain meadows. Although easily completed in one day, there are numerous campsites available along the way. The trail gets its name from the fact that it follows Baby Lake Creek. It does not specifically go to Baby Lake.

On foot from the parking lot, continue south and downhill on a primitive road to the Huston Park Wilderness boundary. The road pre-dates the area's wilderness designation. In 0.5 mile it descends 400 feet to an old sheep bridge across Battle Creek.

The bridge and the Baby Lake Trail are legacies of sheep grazing on national forest lands. Reconstructed in 1962 to provide access for sheep grazing, it now provides access for hikers and backpackers. Sheep use of the Baby Lake area was discontinued in 1986. While hiking this area, notice that most of the trees are relatively young. Huge fires, on the scale of the recent Yellowstone conflagration, killed many of the trees in the Sierra Madre Mountains between 120 and 140 years ago. For about 100 years after these fires the area was relatively open, meaning the trees were small and there was room between them for grass and shrubs to grow. Over the past several

Baby Lake Trail

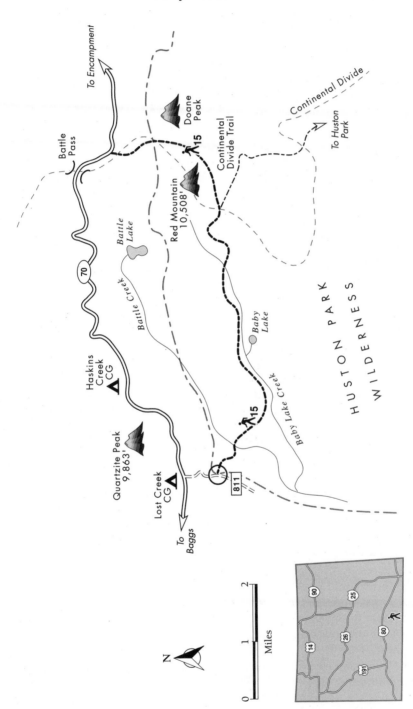

decades, as the trees have grown larger, they have shaded out more of the ground. This shading has gradually decreased the amount of grass and forbs for livestock and wildlife.

After crossing the bridge, bear left up a short hill. Blazes and cairns mark the trail from this point on. For the next hour or so, your hike will be through lodgepole pine forests. In about 2 miles the trail begins to parallel Baby Lake Creek. Out of sight of the trail, the creek is evident by the murmur it makes behind a screen of alder and willows. Baby Lake is located about 0.8 mile south of the trail in a large meadow. The term "lake" is generous.

In a short time the vegetation begins the transition from heavy forest to an area of mixed forest and mountain meadows. The trail across these meadows is often overgrown with lush grass. Be alert for blazes on trees at the far end of the meadow. Cairns and posts also mark the route. These meadows are a favorite bedding ground for the many deer and elk in the area.

After traveling through several meadows, the trail gradually steepens until it reaches the Continental Divide at the low saddle just south of Red Mountain. This can be a turnaround point, or one can continue and turn south onto the Continental Divide National Scenic Trail and into alpine Huston Park. Looking back, one gets a great view of the Snake River Valley. Ahead are lush meadows at the head of Long Peak.

For those who left a vehicle near Battle Pass, continue on and slightly downhill for another 0.25 mile to the junction with the Huston Park Trail. Turning north, it's a short 3 miles to the highway at Battle Pass.

In 1968 the National Trails System Act was passed and included authorization for the study of the Continental Divide National Scenic Trail. The CDNST proposed to be a continuous trail from Canada to Mexico, totaling 3,100 miles, spanning 25 national forests, 3 national parks, 4 BLM districts, endless private land, and 5 basic life zones as it traverses the Rocky Mountains. This trail does not yet exist in completed form, but 45 miles do exist in the Brush Creek/Hayden District of the Medicine Bow National Forest. About 13 miles of the CDNST follow the Continental Divide in the 31,000 acre Huston Park Wilderness. These miles of trail have recently been re-marked and maintained.

—Mike Murphy

Medicine Bow Mountains

THE SNOWY RANGE

Directly west of the flat, dry, high prairie surrounding Laramie, Wyoming 130 climbs to above timberline and into a gorgeous display of alpine beauty. The Snowy Range and its high-altitude flora and fauna sit atop the northern end of the Medicine Bow Mountains. This unique range, with its quartzite cliff faces and many-laked basins, reflects the ancient glacial activity that carved its present physical features and stark beauty. It is so named because snow exists perpetually on some of the mountain slopes.

Lorraine Bonney, author of numerous Wyoming guides and narratives, notes: "The Medicine Bows may be one of the most abused mountain ranges in the country." The entire mountain range—except for the Snowy Range— looks like a checkers game where the surviving forest has had most of its pieces jumped by clearcuts. Recreationists need to loudly voice support for the few remaining roadless areas in these mountains, before logging, oil, gas, and mineral developments hedge out hikers and elk.

Snowy Range high lake country. MIKE GOSSI PHOTO

Except for climbing Medicine Bow Peak, the Snowy Range trails presented in this book mention alternative approaches—via less popular trailheads—to the creek bottoms, ridgetops, and open alpine country of this range. As is the case everywhere, a little cross-country trekking in this glorious mountain land quickly separates you from almost everyone else.

16 Sheep Lake Trail

General description:	A day hike or 2- to 3-day backpacking trip on a relatively untraveled trail.
Distance:	8 miles one way to shuttle.
Difficulty:	Easy to moderate.
Elevation gain or loss:	+250 feet, -700 feet.
Key elevation points:	Brooklyn Lake: 10,550 feet; Sheep Lake: 10,800 feet; Sand Lake: 10,100 feet.
General location:	45 west of Laramie, in the middle of the Snowy Range.
Special attractions:	Deer, elk, coyotes, subalpine parks and wildflowers; good fishing and camping.
Maps:	Hayden section of the Medicine Bow National Forest visitor map; USGS: Sand Lake.
Fees:	$2 user fee, payable at trailhead's self-service station. Campground fees in the area range from $7 to $9.
Manager:	Brush Creek/Hayden Ranger District.

Finding the trailhead: The southern trailhead begins at Brooklyn Lake near the Brooklyn Lake Campground. Signs direct you to this area 4.5 miles east of Snowy Range Pass on Wyoming 130. Here Forest Road 317 exits the highway north at the Nash Fork Campground and winds north just over 2 miles to the Brookland Lake Campground and the trailhead.

The northern trailhead begins 100 yards east of Sand Lake. Sand Lake is accessible from Interstate 80 by taking exit 272 north of Arlington and driving west along the frontage road for 1.2 miles. Here a sign directs you south onto what becomes Forest Road 111. Follow it for 13 miles to the intersection of Forest Road 101. Turn left, or east, here, and 1 mile later you come to the Deep Creek Campground. A road turns south off of this campground and leads to the trailhead. These roads, being well-maintained logging roads, are fine for the smallest compact car. Sand Lake is also accessible from Wyoming 130 by going 2.5 miles west of the tiny town of Centennial to turn onto Forest Road 101. It's a 20-mile northward drive along this gravel road to the Deep Creek Campground.

The hike: Beginning at the Brooklyn Lake Campground and traveling north, the hiker finds a rocky, well-traveled trail rising 250 feet over the 2.5 miles

Sheep Lake Trail

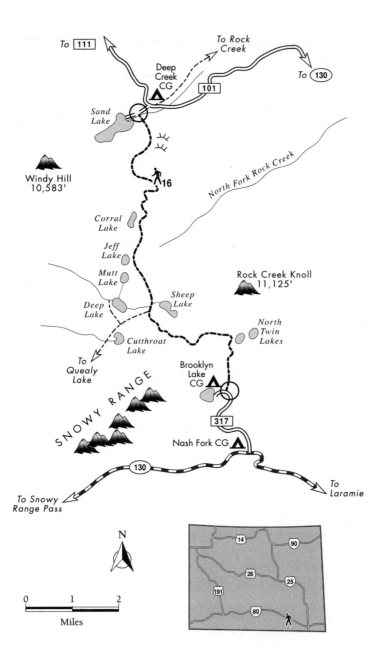

To 111

To Rock Creek

Deep Creek CG

To 130

101

Sand Lake

North Fork Rock Creek

Windy Hill 10,583'

16

Corral Lake

Jeff Lake

Rock Creek Knoll 11,125'

Mutt Lake

Deep Lake

Sheep Lake

North Twin Lakes

Cutthroat Lake

To Quealy Lake

SNOWY RANGE

Brooklyn Lake CG

317

Nash Fork CG

130

To Snowy Range Pass

To Laramie

N

0   1   2
Miles

14

90

26

25

191

80

to Sheep Lake. Don't be surprised to find several hundred sheep grazing along the way, as the land is leased from the Forest Service. Sheep Lake and neighboring Deep Lake are popular day and overnight hikes.

North of Sheep Lake hiker traffic thins considerably and so does the trail. The countryside here is formed from high glacial plains and contains few trees. Jeff Lake provides cover, campsites and fair fishing. Farther north at Corral Lake, the remnants of old horse pens can be found. Here the trail is relatively flat, traveling slightly downhill through lush grass meadows that alternate with forested settings. The final mile before Sand Lake turns into an old jeep track through the timber.

Late season travel is advised in this country if you want to avoid mosquitoes and experience an abundance of wildflowers. Spring comes exceptionally late to this high land. For those wishing to travel longer distances, this trail can be combined with Hike 17 where you continue north past Sand Lake and view the entirety of descending Snowy Range ecosystems.

—Mike Gossi

17 Deep Creek/Rock Creek

General description:	A day or overnight trip on an excellent trail through timbered settings.
Distance:	11 miles one way to shuttle.
Difficulty:	Easy to moderate.
Elevation loss:	2,020 feet (2,020-foot gain if starting at Rock Creek).
Key elevation points:	Deep Creek Trailhead: 10,120 feet; Rock Creek Trailhead: 8,100 feet.
General location:	35 miles west of Laramie, in the northern section of the Snowy Range.
Special attractions:	A wonderful chance to follow a mountain stream from high glacial plains to the high desert floor. Good fishing.
Maps:	Hayden section of the Medicine Bow National Forest map; USGS: Sand Lake, Arlington, White Rock Canyon.
Manager:	Brush Creek/Hayden Ranger District.
Fees:	$2 user fee at Deep Lake Trailhead; none at Rock Creek Trailhead. $7 to $9 per night campground fees.

Finding the trailhead: Follow the access directions to the Deep Creek Campground (Hike 16) for the southern trailhead and a downhill hike. For the Rock Creek access, leave Interstate 80 at exit 272, the Arlington exit, and travel 0.25 mile west along the frontage road. Where the sign indicates the Rock Creek Trailhead, turn left or south on the rougher road and travel 1.5 miles through private land to the northern Rock Creek trailhead and an uphill beginning.

Trail winding along the lower boundaries of Rock Creek

Deep Creek/Rock Creek

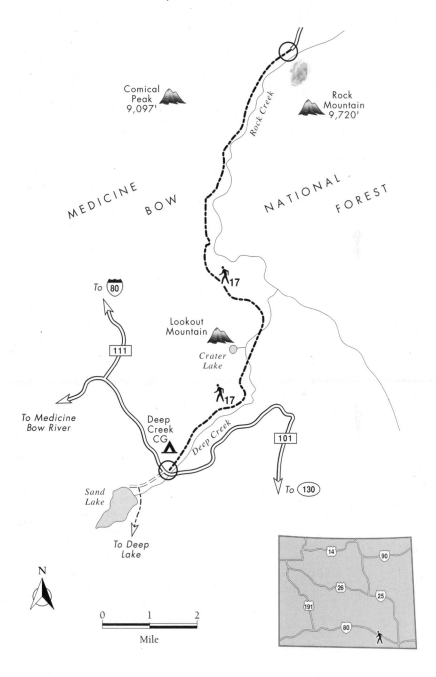

The hike: Deep Creek, which merges with and becomes Rock Creek, can be a point-to-point 11-mile hike. In 1883 this area boasted a major Union Pacific railroad cattle shipping center. Hundreds of carloads of cattle were shipped every day from here to northern Wyoming. Now the area plays a major role in Wyoming's bentonite production.

Beginning at the Deep Creek campground, the trail leads down from open glacial plains into forested canyons. Downstream 3.5 miles an unofficial trail cuts to the west and heads to Crater Lake. Here the hiker enjoys some nice campsites and good fishing. Despite its name, Crater Lake is glacially formed and spring fed.

Slightly over a mile farther the trail crosses Deep Creek and joins the western side of the larger Rock Creek drainage. There's an incredible overview of the forested country at this point. Then the trail travels downward through fir and spruce forests and into thinner pine forests as the canyon bottom nears the forest boundary. The rocky scenery is impressive here, and many old mining remnants in the form of cabins, ore car tressels, and mining pits exist on these mountainsides. The northern end of the trail is heavily used by joggers and day hikers. Fishing opportunities abound.

—Mike Gossi

18 Medicine Bow Peak

General description:	A good day hike that can be done as a loop and includes a scenic peak climb.
Distance:	4.5 to 7 miles.
Difficulty:	Easy to moderate.
Elevation gain and loss:	+1,513 feet, -1,813 feet if hiked as a loop from Mirror Lake to Lake Marie; +1,213 feet if hiked from Lewis Lake.
Key elevation points:	Mirror Lake trailhead: 10,500 feet; Medicine Bow Peak: 12,013 feet; Lake Marie Trailhead: 10,200 feet.
General location:	35 miles west of Laramie, near the Snowy Range Pass crest, in the Medicine Bow Mountains.
Special attractions:	Ready access plus fairly short and easy hiking for such unparalleled views and alpine peak grandeur.
Maps:	Hayden section of the Medicine Bow National Forest map and/or USGS: Medicine Bow Peak quad.
Fees:	$2 day use fee, self service at the trailhead.
Manager:	Brush Creek/Hayden Ranger District.

Finding the trailhead: The peak can be accessed from three locations. Sugarloaf Recreation Area, 0.5 mile east of Snowy Range Pass on Wyoming 130, provides the shortest route. Begin from the trailhead at Lewis Lake, which is reached by following the signs and driving 1 mile north of the main highway into the Sugarloaf Recreation Area.

Medicine Bow Peak

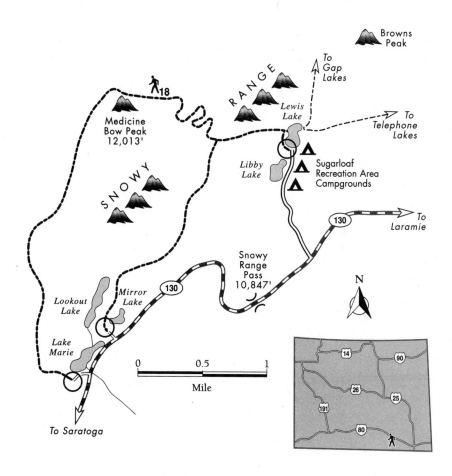

The hike: Medicine Bow Peak, at 12,013 feet, forms the highest summit in the Snowys. One of the area's first fire lookouts was built atop this lofty mountain, but it was eventually abandoned and dismantled because it was in the clouds most of the time. The well-marked and well-used path rises almost 1,300 feet to the summit in less than 2 miles.

Hiking from the Lake Marie Trailhead, located 1.5 miles west of Snowy Range Pass, adds an extra 300 feet elevation gain to the climb. This trail is not quite as steep as the Lewis Lake access and follows the gentle back side of the Snowy Range, providing great views to the north and west.

Mirror Lake Campground is the third access point. It's located about 1 mile west of Snowy Range Pass. Starting at this point, the hiker passes

A view from Medicine Bow Peak. MIKE GOSSI PHOTO

beside many small lakes and beneath the east face of Medicine Bow Peak. This Mirror Lake Trail joins the Lewis Lake Trail after a couple of miles, and it's about a mile to the top from this point.

—Mike Gossi

Central and Southern Wyoming

This vast and somewhat barren-looking section of high plateau desert composes much of Wyoming. Here the roads are many and long, and the trails, where they exist at all, are short. The mountain ranges that rise in this area haven't gained the attention that a national forest might bring to them. The extensive flats, rolling hills, and intermittent ravines of this country are known mostly to local ranchers and, more recently, by developers and ATVers.

But some hiking treasures do exist here for the people who know both where to seek them out and how to appreciate them for what they are. A large-scale topographical map of the area reveals endless hills and mini-mountain ranges, and a plethora of washes, many with alluring contours and names. A BLM surface map of the area shows who owns what and reveals that a majority of the land boasts federal or state government ownership. A trustworthy vehicle and an adventuresome spirit can place you in the middle of some of the wildest, most spectacular, and least known scenery in Wyoming.

The BLM is the majority stockholder on these lands, controlling nearly one-eighth of this country's land area. The 1976 Federal Land Policy and Management Act (FLPMA) authorized the agency to pursue multiple-use management directions, and lately the BLM appears to be taking a more balanced management approach. Recreation, habitat preservation, endangered species protection, and wilderness are found in the BLM's active vocabulary. Trails, wilderness study areas, and riparian rehabilitation areas are now being put together on these lands that "no one else wanted."

19 Garden Creek Falls

General description:	A steep and spectacular day hike to an impressive waterfall.
Distance:	2.5 miles round trip.
Difficulty:	Moderate.
Elevation gain:	270 feet.
Key elevation points:	Trailhead: 6,230 feet; top of waterfall: 6,500 feet; surrounding ridgetop: 7,760 feet; town of Casper: 5,250 feet.
General location:	A few miles directly south of Casper, on Casper Mountain.
Special attractions:	Great photo opportunities around an impressive waterfall. Although quite steep, there is some nice cross-country ridge hiking with good views.
Maps:	BLM Casper surface land management map; USGS: Casper.
Manager:	BLM Platte River Resource Area.

Finding the trailhead: After leaving Interstate 25 on exit 185, near the east end of Casper, turn south onto Wyoming 258 or Wyoming Boulevard. Circle the southern end of Casper for 6.5 miles on this road. Here, at a stoplight, a Casper Mountain Road sign and a Wyoming 251 sign point the direction southward. Drive uphill for 2 miles to the Wyoming 252 junction where you turn right or west and follow Wyoming 252 for 0.3 mile. A blue Rotary Park sign labels a paved road that veers off to the left. After 0.7 mile on this road you arrive at a graveled parking lot and the Garden Falls trailhead.

The hike: Anyone who has driven Interstate 25 south through Wyoming has noticed this alluring, timbered mountain rising above the prairie south of the city of Casper. Although most of Casper Mountain is privately owned and inaccessible, this small Rotary Club park affords the opportunity to explore a part of the steep topography overlooking the city. Garden Creek Falls, especially in the spring, is a sensational waterfall for this part of the world.

There are 2 ways to view these falls. Southeast of and before crossing the bridge over Garden Creek, a maintained trail wanders up the creek a short distance to the best overall vista of the waterfall. Across the bridge and along the western shore of Garden Creek, a second trail follows the water and soon climbs the steep cliffs surrounding the falls. This trail branches into many paths across the mostly vertical cliffs, but a main course does exist. NOTE: the trails on this side of the falls are unofficial. They sharply climb beside and above the 120-foot waterfall and offer some interesting views. A nice picnic area sits near the stream above the falls.

The "trails" that lead to the head of the falls are exceptionally steep and

Garden Creek Falls.

quite exposed. If you have a fear of heights, these are not for you. Also note that the area, being so near a larger city, is a party hotspot. Early morning is the best time to visit the country and view the falls.

An exciting addition to this short hike are the human "game" trails that break away from the paths on the west side of the creek and lead to a nice, less steep ridge walk that overlooks Casper and the prairie beyond. These access trails to the ridgetop are steep, but the ridge is unpopulated and worthy of exploration. Another opportunity to cross-country exists above the falls. Most folks quit hiking just beyond where the falls begin. But a sweet little path does trace its way up the canyon and through a woodland along the western side of the creek.

Garden Creek Falls

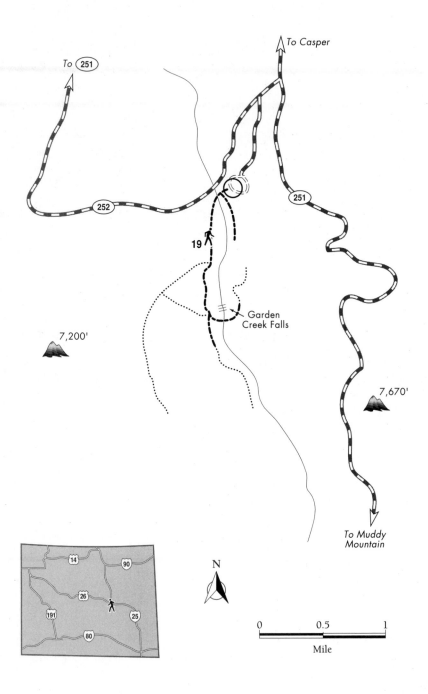

To (251)

To Casper

251

252

19

Garden
Creek Falls

7,200'

7,670'

To Muddy
Mountain

N

14   90

26

191   25

80

0   0.5   1
Mile

Be aware that cross-country paths leading to the top of the falls do exist on the eastern side of the creek, but they are steep, slippery, and dangerous. Map aficionados will notice that something labeled "Asbestos Spring" is located near the headwaters of Garden Creek. Perhaps you should carry your own drinking water to the park.

20 Muddy Mountain

General description:	A family and wheelchair-accessible hike on well-maintained interpretive trails.
Distance:	0.25 to 2.5 miles.
Difficulty:	Easy.
Elevation gain or loss:	Less than 200 feet.
Key elevation points:	Muddy Mountain: 8,200 feet.
General location:	18 miles directly south of Casper, in the Laramie Mountains.
Special attractions:	A flat mountaintop offering striking views of rolling Wyoming prairies; a chance to stroll through those prairies.
Maps:	BLM-Casper, 1:100,000 surface management map. USGS: Freeland, Crimson Dawn, Otter Creek.
Manager:	BLM Platte River Resource Area.

Finding the trailhead: Hike 19, Garden Creek Falls, gets you south of Casper and onto Wyoming 251. Continue along this paved road south and up the breathtaking switchbacks on Casper Mountain. Stay on the main road through a series of 3 county and Lions Club parks, finally topping a ridge and reaching the end of the pavement. Descending a couple of miles through spectacular country places you at the intersection of Natrona County 505 and Muddy Mountain Road. It's another 4.4 miles south and uphill to the Muddy Mountain Special Resource Management Area. Most of the prairie country to the west and along the county road is public land.

The hike: With a couple of campgrounds and several parking areas, this small, mountaintop, natural interpretive area offers easy access to some pretty sites. The northern boundary—the Rim Overlook Trail—affords astounding overviews of prairie drainages 1,200 feet below, which gradually spread out into the vast and rolling Wyoming countryside. The W.E. "Bill" Sauer Nature Trail system loops through several lodgepole forests settings, offering occasional interpretive information signs along the way.

West from the area's mountaintop, or from almost anywhere along Natrona County 505 toward Wyoming 487, you can spend a half day or more wandering from gully to ridge to ravine to prairie flat. Lodgepole forests give way to thinner pine settings, which yield to scrubby brush environments,

Muddy Mountain

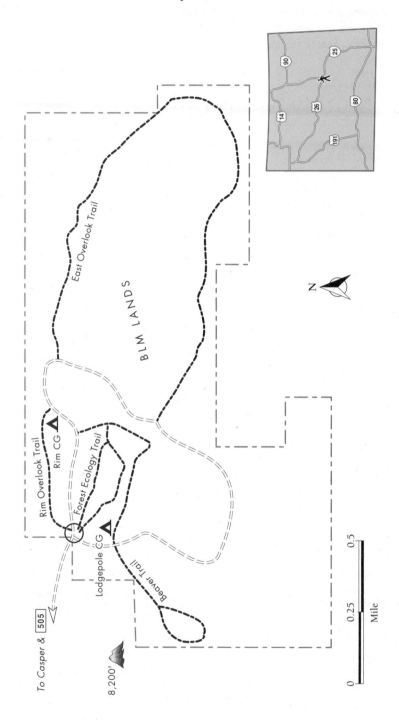

which lead into grasslands and sagelands, which transform into alkali flats and gulch bottoms. It's rugged country: you need to be both sure-footed and able to find your way back. But the unique flora and fauna are reminiscent of a land and a type of wandering that used to be more available. Be sure to carry drinking water, both on the mountaintop trails and along its untrailed flanks.

21 Ferris Mountains

General description:	A trail-less, virtually unknown mountain range.
Distance:	N/A.
Difficulty:	Expert hikers only.
Elevation gain or loss:	N/A.
Key elevation points:	Ferris Mountains Wilderness Study Area boundary: 7,500 feet; area peaks range from 8,039 feet to 10,037 feet.
General location:	45 miles north of Rawlins, near a high desert pass and small settlement called Muddy Gap.
Special attractions:	Solitary hiking; unknown deep canyons; high mountain ridges and peaks; all of it untrailed.
Maps:	BLM BAIROIL 1:100,000 surface management map; USGS: Spanish Mine, Youngs Pass, Muddy Gap.
Manager:	BLM Rawlins District.

Finding the trailhead: Driving north from Rawlins on U.S. Highway 287 for 45 miles places you at the one-gas-station town named Three Forks or Muddy Gap. South and east of this highway junction area lies the little-known range of the Ferris Mountains.

Currently it takes a real bloodhound to nose out the legal byways into this range. The only legal access into the Ferris Mountains at this time is via county and offshoot BLM roads on the north side of the range. In several places even the county roads have no signs, but they seem to be the more gravelly ones that intersect the main highway with stop signs. The BLM roads are primitive, high clearance, and barely maintained. One person driving on a road when it is too wet can leave rut damage and make it less passable for others. The map accompanying this area describes road access as it stands in 1998, but the recreation director's major recommendation is for individuals to contact the Rawlins BLM office before heading into the Ferris Mountains.

The hike: The absolute hardest chore a guidebook author faces is deciding whether or not to reveal to the hiking crowd the biggest secret he has discovered. The Ferris Mountains form a BLM wilderness study area of 22,245 acres, one of the largest untouched areas the BLM owns. Forested peaks up

Ferris Mountains

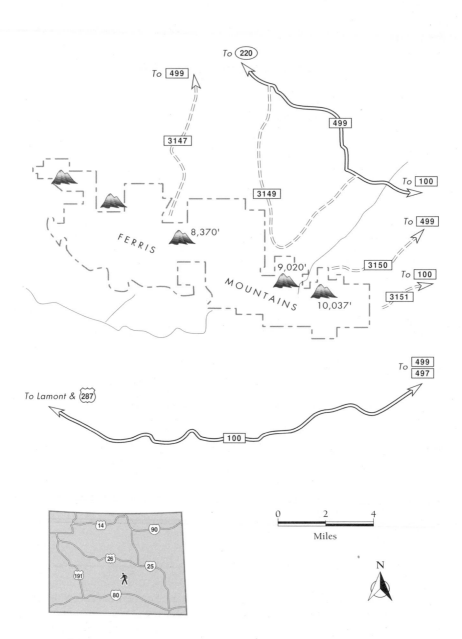

To (220)

To [499]

499

3147

To [100]

3149

To [499]

3150

To [100]

3151

FERRIS

8,370'

9,020'

10,037'

MOUNTAINS

To [499]
[497]

To Lamont & (287)

100

0   2   4
Miles

14   90

26   25

191

80

N

to 10,000 feet high hide the shrub-covered and unforested slopes, the grassy meadows, and the riparian zones that are present in the many open parks of this range. The mountains are rugged, quite steep, and essentially roadless. Wildlife abounds here, as does unusual geology.

The greatest joy of the Ferris Mountains is that they exemplify wilderness as wilderness used to be. Not only are they unscarred by roads, but they also contain no trails. The hiking experience of the Ferris Mountains is one of driving to the area, parking near the scenery or landscape that attracts you the most, and just wandering anywhere the calling takes you. I can't draw a map of a specific hike because there is none. This area is a vast playground without any of the confines (i.e., trails) we've allowed to dominate most other hiking playgrounds. Variety and surprising beauty rule this country. I wandered aimlessly for a day in the northeastern corner of the range and experienced vast, untrammeled valleys, crystal creeks, sandstone hogback ridges, flowers beyond comparison, juniper/pinyon forests, and snow-dappled forested mountaintops that sport incomparable views in all directions.

A trip into the Ferris Mountains is recommended for those who have strong map and compass skills. It is not for the novice hiker. The place offers you both the chance to grab a topo and test your orientation skills and the chance to test your luck at wandering into something new and surprising. (NOTE: There are some private land parcels in the mountains. Permission should be obtained from private landowners before using their lands—see Appendix I.)

The water in these mountains is good, which is to say that it's not alkali, as is most of the water in this section of Wyoming. However, lots of cattle roam this country. Also be aware that if it rains and your rig is off the county road, where you are will be home until the sun gets a chance to shine for a few hours.

The Ferris Mountains area has been recommended for wilderness classification by the BLM and the president. It now must gain similar approval from our "wilderness-loving" Republican Congress. Letters and loud voices are needed if this wild land is to remain that way.

22 Fossil Butte National Monument

General description:	A historic, geologically fascinating place to spend a day hiking.
Distance:	1.5 and 2.5 mile loops.
Difficulty:	Easy to moderate.
Elevation gain and loss:	Fossil Lake Trail: none. Quarry Trail: +600 feet.
General location:	12 miles west of Kemmerer along U.S. Highway 30.
Special attractions:	Fossils amid limestone cliffs, all deposited from an ancient lake bed. Open sagebrush country and picturesque buttes with excellent views.
Maps:	The Fossil Butte National Monument activities handout; USGS: Rock Slide, Nugget, Fossil, Kemmerer Reservoir.
Manager:	Fossil Butte National Monument.

Finding the trailhead: Fossil Lake Trail: From Kemmerer, drive west on U.S. Highway 30 for 10.5 miles. A sign here directs you north toward the national monument on paved Lincoln County 300. After 2.5 miles of westward driving, another sign points north and a paved road takes you 1 mile to the visitor center. Beyond the visitor center, continue following the paved road north and uphill for 2 more miles. A picnic ground is situated among a grove of aspen trees to the right, and 0.3 mile beyond this point a small parking lot marks the Fossil Lake Trailhead.

Quarry Trail: About 1 mile along Lincoln County 300, after you've turned off the main highway, a sign notes the location of the historic quarry trail, and a short paved road leads northward to a parking lot with vault toilets.

The hike: The Wyoming sagebrush-grasslands assume a new and exciting countenance in the state's southwestern corner. Here, white limestone and reddish shale buttes rise and fall like land-locked waves. Actually, waves is an apt description, because 50 million years ago this entire area was a vast subtropical lake teaming with multiple varieties of fish, insects, and plants. The ancient flora and fauna were perfectly preserved en masse by the calcium carbonate particles that covered them with a protective blanket. The site is now preserved by national monument classification, and here paleontologists still seek answers to questions about the past.

Highly recommended is a tour of the visitor center. The monument, has 2 separate hiking trails, and they serve as a nice introduction to the area. But a real joy for the hiker is to cross-country it to a high butte top and bask in the spacious and rolling sagebrush country scenery. The Park Service allows cross-country hiking.

NOTE: Within the monument everything, from fossils to flowers, is protected. It is illegal to remove any fossils. I did listen to stories of people

Fossil Butte National Monument

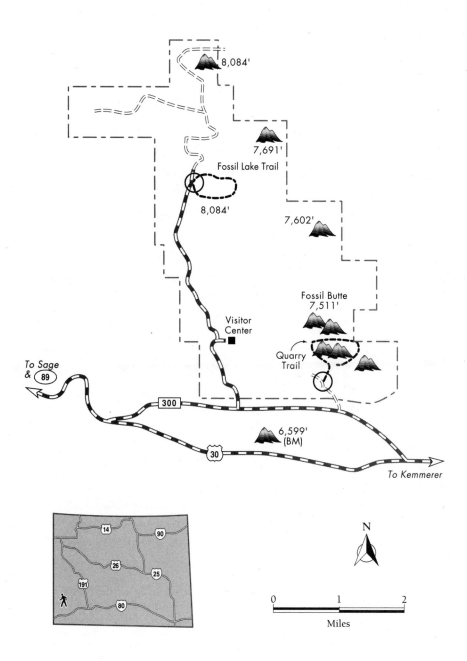

8,084'

7,691'

Fossil Lake Trail

8,084'

7,602'

Fossil Butte
7,511'

Visitor
Center

Quarry
Trail

To Sage
& 89

300

6,599'
(BM)

30

To Kemmerer

14

90

26

25

191

80

N

0   1   2
Miles

Limestone buttes contain fossilized flora and fauna, Fossil Butte National Monument.

spending time in jail for removing fossils they found lying on the ground.

Fossil Lake Trail: This 1.5 mile long, relatively easy trail offers the hiker a closeup view of the fauna and flora in the park. Musical and abundant aspen groves, high desert landscapes, even trickling springs and beaver ponds, can all be found on the hillsides this trail traverses. This loop trail also offers some of the best views in the park. The trail circles beneath the old quarry cliffs and then descends the steep hills through a thick and mature aspen grove. It ends at the picnic ground.

Quarry Trail: This 2.5 mile loop climbs to a historic fossil quarry on the face of Fossil Butte. Evidence of "fishermen," as the turn-of-the-century fossil collectors were called, can be seen along the route. This is an interpretive trail, and several unobtrusive markers explain the highlights of the history, geology, and wildlife of the area. The trail gains more than 600 feet elevation in a short distance. If the loop part of the trail is traveled clockwise, the uphill slope is not as steep. If it rains while you're hiking, count on sliding through some honest gumbo.

At the high northwest corner of the loop, a short side trail switchbacks up the butte's face to the old quarry site. West of this trail is the best place to cross-country hike to the top of Fossil Butte and into the scenic high sagebrush-shrublands. Bring a bottle of water, especially during summer. Also carry some binoculars, for wildlife and raptors are abundant.

23 Bear River State Park

General description:	A half-day saunter along river bottom trails. Also a 6-mile Volksmarch-accredited trail that follows a greenbelt area along the Bear River and into the city of Evanston.
Distance:	1 to 6 miles round trip.
Difficulty:	Easy.
Elevation gain and loss:	Less than 50 feet.
Key elevation points:	Visitor center: 6,748 feet.
General location:	1 mile east of Evanston, in the extreme southwestern corner of Wyoming.
Special attractions:	Cottonwood tree river bottom habitat and lots of birding.
Maps:	The Bear River State Park handout map; USGS quads aren't needed, but they would be Evanston and Millis.
Manager:	Bear River State Park.

Finding the trailhead: Drive to exit 6 on Interstate 80, 1 mile east of Evanston's main exit, and head south on paved Bear River Drive. After 1 block you'll see a large park sign directing you right, or west, and into the park. One trail begins immediately to the right by some restrooms; another begins about a quarter of a mile down the road, and a third trailhead starts at the southern end of the road in a picnic area.

The hike: Evanston, I'm told, used to exist several miles up the Bear River. But it became "just too wild a place," beyond hope, and a group of "decent" citizens burned it down and rebuilt the town in its current location. Bear River State Park's 280 acres were opened to the public in 1991. It's a pretty and peaceful place, and offers a bit of leg stretching and wildlife watching

Bear River State Park

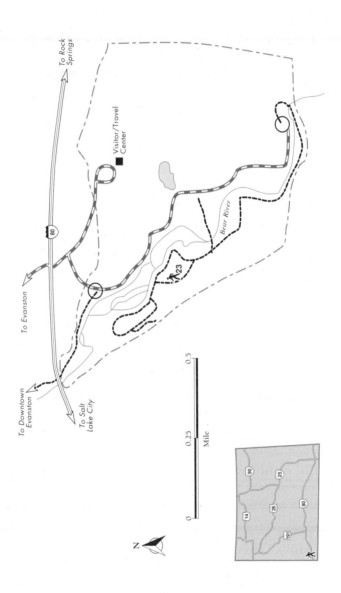

To Rock Springs

Visitor/Travel Center

80

Bear River

23

To Evanston

To Downtown Evanston

To Salt Lake City

N

0   0.25   0.5
Mile

90

25

14   26   80

191

in a corner of Wyoming where hiking trails are scarce.

Currently, the park itself has nearly 2 miles of trails. It's quite nice to wander the gravel loops on the west side of the river. One does get an idea of what riparian life in southeast Wyoming was like before it all became developed.

The Duncomb Trail, the first trail on the north end of the park, is paved and wheelchair accessible. Recently, this trail has been tied into a greenbelt project and extended under the interstate, along the river and through the city. Via the Evanston City BEAR (Better Environment And Recreation) project, it has evolved into a 6 mile Volksmarch-accredited trail (see Hike 2) that offers hikers a nice half-day journey.

North-Central Wyoming

THE BIG HORN MOUNTAINS

Wyoming boasts 50 peaks that tower more than 13,000 feet above sea level. Only 3 of these giants reside outside the Wind River Range, one of them being 13,167-foot Cloud Peak in the Big Horn Range. Blacktooth Mountain, at 13,005 feet, is another Big Horn summit. These impressive mountains sweep in a crescent arc from southern Montana toward the center of Wyoming where they nominally merge with the Owl Creek Mountains. The Big Horns offer granite summits, timbered slopes, crystalline water sources, and valuable habitat in the midst of the monotonous sagebrush prairies of the Powder River Basin to the east and the dry plains of the Bighorn Basin to the west. These basins, rich in uranium, oil, and coal, propose to devour much of the precious water supplied by the Big Horns.

Three Indian tribes, the Cheyenne, Sioux, and Crow, journeyed into these mountains for solitude and spiritual inspiration. The Crow Indians especially defended the Big Horns as hunting grounds and sacred areas. Today's Big Horn battles focus on the remaining pieces of the range's original structure, as industry, roads, and people all compete for a share of what's left of the mountain pie.

These mountains, 120 miles long and 50 miles wide, are dazzling in their recorded history, wilderness grandeur, spectacular alpine lakes, and hiking and exploration possibilities. More than 1,500 miles of trails offer a lot of access to these mountains and the surrounding areas.

24 Sykes Mountain/ Bighorn Canyon National Recreation Area

General description:	A half-day expedition into some harsh and seldom visited Wyoming landscapes.
Distance:	2 to 4 miles round trip.
Difficulty:	Moderate.
Elevation gain:	800 feet.
Elevation key points:	Bighorn Lake: 3,640 feet; Sykes Mountain Trailhead: 3,800 feet; Crooked Point: 4,618 feet.
General location:	12 miles north of Lovell, by the western shores of Bighorn Lake in the Bighorn Canyon National Recreation Area.
Special attractions:	Untrammeled desert country; great views of the Bighorn Basin, the Big Horn Mountains and the Pryor Mountains extending into Montana.
Maps:	USGS: Sykes Spring.
Fees:	$5 per day use fee; $30 annual pass.
Manager:	National Park Service, Bighorn Canyon National Recreation Area.

Finding the trailhead: Two miles east of Lovell on U.S. Highway Alternate 14 (14A), Wyoming 37 ventures north and into the recreation area. Follow this paved road about 10 miles to the well-signed Horseshoe Bend turnoff. For the last couple of miles, a mound of reddish rock will be visible to the east. This unimpressive (from the road) hunk of nothing is Sykes Mountain. An aging camp store on the west side of Wyoming 37 (just south of the Horseshoe Bend Road) is one place to park. Since this store was recently bought by the National Park Service and its fate is undecided, the ranger suggests parking at or north of the national recreation area entrance sign.

The hike: The Sykes Mountain cross-country adventure is certainly not a hike for everybody. It is geared for trekkers well versed in cross-country travel. Those who love to wander will probably enjoy this bizarre piece of landscape. I guarantee your first thought after parking will be, "Why on earth would I want to hike on this dismal pile of rubble?" I also guarantee that appearances are deceiving.

The easiest access to this desert mountain follows the first dry, unnamed little north-south drainage that intersects the Horseshoe Bend Road. Hike about 0.1 mile east of the Wyoming 37/Horseshoe Bend Road intersection and turn south and into the first canyon. If you cut up the second north-south drainage to the east, you'll soon be up against an impassable cliff. A

Sykes Mountain/Bighorn Canyon
National Recreation Area

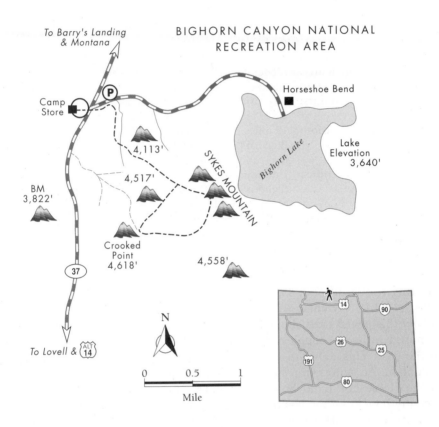

great game trail exists on the west side of this first drainage, and you can follow it into the canyon. Where a rockslide heaps into the canyon bottom, the game trail crosses to the east side of the drainage and continues its upward climb. This is the last game trail clue I can offer, for the canyon and climb now become a fascinating piece of cross-country work in finding your way upward through a maze of miniature canyons, scrub juniper, and ragged rock formations. The journey is never too difficult, but it is always rugged and climbs a series of rocky stepping stones.

After a mile weaving upward, you face a gaping canyon whose ridge forces the journey eastward. (A park ranger notes that this canyon forms an alternative pathway to ascend to the escarpment from the road.) Traveling eastward as far as possible, you come to a steep escarpment that overlooks the Horseshoe Bend area of Bighorn Lake, the Bighorn Canyon area and the Pryor Mountains to the north. From here the highest point of the mountain, Crooked Point, is visible. It's worth it to wander across the rock and sand flats and up the hillside to this summit. Unusual weathered sandstone formations can be found atop that point, and the 360-degree view of the Bighorn Basin is astounding.

This land is harsh and stark. First appearances dictate that nothing could live up here. But after a few hours and several miles of wandering, I saw herds of mule deer, jumped from a few rattlesnake buzzes, and witnessed unique flowers that possibly grow only in that spartan environment. Plus, as the park ranger says concerning this particular hike: "On a nice, cool, September day, when the lake is full and the lake surface is like a mirror, the view north from the escarpment over Horseshoe Bend is special indeed."

Nice hiking west of the rim of the canyon also exists near the Montana/Wyoming border. Although the most dramatic part of this west-rim hiking lies north of the state line, it is accessible only by going through Wyoming.

Bring water on these hikes. It's dry, hot country. For that reason, early morning and early or late season are the best hiking times. These are not tennis shoe hikes—the terrain is far too rugged. And although there were a few rattlesnakes, they were quite friendly. They warned me of their presence long before I could have stepped on them.

25 Paint Rock Creek

General description:	A nice day or overnight hike into an exceptional canyon-country drainage on the western slopes of the Big Horn Mountains.
Distance:	16 miles round trip.
Difficulty:	Easy to moderate.
Elevation gain and loss:	1,100 feet.
General location:	50 miles northeast of Worland, in the BLM lands bordering the western Big Horn Mountains.
Special attractions:	Unique country—towering limestone cliffs above a pristine riparian creek setting. Excellent stream fishing.
Maps:	Bighorn National Forest visitor map, BLM Worland surface map, and/or USGS: Hyatt Ranch and Allen Draw quads. Lake Solitude quad is optional.
Manager:	BLM Worland District Office.

Finding the trailhead: Between Worland and Greybull, scenic Wyoming 31 travels east toward the Big Horn Mountains and to the tiny farming burg of Hyattville. One-half mile north of this town a paved road—the Alkali-

Canyonlands-type cliff tower above Paint Rock Creek.

Cold Springs Road—continues the journey. Stay on the Cold Springs paved road when the Alkali part of this road turns to gravel and jogs off to the north. The pavement ends 5 miles later. Here the Cold Springs Road goes left or north up a hill, and Hyatt Lane shoots right or south. Less than a mile beyond this intersection, along the Cold Springs Road, stands a sign marking the Paint Rock Creek Parking area.

Paint Rock Creek

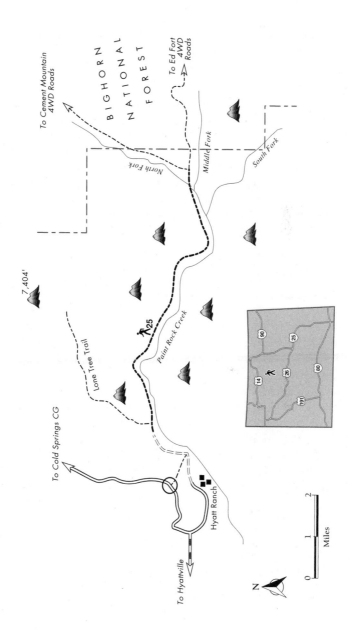

The hike: Paint Rock Creek possibly derived its name from the Indian tribes that used the multi-colored clay found on the creek's banks for ceremonial and war paint. Another story states that the creek was called Paint Rock for the Indian pictographs found on a nearby cliff.

The first level mile of this trail is on BLM land; then you hike 0.7 mile on private land graciously opened to public access by the Hyatt Ranch's owners, Grigsby Enterprises. Stay on the road that skirts the north side of several grassy hay fields. And be sure to close all gates you pass through. Near the towering cliffs of the mouth of the canyon, BLM land is again noted by a sign and a fence. Hiking now becomes ideal for the next 6 miles. The roadbed turns into a wide trail that is being reclaimed by returning vegetation. The walking is smooth and mostly level. The creek flow becomes quite large and has a powerful voice. But the most prominent feature of this journey is the castle-like, massive limestone cliffs.

One can camp almost anywhere in this canyon. One can also fish the stream or steeply climb and explore the various breaks in the canyon's walls. The forested bottom contains some of the largest junipers I've seen. Near the Forest Service boundary, North and Middle Paint Rock Creeks merge, and one can hike either stream a few miles and into a confusion of four-wheel-drive roads that surround the area. If you are in this canyon near sunset, be sure and look up. There is an amazing amount of eagle, hawk, falcon, and swallow activity between the lofty cliffs.

It's advisable to hike this area earlier in the year. For one, the ranch only allows access from April through September. Also, the summer is hot and the deer flies are profuse during late June and July. Another inarguable reason for early season visitations is that the main plant reclaiming the old roadbed is cheat grass. Most folks from the West know the havoc cheat grass plays with socks when it is dry.

Paint Rock Creek affords a Canyonlands-like experience in the middle of Wyoming. A corollary experience can be found in nearby Medicine Lodge State Archaeological Site, where pictographs and petroglyphs abound.

You might consider writing Grigsby Enterprises via the Hyatt Ranch (Hyattville, WY, 82428) and thanking them for allowing us access to such a unique area.

26 Middle Fork Powder River

General description: Extremely rugged landscape that offers myriad exploration opportunities.

Distance: 3 or more miles round trip for each of the 3 hikes.

Difficulty: Experts only.

Elevation gain and loss: -300 to 600 feet.

Key elevation points: Middle Fork Powder River: 5,200 feet; Fishing trail start: 5,600 feet; Outlaw Cave Trail start: 6,000 feet.

General location: 17 miles west and 6 miles south of Kaycee, on the very southern fringe of the Bighorn Mountains.

Maps: USGS: Poker Butte, Gordon Creek, Roughlock Hill, First Water Draw. Better overview topo maps from the BLM's 1:100 000 surface management maps include Kaycee and No Water (the latter for the upper portions of the river drainage). Since 20 percent of the land in this area is privately owned, these maps help one plot adventures without the threat of trespass.

Special attractions: Great fishing; prehistoric archaeological caves and historic outlaw legend caves; unpopulated country.

Manager: BLM Buffalo Resource Office.

Finding the trailhead: North of Casper 66 miles, or 46 miles south of Buffalo, take exit 254 off Interstate 25. This places you in the tiny cowman's town of Kaycee. Head directly west for 0.5 mile and turn left onto Wyoming 190 toward Barnum. At Barnum (a one-trailer town), 17 miles of paved road later, the pavement ends and the road divides. A "Middle Fork Powder River" management sign directs you south onto a gravel/dirt road. (NOTE: rain mixed with this road yields goosh, which is beyond mud, and two-wheel-drive rigs aren't going to traverse it.) Travel southward, paralleling gorgeous red sandstone hogbacks, through several private ranches for 5 miles to another BLM sign that points west and advises that passenger cars travel no further. One mile west and uphill was as far as my two-wheel-drive truck could travel, placing me at a parking area for the first fishing trail.

The hike: Once again, this particular hike description can only introduce you to some awesome country that can't be defined by regular hikes and trails. Geology has gone bonkers in this landscape, trying to decide if its goal is mountainous, prairie, or canyon country, and the result is a grand motif of all three. The Middle Fork of the Powder River forms a fascinating slit in the rolling prairie-hill lands, with dominating cliffs defining its snakelike parameters. The earth here, like Canyonlands National Park in Utah, is a lot of horizontal land interrupted by a lot of vertical land. You get to explore it.

Three "trails" access the river bottom along this Outlaw Cave BLM Road (Road 6217). The first drops 300 feet in about 0.5 mile. It is extremely

Middle Fork Powder River

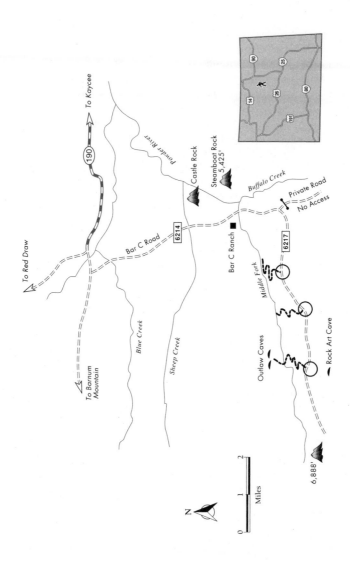

rugged and is difficult to follow due to the endless game and cattle trails jotting off of it. A second fishing access trail, 1 mile up the road, descends more than 350 feet and is extremely steep and rugged in its lower half. When you get to the river, unless you've brought rubber boots, or wading shoes and a stout walking stick, travel will be severely curtailed by thick brush and river-meeting cliffs.

Travel again 1.5 miles farther uproad to a primitive campground and access trail to the Outlaw Cave. This best-of-the-three but still rough trail drops 600 feet to the river bottom, and then requires a wade to reach the cave. Be aware that the Middle Fork Powder River, especially in spring and early summer, is swift and cold and large.

Much of my time in this gorgeous area was spent randomly wandering the top sides of the cliffs that surround and overlook the river, and seeking uncharted ways into the main river canyon via side canyons. Lots of 4th-class scrambling placed me in some amazing settings. Also, directionless hiking over the surrounding prairies and ridges afforded unbounded panoramas of Wyoming at its best. The valleys of the Middle Fork Powder River were used by outlaws for grazing their rustled cattle. The outlaw Butch Cassidy and his gang immortalized the Hole-In-The-Wall area (on private land, closed to public access). Spending time here will make you want to be an outlaw so you, too, can hide out in this country.

27 Mirror Lake and Lost Twin Lakes

General description:	A long day hike or 2- to 3-day outing into high alpine lake settings in the southern end of the Cloud Peak Wilderness.
Distance:	10.5 miles round trip.
Difficulty:	Moderate to difficult.
Elevation gain and loss:	1,270 feet.
Key elevation points:	Trailhead: 9,250 feet; Mirror Lake: 9,850 feet; Lost Twin Lakes: 10,520 feet.
General location:	50 miles east of Worland, in the southwestern sector of the Bighorn National Forest.
Maps:	Bighorn National Forest visitor map; USGS: Lake Angeline, Lake Helen.
Special attractions:	Awesome 1,000-foot cliffs that tower above the south shore of the Lost Twin Lakes.
Manager:	Tensleep Ranger District.

Finding the trailhead: From the tiny town of Ten Sleep (26 miles east of Worland on U.S. Highway 16) drive east on U.S. Highway 16 through spectacular Tensleep Canyon for 18 miles. At mile marker 44 turn left onto

Towering cliffs surround lower Lost Twin Lake.

Forest Road 27. A huge "West Tensleep Lake" sign marks the road. Drive north 7 miles along this wide gravel road until you come to another sign pointing left to the campground and right to the trailhead. There is a parking lot here, and at its north end an information board and sign notes the Middle Tensleep Trailhead.

The hike: West Tensleep Lake and Campground serve as beginnings for the most popular hikes into the Cloud Peak Wilderness Area. A few days of hiking in this beautiful section of the Big Horns will explain its notoriety. Tensleep Canyon and Creek inherited their names from an old Indian campsite that was "ten sleeps" or ten days of travel from important points like Yellowstone and Fort Laramie.

Up a closed road 0.1 mile, a small "Mirror Lake" sign points north or left toward the trail whose first miles trace along a gentle lodgepole forest ridge. The trail then switchbacks down to an easy creek crossing. Tank up here, because the next mile is a steep and steady incline to a ridgetop. At 2.7 miles the trail crosses Tensleep Creek. In late June this means a wade, but it becomes a rock hop later in the year. Mirror Lake actually seems like a lost lake, because after crossing the creek you have to leave the trail and hike a grassy ridge east for 0.2 mile to reach its shores. Good camping exists on the west shore of this pretty lake.

The trail now becomes a mellow walk through alpine meadows and forests. Sometimes, Tensleep Creek races wild and rushing; and sometimes it just lazes along through the gorgeous scenery. At 4.7 miles another creek

Mirror Lake and Lost Twin Lakes

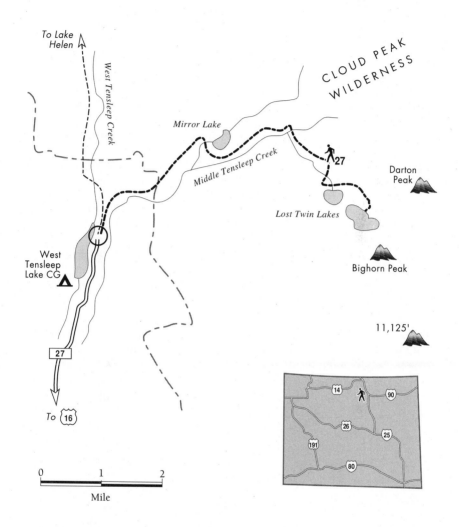

crossing (or wade, depending on how far you can jump) marks the last leg to Lost Twin Lakes. After this crossing, the trail is hard to see, but simply leave the creek by journeying due south into the forest. For another 1.5 miles the trail climbs steeply to the first Lost Twin Lake. The 1,000-foot cliff faces dropping into the peaceful and enclosed lake setting offer an astounding area in which to camp.

This is simply a very nice high country hike. The area shows little sign of overuse. Using the lake as a base camp, one can climb to the tops of the surrounding peaks.

28 Mistymoon Lake

General description:	A rugged 2- to 3-day hike into the alpine lake country of the Cloud Peak Wilderness.
Distance:	12 miles round trip.
Difficulty:	Strenuous.
Elevation gain:	1,125 feet.
Key elevation points:	Trailhead: 9,250 feet; Lake Helen: 10,050 feet; Mistymoon Lake: 10,375 feet.
General location:	50 miles east of Worland, in the southwestern sector of the Bighorn National Forest.
Special attractions:	Alpine lakes and high peak scenery. Good fishing.
Maps:	Bighorn National Forest map; USGS: Lake Helen.
Fees:	Area campgrounds: $8 to $10 per night. No wilderness user fee.
Manager:	Tensleep Ranger District.

Finding the trailhead: Driving directions are the same as those to Mirror Lake/Lost Twin Lakes (Hike 27). At the north end of the hiker's parking lot, the West Tensleep Trail begins right beside the Middle Tensleep Trail. A sign notes that Mistymoon Lake is 6 miles away.

The hike: Mistymoon is such a magical, alluring name. In fact, I visited the lake under a full moon on a windless night, and magical only begins to describe the experience.

Don't let the 6-miles-distance sign fool you. This is a rough trail and seems like a much longer hike. Also, another sign notes that no fires are allowed at the lake. Camp stoves are in order.

The first 2 miles of the West Tensleep Trail are gentle. The next couple of miles become amazingly long and rugged, and by the time you reach Lake Helen at 4 miles, you may decide to camp there and hike to Mistymoon Lake the next day. The splendid scenery begins here at Lake Helen, with rocky subalpine bowls merging into high peak vistas. The trail rounds the western side of Lake Helen and 1 mile later does the same at Marion Lake. Campsites are not lacking and water is everywhere. The final mile to Mistymoon Lake climbs somewhat steeply, breaking above the timberline and into short tundra and stark granite rock. It's a fragile, harsh, and beautiful environment here, and Mistymoon Lake is a real gem. Its popularity is well deserved.

The best camping at this lake is found off the trail before and below the shelf on which the lake sits. The land around Mistymoon Lake is quite exposed and carries a good slope. Dawn and sunrise by these waters, when the air is calm and the surrounding jagged peaks mirror themselves on the lake's surface, is a great time to be awake and alive. From here one can travel east to Florence Pass and into the eastern drainages of the Big Horns,

Mistymoon Lake

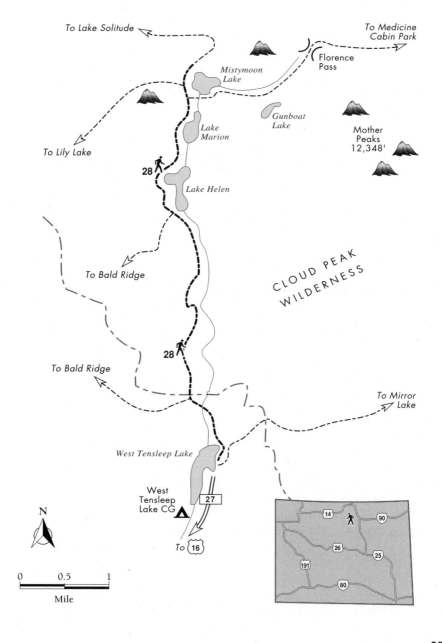

or dayhike the Lake Solitude/Lily Lake loop to the west. Mistymoon Lake is also a good base camp for an ascent of Cloud Peak (Hike 29).

Please walk with respect on this fragile environment.

29 Cloud Peak

General description:	An exciting and especially beautiful ascent to the highest peak in the Big Horn Range.
Distance:	11-mile round trip from Mistymoon Lake (Hike 28).
Difficulty:	Strenuous; some climbing experience recommended.
Elevation gain and loss:	2,818 feet from Mistymoon Lake (Hike 28).
Key elevation points:	Mistymoon Lake: 10,357 feet; Cloud Peak: 13,175 feet.
General location:	50 miles east of Worland, in the southwestern sector of the Bighorn National Forest.
Special attractions:	The ascent of the highest peak in the region, and spectacular scenery
Maps:	Bighorn National Forest map; USGS: Lake Helen, Cloud Peak.
Manager:	Tensleep Ranger District.

Finding the trailhead: Same as for Hike 28.

The hike: Since a round trip from Mistymoon Lake to the top of Cloud Peak and back is an 8 to 10 hour proposition, this description assumes you have followed the directions in Hike 28 to Mistymoon Lake and are beginning the journey from there. Before undertaking this climb, scan this brief safety checklist:

•You need to be somewhat acclimated to higher elevations.

•You need to be in fairly decent physical shape.

•Start early in the morning to beat the afternoon thunder and lightning storms, and to allow yourself a leisurely pace.

•Carry good wind and weather gear along. Also take sunscreen, lunch, and lots of water.

•Heavy waterproof boots are a necessity.

•An ice axe or a stout walking stick may be needed for the snow fields that last into August.

•BE SKILLED AT ROCK-HOPPING. This ascent requires some extreme rock-hopping. Make sure EVERY ROCK you use will provide a solid step. A twisted or broken ankle in these isolated environs is a serious affair.

Park at West Tensleep Lake trailhead. Hike to Mistymoon Lake. From the lake it is 5.5 miles and 5 hours to the summit of Cloud Peak. From Mistymoon Lake go north on the Solitude Loop trail to the top of the ridge. Descend a

Cloud Peak

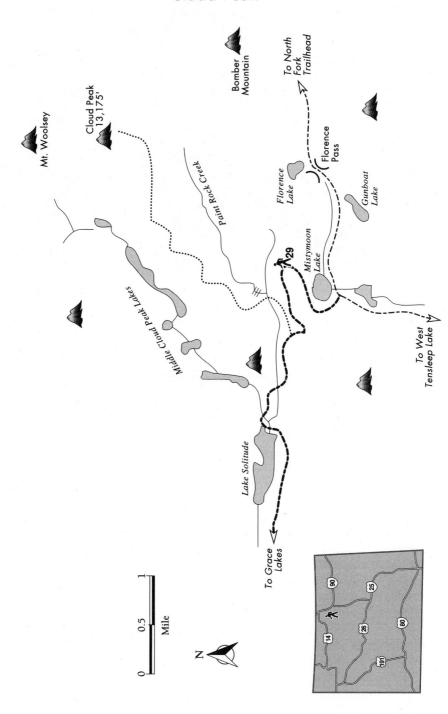

Mt. Woolsey

Cloud Peak
13,175'

Bomber
Mountain

To North
Fork
Trailhead

Paint Rock Creek

Florence
Lake

Florence
Pass

Gunboat
Lake

Mistymoon
Lake

29

Middle Cloud Peak Lakes

Lake Solitude

To West
Tensleep Lake

To Grace
Lakes

N

0   0.5   1

Mile

90

25

14

26

80

191

A view from Cloud Peak.

short distance, then leave the trail and cross Paint Rock Creek heading north for the waterfall. The easiest descent is to follow the main trail west from this ridgetop for almost 0.5 mile. Here you can look due north and see both the waterfall and an ascending trail in the rocky hillside to the left of it. Head north for that waterfall, cross Paint Rock Creek, which in early season may be an icy wade, and begin the seemingly perpetual climb to the top.

The main rule now becomes "head northeast and up." There are some cairns marking the way, but you'll probably be too busy watching your own rock-hopping footsteps to catch them all. The higher you get up the mountain, the easier it is to view the ridge you have to follow to the top.

The steep climb and rough country are not the only reason this hike takes so long. It is so spectacular that you tend to stop every 30 feet and gaze at the scenery. This country is the essence of the Cloud Peak Wilderness Area.

I didn't quite make it to the summit. After pausing for a moment to add another note to the advice checklist ("Don't be too proud to turn back if the weather changes"), I then looked up and saw the thunderclouds building rapidly. I suddenly found it necessary to follow my own advice. This country is too exposed to risk getting caught in a storm, and the lichen-covered granite is treacherous when wet. Remember that, even in dry conditions, the return trip's downhill rock-hopping is harder and more dangerous than the uphill scramble.

If Cloud Peak seems a bit too difficult for you, there is no shortage of gentler summits surrounding Mistymoon Lake.

30 Circle Park/Willow Lake

General description:	An overnighter into the open subalpine country beneath the bare, granite faces of the southern Bighorns.
Distance:	8 miles round trip.
Difficulty:	Moderate to strenuous.
Elevation gain:	1,590 feet.
Key elevation points:	Circle Park Campground: 7,900 feet; Sherd Lake: 8,500 feet; Willow Lake: 9,490 feet.
General location:	17 miles south of Buffalo, in the very southeastern corner of the Cloud Peak Wilderness.
Special attractions:	Good fishing in scenic lakes beneath magnificent rock faces.
Maps:	Bighorn National Forest visitor map; USGS: Brokenback Narrows.
Fees:	Area campgrounds cost $8 to $10 per night. No user fees for hikers.
Manager:	Buffalo Ranger District.

Finding the trailhead: U.S. Highway 16 directly west from Buffalo climbs into the scenic Bighorn Mountains for nearly 15 miles before the graveled Circle Park Road, Forest Road 20, forms a junction with it. This road heads directly west for 2.5 miles to the Circle Park Campground, but the turnoff to

The Big Horn Mountains rise elegantly from the shores of Willow Lake.

Circle Park/Willow Lake

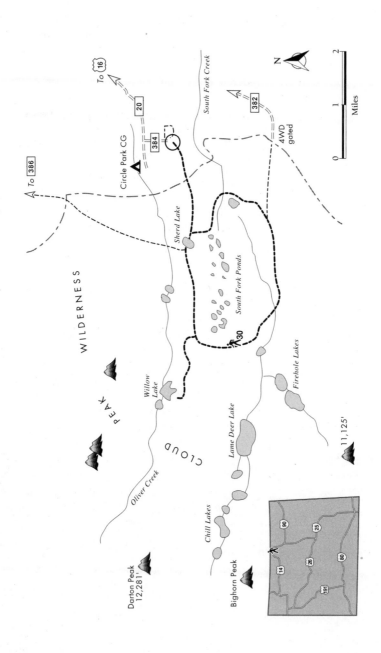

the trailhead comes 0.5 mile before you get to the campground. Go south onto Forest Road 384 and after about 0.5 mile you'll arrive at a self-registration station (required to enter the wilderness).

The hike: It's only 4 miles from the trailhead to Willow Lake, but the trail is so rocky and rugged that the distance feels much longer—thus the overnight rating. A wonderful woodland loop return trip is possible here, and the neighboring drainages in this area abound with cross-country and subalpine lake exploration possibilities.

The beginning of this rocky trail is through a lodgepole forest. At 0.7 mile, an unmarked intersection appears; keep heading west or left, and 0.2 mile later you'll enter the Cloud Peak Wilderness. Just after this boundary, you'll encounter another trail junction offering to return you to the Circle Park Campground.

Sherd Lake, a glassy foreground for the bald tops of the Bighorns, is located 2 miles from the trailhead. Here the loop around the South Fork Ponds begins, with Willow and Long Lakes accessible via the trail to the right. But 200 feet along this trail another intersection appears. Willow Lake lies up the trail to the left. This viewless and steep 1.2 mile trail eventually places you on a fire-burned ridgeline that offers incredible alpine and eastern prairie views. Follow this ridge for about half a mile to another unsigned intersection. Willow Lake requires a right or northward turn along the obviously main trail; the south trail is the South Fork Ponds Trail.

Now a 0.75 mile wooded descent places you on a flatter benchland that overlooks Willow Lake. One pretty much must camp on this bench, both because of a 100-foot-from-water wilderness camping regulation and because most of the lakeshore is encased in rock. Makeshift trails do lead from the bench to the lake. One very tiny patch of willows on the northwest end of the lake must be responsible for its name.

The entire country above the lake offers tricky, alpine rock-hopping that can lead to some great summit climbs and day hikes.

31 Tongue River

General description:	A rugged day hike or—more practically—a 2- or 3-day journey into several different, impressive mountain settings.
Distance:	18.2 miles round trip.
Difficulty:	Strenuous.
Elevation gain:	3,280 feet.
Elevation key points:	Amsden Creek Trailhead: 4,500 feet; Sheep Creek intersection: 5,400 feet; Horse Creek intersection: 6,300 feet; Horse Creek Pass: 7,350 feet; trail rejoining Tongue River: 7,220 feet.
General location:	9 miles west of Ranchester, in the northeastern Big Horn Mountains.
Special attractions:	Fishing, limestone caves, lots of wildlife.
Maps:	Bighorn National Forest visitor map and USGS Dayton South and Skull Ridge quads.
Manager:	Bighorn National Forest, Tongue River Ranger District.

Finding the trailhead: Take exit 9 off Interstate 90 onto U.S. Highway 14 just east of Ranchester. Head west toward Dayton. After this highway passes the junction of Wyoming 343, at the 5-mile mark and just east of (before) the highway bridge crossing the Tongue River, a paved road—Sheridan County Road 92—jots to the west (right). A brown recreation sign here points to the Tongue River area. After about a block, the road becomes gravel and travels through some lovely farm country for 2 miles, where it intersects Sheridan County 90. Stay to the left on Sheridan County 92 and follow the narrow roadway for another 1.5 miles into the head of the Tongue River Canyon where it ends at a parking area and trailhead. This is the Amsden Creek Big Game Winter Range, which is a locally popular fishing and picnicking area.

The hike: Everyone visiting *I-tan-i-ho,* a Cheyenne Indian name meaning "tongue," will immediately be struck by the gorgeous river gushing through cottonwood bottomlands surrounded by towering limestone cliffs. The trailhead shows a lot of usage, but many casual hikers are simply trucking 0.25 mile to the first trail intersection at a steel bridge across the river, where a 0.75 mile trail switchbacks up the south cliffs to a rather large cave in the limestone rocks. This forms a fun little side journey with quick elevation gain—just try to ignore the twentieth-century pictographs (spray paint). The cave cuts 40 feet back into the earth, and because it's pretty dark with lots of holes and stepoffs, you'll need a flashlight if you want to explore.

For 1.5 miles west from the bridge, the trail is deeply immured beneath towering limestone cliffs. There is moderate elevation gain and nice views of the river below. After a while, huge ponderosa pines invade the setting, interspersing themselves among the massive limestone boulders that have

Tongue River

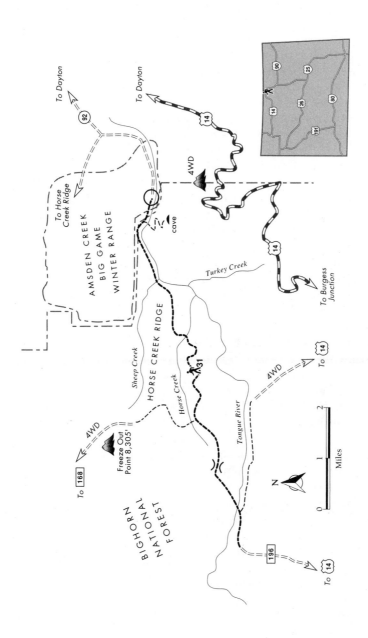

tumbled down the cliffs over the eons. At 2 miles this landscape yields to some huge meadows. The first real campsites are encountered here, although the trek to water would be a steep journey downhill to the river. Anywhere you go in this area you will be competing with livestock and a sprinkling of poison ivy.

Now the trail steeply descends 0.5 mile to again be near the river and to cross (via a log) rambunctious Sheep Creek. Sheep Creek, Horse Creek, Turkey Creek—these names really make one want to purify the water before drinking it.

This Sheep Creek intersection area is a great place to camp, and for folks on their first hike of the season, that may be good advice. The next 2.5 miles consist of some of the steepest trail hiking I've ever done. The route leaves the river and a rocky gorge called Box Canyon and heads northwest, almost straight up toward an intersection with Horse Creek. This part of the trail is responsible for the "strenuous" rating. But with every step the country gets more grand. The limestone cliffs recede to distant heights, the river is relegated to remote and impressive views, aspen groves begin claiming the meadowed landscape. . . this is quintessential Big Horn hiking.

At 4.7 miles the trail cuts across Horse Creek, and for another mile it wanders steeply uphill. Sometimes it blasts through fields of neck-high grass; often it's an easy-to-follow path across meadows. There is a fence gate atop a minor pass at 5.8 miles that needs to be closed. A slight downhill trek places you below mighty Horse Creek Ridge where the views become even more intense.

In this spacious, high-mountain drainage, cowboys have been rounding up livestock with ATVs, and the resulting two-track trail now heads north. The ATV trail cuts up open Horse Creek Ridge to the north while the main Tongue River Trail all but disappears. After you cross now-tiny Horse Creek (to its northern side), and before the fence gate that the ATV trail cuts through, look to the southwest, toward a pass, and head generally west, again crossing the creek to the south shore. Here it's a matter of hiking generally westward toward an easy-to-distinguish pass. The trail intermittently appears and disappears, but your goal remains a gate in yet another fence that sits at the top of the unnamed pass directly to the west. This landmark measured 7.3 miles on my pedometer.

Now begins a gentler trek downhill to rejoin the river shores. This more fragile country has succumbed to the whims of the many bovines grazing here, and trails wander everywhere. Someone did set some fence posts with blaze markings along the real trail, but half of them are rubbed down by the cattle and can in no way be guaranteed as guideposts. Landmarks become the guide now. Look below (southwest) to the Tongue River drainage and you'll observe an obvious canyon—the South Fork of the Tongue River—entering the main drainage. Just west of that junction is where the official trail meets and crosses the Tongue River. It's now a simple matter of following some of the many trails downward for about 1.5 miles to that point in the river.

After all this—9.1 miles of hiking—you'll find yourself sitting on the shores of a beautiful mountain stream. If you carried your pack to this point, endless camping possibilities exist on both sides of this easily fordable river. Fishing opportunities abound. It's a peaceful place to spend a day or two. There is a trail on the south shore that eventually leads back to the highway.

Remember, this is an 18.2-mile round trip, and the first part of the return journey is uphill.

32 Bucking Mule Falls National Recreation Trail

General description:	A fairly long and rugged overnight hike along the rim of a spectacular canyon; or, a 1 mile, half-day hike to the falls.
Distance:	11 miles one way to shuttle.
Difficulty:	Strenuous.
Elevation gain and loss:	1,200 feet.
General location:	40 miles east of Lovell, in the northwestern Big Horn Mountains.
Special attractions:	A towering waterfall and scenic mountain panoramas.
Maps:	Bighorn National Forest visitor map and/or USGS: Mexican Hill, Medicine Wheel and Bald Mountain quads. Boyd Ridge quad is optional.
Manager:	Medicine Wheel Ranger District.

Finding the trailhead: U.S. Highway Alt. 14 (U.S. 14A) east of Lovell is an awe-inspiring drive across a polychromatic prairie that rises to meet the Big Horns. About 40 miles east from Lovell, turn north on Forest Road 14 (this used to be the Sheep Mountain road, which used to be Forest Road 11) and drive 3.5 miles to its intersection with Devils Canyon Road (still Forest Road 14). Travel west on Devils Canyon Road for 7 more miles to the trailhead parking lot.

The hike: Bucking Mule Falls is a spectacular cascade that tumbles 600 feet. Devils Canyon is rocky, water-carved land. Its rugged beauty makes the steep hiking pitches along this well-maintained trail worth the effort.

The shorter version of this hike is an easy walk, perfect for families, that skirts the rugged southern rim of Bucking Mule Canyon. From the thick lodgepole pine and Engelmann spruce forest at its beginning to the incredible overhanging rock ledges and an awesome view across the canyon and down onto the crashing waterfalls at the end, this hike fascinates every step of the way. It's about 1 mile to the falls from the trailhead, and a round trip journey takes a couple of hours.

Bucking Mule Falls National Recreation Area

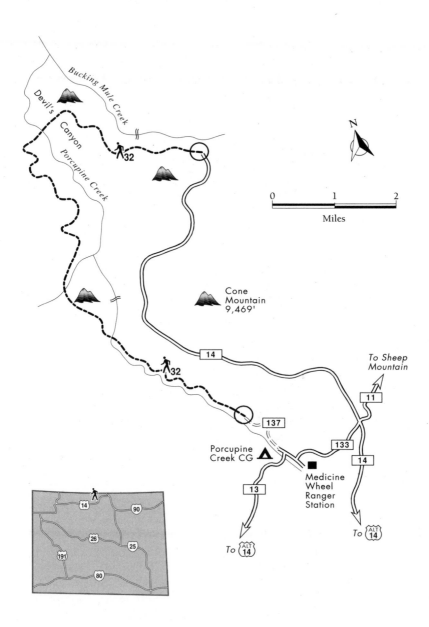

For those who wish to journey the entire 11 miles of the trail, the path is well maintained and easy to follow as it continues to skirt Bucking Mule Canyon and then drops steeply down into Devils Canyon, a stretch of the Porcupine Creek drainage. This crossing is your only chance to enjoy fresh water for the next 4.5 miles, as the trail climbs steeply out of Devils Canyon and traces the southern rim of Porcupine Creek Canyon. The views that accompany this walk are spectacular. Finally the trail again drops into the upper reaches of Porcupine Creek and follows its northern banks to the Jaws Road, ending a bit more than a mile below Porcupine Campground. Here you can try and catch a ride back to the original parking lot, or gain an entirely new perspective on this wild country by retracing your steps.

A large number of horsepackers use this trail. Also, due to cliffy terrain and thick timber, camping is limited. The upper stretches of Porcupine Creek boast fair fishing.

—Susan Gilmore

33 Five Springs Area/Medicine Mountain

General description:	A long but enjoyable day hike to a mountain summit with a considerable gain in elevation. Also, opportunities for short hikes abound.
Distance:	12 miles round trip.
Difficulty:	Moderate.
Elevation gain and loss:	2,762 feet.
Key elevation points:	Five Springs Campground: 7,200 feet; Medicine Mountain summit: 9,962 feet.
General location:	25 miles east of Lovell, on the western fringes of the northern Big Horn Mountains.
Special attractions:	Primitive hiking in a little-used area; a gorgeous waterfall; nearby proximity to the enigmatic Medicine Wheel archaeological site.
Maps:	Bighorn National Forest visitor map; USGS: Medicine Mountain.
Manager:	BLM Worland District.

Finding the trailhead: Located 25 miles east of Lovell on U.S. Highway Alternate 14 (14A), the BLM Five Springs Road leads to a nature trail at Five Springs Falls, where there is water and a few camping and picnic sites. This road is exceptionally steep and potholed, and has some incredibly sharp curves. The Medicine Mountain trail begins a mile or so past the campground, at the end of the road.

The hike: Although inside the Bighorn National Forest boundaries, the

Five Springs Area/Medicine Mountain

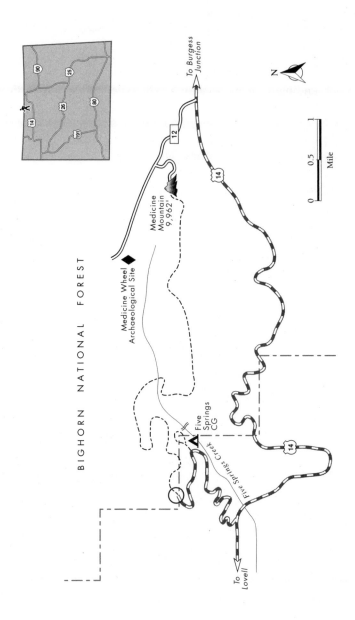

To Burgess Junction

N

0   0.5   Mile

12

14

BIGHORN   NATIONAL   FOREST

Medicine Mountain 9,962'

Medicine Wheel Archaeological Site

Five Springs CG

Five Springs Creek

14

To Lovell

90
25
80
26
191
14

Medicine Mountain hike is not an established Forest Service trail and is not maintained as such. Medicine Mountain looms over a Sheepeater Tribe's stone medicine wheel, a prehistoric wonder located on the northwest side of the mountain. The origin and significance of this stone relic is still unknown, but it is believed to be part of ancient religious ceremonies. Crow Indian legend states that the wheel was built by "people who had no iron." The wheel is an almost perfect circle of stones 70 feet in diameter; 28 stone spokes radiate out from a central stone cairn. Discovered in the 1880s, the site has recently been so vandalized and molested by souvenir hunters that a protective fence now surrounds the monument. Though not visible from the top of the mountain that it sits upon, the site is certainly worth a visit.

At the Five Springs Campground—a beautiful spot tucked beneath tortured cliffs and beside a gushing stream lined with deciduous trees—a half-mile loop trail guides you to a fascinating view of a waterfall tumbling down pinkish-gray cliffs. The area forms a great base camp for both the Medicine Mountain hike and other hikes in the nearby Big Horns.

Following the road beyond the campground to a gated dead end places you on a south-facing mountain slope and atop an old roadbed that has completely returned to trail status. Striated limestone cliffs rise to the north, and granite structures loom ahead. The trail itself fades in and out, but the old roadbed is easy to follow for nearly 3 miles. This path does recross Five Springs Creek, so there is some water along the way.

After this crossing the trail heads south and toward U.S. Highway 14A. Here the trail can be confusing. The countryside is heavily forested and also heavily roaded. One old roadway will eventually cut straight west toward the summit of Medicine Mountain. From this point to the top, it's a decent climb requiring good lungs.

A road does ascend Medicine Mountain from its eastern flanks, and a space-age FAA radar geodesic dome stands atop the mountain, monitoring air traffic in a 3-state area. But the wonderful 6-mile climb to the top of the mountain via this little-used trail offers spectacular vistas of the Big Horns from the nearby cliffs to the west of the Medicine Wheel. The trail climbs steeply and continuously through open meadows and sporadic timberland to the summit of 9,962-foot Medicine Mountain. Carry some water for the last half of this hike.

Note that BLM responsibility ends at the campground, and the Medicine Wheel District of the Big Horn National Forest is basically unaware of or trying to forget this trail. The path's only maintenance is done by hiker and horsepacker usage, and that is quite light.

—Susan Gilmore

West-Central Wyoming

THE WIND RIVER RANGE

Welcome to the roof of Wyoming. For over 100 miles, from Togwotee Pass on U.S. Highway 287 to South Pass now straddled by Wyoming 28, the Wind Rivers form an unbroken and supreme expression of mountain beauty, geology, glaciers, wildlife, and wilderness. Forty-seven peaks touch or exceed the 13,000-foot elevation barrier; 63 glaciers in this range cover a total of 17 square miles of mountain.

Geology buffs can study thrust faults that were so severe the rock folds literally faulted over on themselves. Tremendous Ice Age glaciation bulldozed large canyons into the range while sculpting the granite peaks into an awesome display of cliff art. And speaking of granite cliffs, rock climbers have found their Shangri-la in the towering and varied headwalls, spires, chimneys, and sheer summits of the Wind River Mountains.

The human history of these mountains, from Native American to fur trapper to late nineteenth century-immigrants and gold miners, is far richer than the accumulated bounty of fur pelts and precious minerals extracted from the land. More than 300,000 people and their horse-drawn wagons poured through South Pass between 1843 and 1863, following hopeful promises and improbable dreams.

But by far the greatest contemporary treasure of the Wind Rivers lies in its vast acreage of officially classified wilderness. Three major wilderness areas plus the de facto wilderness of the Wind River Indian Reservation create more than 1 million acres of contiguous wilderness.

Environmental Protection Agency studies have concluded that the high wilderness lakes in the Wind Rivers are susceptible to damage and contamination from acid rain. The pure waters have a low alkalinity and sport little ability to buffer the nitrates and sulfides of the nearby coal-fired Jim Bridger electric plant. A second, more immediate threat challenges these mountains in the form of human hikers coalescing in greater numbers than an area can accommodate. Even the roof of Wyoming, classified and protected as it is, needs help if it is to survive as a viable remnant of wild country.

Keep a few general considerations in mind when planning any journey into the Wind River Range. The western side of the Wind Rivers fall under the auspices of the Bridger-Teton National Forest. The forest maps of this national forest are the finest maps any individual forest offers. The eastern slopes of the Wind Rivers are administered by the Shoshone National Forest. Be sure to obtain the NEW version of the Shoshone Forest's south visitor map. They lack great detail, but do portray the roads and trails and creek drainages and a few high mountain points.

Understand that *Hiking Wyoming*'s section on the Wind Rivers contains but a very few introductory trails into the Wind River's wilderness areas and its more than 700 miles of trails. Falcon Publishing also offers a comprehensive guide titled *Hiking Wyoming's Wind River Range,* by Ron Adkison. Ron's book can help you plot a week or a month or a summer of hiking in this most superlative area.

The recreational forester of the Pinedale District in the Bridger National Forest notes that black bear encounters in the Wind Rivers have been a real problem for the past 10 years. She says using proper food storage techniques is paramount if this trend is going to be reversed. The Pinedale District loans food storage tubes on a deposit/donation basis as a means to help this process. ALSO, she states that there have been *confirmed* grizzly bear sightings in the Bridger Wilderness. She imagines they will be seen in the Fitzpatrick Wilderness soon. The ranger patrols and trail crews are required to carry pepper spray with them when on the trails.

34 Sinks Canyon

General description:	A gentle day hike that explores the foothills of the eastern Wind River Mountains.
Distance:	6 miles round trip.
Difficulty:	Easy.
Elevation gain and loss:	600 feet.
Key elevation points:	Trailhead: 6,600 feet.
General location:	7 miles southwest of Lander, on the Middle Fork of the Popo Agie River.
Special attractions:	Disappearing rivers and other extraordinary geological features. Also, diverse lower mountain settings.
Maps:	Obtain a Sinks Canyon Volksmarch Trail Map from the state park visitor center. USGS: Fossil Hill.
Manager:	Sinks Canyon State Park.

Finding the trailhead: U.S. Highway 287 forms the main drag of Lander. On Fifth Steet, which is also Wyoming 131, turn south. It's a simple matter of following the Wyoming 131 and Sinks Canyon Park signs for 7 miles to the park boundaries.

The hike: This hike constitutes another of the Wyoming State Park Volksmarch walks (see Hike 2), and it is one of the best. The park is founded around a natural phenomenon where the entire Middle Popo Agie River plunges and disappears into a limestone cavern, The Sinks. The river reappears 0.5 mile later as a large spring named The Rise. It's interesting to note that the volume of The Rise is greater than the water volume vanishing into

Sinks Canyon

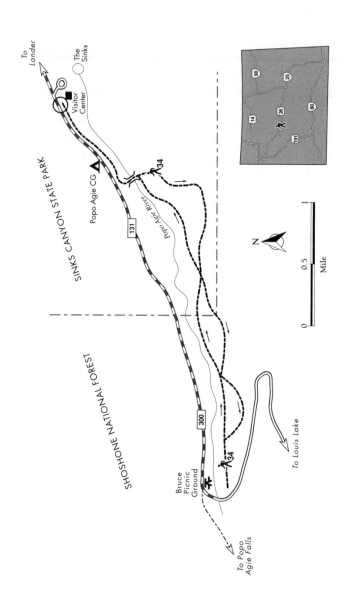

The Sinks. When a harmless dye was released into The Sinks, it took over two hours before it reappeared at The Rise. Where the extra water comes from, and why the swiftly moving river requires such a time period to travel a half mile, remain mysteries.

The trail officially begins at the visitor center. Here also you can hike a short distance to the river and view where the earth swallows the cascading waters.

Like several State Park Volksmarch trails, this one incorporates a bit of roadway into it. The first 0.6 mile traces the main highway west to the Popo Agie Campground. Then you must follow the campground gravel roads west as far as possible (0.2 mile) to the Nature Trail parking area. Here a wild suspension bridge spans the river, and the true hiking trail begins with a standard IVV (Volksmarch) brown and yellow sign. If one is not after Volksmarch accreditation, one could eliminate over a mile of this trail by driving to the parking lot and starting at the suspension bridge.

The trail is a figure 8 with a third loop attached to it. The main rule to follow at trail intersections is to always go left. Arrows on IVV signs point the way, but if there's any doubt, go left. The first mile has a slight climb as you journey into the unique habitats of the Wind River foothills. It's actually country few people see, having set their sights on the high peaks to the west. It's also a country that is splendid in its own special way. Lush meadows (by Wyoming standards), gentle forests, riparian aspen groves, and extended views of cliff-encompassed Sinks Canyon keep the hiker entranced. In late June the river wears a wild white robe and the flowers almost overdecorate the meadowed hillsides. Where the trail is a bit difficult to follow, look for the IVV signs and for blue diamond ski trail markers.

The trail turns back on itself at Bruce Picnic Ground. Much of the return journey treads through special river environments. The only slightly confusing area occurs at the return end of the western loop near the University of Missouri's geology camp. Cross the little log foot bridge that spans an offshoot rivulet, but don't cross the suspension bridge over the main river. Continue on the trail parallel to and on the south side of the river.

This is a most enjoyable hike. It can be used to get the legs into shape for the long and rugged trails into the nearby Popo Agie Wilderness Area. It also forms a great trek for easy walking, open views, and welcome solitude.

Sinks Canyon State Park sports two other short nature/interpretive trails. Descriptive pamphlets are available at the visitor center, which is open Memorial Day through Labor Day.

35 Middle Fork of the Popo Agie River/Tayo Park Loop Trail

General description:	A rugged, 5-day or longer backpack into high country lakes surrounded by majestic peaks.
Distance:	28 miles round trip.
Difficulty:	Strenuous.
Elevation gain:	3,500 feet. Add 2,400 feet if climbing Wind River Peak.
Key elevation points:	Trailhead: 7,200 feet; Popo Agie Falls: 7,800 feet; Three Forks Park: 9,000 feet; Pinto Park: 10,100 feet; Deep Creek Lakes: 10,700 feet; Tayo Park: 9,800 feet.
General location:	Begins 12 miles southwest of Lander.
Special attractions:	Astonishing vistas of panoramic peaks and alpine lake settings. Deep Creek Lakes are rumored to contain golden trout.
Maps:	Shoshone National Forest south half visitor map. USGS: Fossil Hill, Cony Mountain, Sweetwater Gap. Also, Earthwalk Press has an excellent overview topography and trail map of the Southern Wind Rivers. It's available at most local sporting goods and outfitting stores.
Manager:	Washakie Ranger District.

Finding the trailhead: Wyoming 131 (the Sinks Canyon State Park road, described in Hike 34) leaves Lander at Fifth Street, and the entire 11 miles west to the trailhead is paved. Just past the Bruce Picnic Area the road turns south and crosses the Middle Fork of the Popo Agie River. South of and across the bridge is a several acre parking lot geared to accommodate the many hikers, packers and horse packers that now use the trail.

The hike: It was in 1971 when I first traveled this major access trail into the then Popo Agie Primitive Area. Then, a grimy little dirt road out of Lander led to an unmarked and obscure trailhead. A few horsepackers and a survival school named NOLS were practically the only users of the wilderness. For 5 weeks we traveled these mountains, meeting almost no people and experiencing wild beauty beyond comprehension. Gone are the days. This is now a bustling trailhead.

The Middle Fork Trail not only serves as a gracious introduction to the Wind Rivers, but it forms the major access route into the entire Popo Agie Wilderness. A map posted on the trailhead sign shows a system of 28 different trails, with this 1 trailhead as the gateway to all. Bear in mind that the hike to Popo Agie Falls, the first mile of the trail, is the goal of over half the people using the trail.

The steep and rocky beginning, in a mile, takes you 600 feet higher to

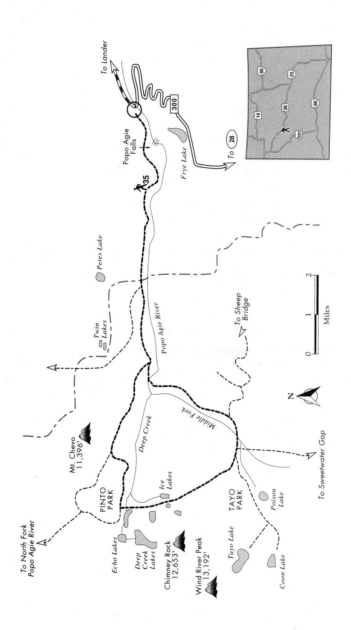

To Lander

Popo Agie Falls

300

To 28

Frye Lake

35

Petes Lake

Twin Lakes

Popo Agie River

To Sheep Bridge

Mt. Chevo 11,396'

Deep Creek

Middle Fork

Ice Lakes

To Sweetwater Gap

PINTO PARK

TAYO PARK

Poison Lake

To North Fork Popo Agie River

Echo Lakes

Deep Creek Lakes

Chimney Rock 12,653'

Wind River Peak 13,192'

Tayo Lake

Coon Lake

N

Miles

0   1   2

90

25

26

80

14

191

where a short side trail journeys off for a view of the impressive Popo Agie Falls.

Periodic decisions need to be made—if you haven't pre-planned your trip—on which side trails to take. I present this hike as a journey up the Middle Fork to Three Forks Park, a jog along the Pinto Park Trail, a slice over to the Deep Creek and Ice Lakes, a journey into Tayo Park and a loop back down the Popo Agie Middle Fork, again to Three Forks Park and out the main trail. But this itinerary forms a basic introduction, and many other possibilities present themselves along the route.

The wilderness boundary begins about 6 miles after the trailhead. This wilderness has a "no camping within 200 feet of trail, lakes and streams" rule, and between that and the extremely rugged, rocky, and timbered countryside, it's another 4 miles to good camping at Three Forks Park. The trail is well signed from here to Pinto Park. Go 4 more miles and the Deep Creek Cutoff Trail jogs south, where the rewards for your long hiking efforts begin. The Deep Creek Lakes, the Ice Lakes, and upper Tayo Park are set in almost dreamlike high alpine meadows that lie beneath the base of giant peaks and shear granite cliffs.

Wind River Peak, at 13,192 feet, affords a challenging cross-country peak climb without any technical gear required. Its gentle ridges are accessible from the southern shores of the upper Deep Creek Lakes. Be aware that there are several creek crossings between the Echo Lakes and Tayo Park, and a major creek crossing occurs on the Middle Fork Trail before you re-enter Three Forks Park from the west. These waters are swift and icy. In fact, Ice Lakes can still be frozen solid in mid-July. Wind River Peak may be a snow climb up to that time, and an ice ax can be useful.

It would take a book-length description to do justice to the vast beauty encompassed by this hike. It is an excellent first taste of the southern Wind Rivers and will surely pique your adventure buds into wanting more. The trail intersections are well signed, but it's still advisable to carry a topo map. Signs do have a habit of disappearing.

36 South Pass City

General description:	A historic day hike in high altitude, rolling prairie country.
Distance:	6 miles round trip.
Difficulty:	Easy to moderate.
Elevation gain and loss:	Less than 400 feet.
Key elevation points:	South Pass City: 7,980 feet.
General location:	35 miles south of Lander, in the southernmost foothills of the Wind River Range.
Special attractions:	A chance to explore the dazzling mining and settlement history of Wyoming.
Maps:	Obtain a Volksmarch map from the supervisor of the South Pass City Historic Site. The topography is located on USGS South Pass City quad.
Manager:	South Pass City State Historical Site.

Finding the trailhead: Leave Lander driving south on U.S. Highway 287. Wyoming 28 forks west 9 miles from town. This scenic highway takes you 25 miles to a South Pass City State Historical Site sign where you turn south and follow a well-graded gravel road for 2.5 miles to a large parking lot beside the historic city.

The hike: Wyoming has made excellent efforts to preserve its heritage, and

High Wyoming Prairie near South Pass City.

117

South Pass City

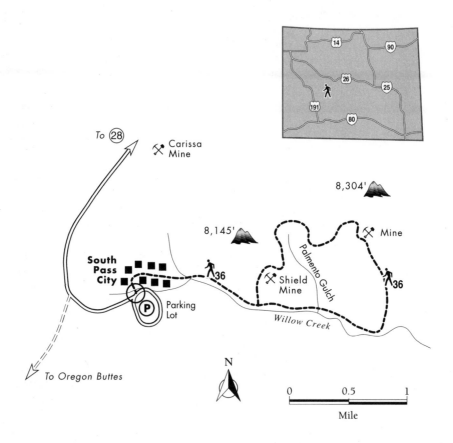

here is an area where history and hiking now merge. In the late 1860s the Carissa Mine began producing gold, and a rush to the South Pass area began. Within 2 years South Pass City, Atlantic City, and a burg named Miner's Delight were built. As businessmen arrived to meet the prospectors' needs, the South Pass area soon boasted over 2,000 inhabitants. Mining busts and booms bounced the population of the area up and down for nearly 100 years. Today, few mines are active. But a fascinating restoration of South Pass City has created a unique piece of living history. What I consider the best of the state's Volksmarch trails has been added to the site (see Hike 2).

The 6-mile Volksmarch trail begins in the townsite, and for a complete exploration of all aspects of this area, leave enough time to explore the restored buildings and historical markers. You can obtain information, maps, and if desired, official Volksmarch trail registration at the 1848 Smith-Sherlock Co. Store on "Main Street" (open Memorial Day through Labor Day, usually until 6 P.M.).

Volksmarches are nice because they create trails in country where there would otherwise be no hiking. Just east of the townsite, well-signed by the brown and yellow IVV signs, the trail follows aptly named Willow Creek for nearly 2.5 miles. Here is a landscape where the last of the Wind River Mountains and the first of the high prairies seem to be competing with each other for dominance.

Then the trail leaves the creek, climbs an aspen-lined ravine to the north and enters the windswept, short-grass sage prairie that rules so much of Wyoming. Topping a ridge, the trail passes by an old mine where one fissure was so deep I couldn't hear a dropped rock hit the bottom. You need to be extremely careful around mine shafts.

An old roadbed now constitutes the trail and guides you into the headwaters of Palmento Gulch with its musical aspen groves and copious evidence of beaver activity. Another rocky ridge, another mine, and a staggering view of Willow Creek surrounded by the prairie it cuts through, and the trail returns to the creek bottom and back to South Pass City.

This is a day hike worth seeking and hiking. Its uniqueness and beauty won't disappoint you. Be advised that this is probably some of the windiest country in the world.

37 Sweetwater Canyon

General description:	An isolated, cross-country, 2 to 3 day expedition into a little known prairie canyon.
Distance:	Up to 20 miles round trip.
Difficulty:	Strenuous; experts only.
Elevation gain and loss:	Less than 300 feet.
General location:	40 miles southeast of Lander, along the banks of the Sweetwater River.
Special attractions:	A prairie wilderness river that few people know about. Excellent fishing, remarkable geology.
Maps:	Bureau of Land Management South Pass and Lander 1:100,000 surface management maps and USGS: Lewiston Lakes and Radium Springs quads.
Manager:	BLM Lander Resource Area.

Finding the trailhead: I highly recommend contacting the Lander BLM office for directions before journeying into this country. Be also aware that a drive to Sweetwater by whatever route requires a high clearance vehicle, good rut driving skills, and an awareness that if it rains, there you will be stuck until the sun again shines.

Following the directions from Lander to South Pass City (Hike 36), drive to the abandoned Carissa gold mine. Here, instead of continuing toward South Pass City, a graveled and graded county road journeys eastward toward Atlantic City. About 2 miles later on this road, by another abandoned mine and totally dilapidated shack, the Pickaxe Road is signed and journeys south. Follow this graded road 4.9 miles to an intersection labeled the Lewiston Road. Even though the sign here notes that the Sweetwater River is 6 miles further south on Pickaxe Road, turn east onto the dirt Lewiston Road. This road, as the miles pass, deteriorates in width and quality.

After 7.6 miles, at a concrete Oregon Trail/Pony Express historical marker, Lewiston Road branches into 3 equally unalluring directions. The only landmarks noting this intersection are 2 log cabins directly to the north that cannot be seen from the intersection but are visible 0.5 mile before the described junction. Turn right, or south, onto a two-track road and head up a hill. At the top of the hill, take the two-track to the left, and 0.25 mile later take the fading two-track that goes right. Three quarters of a mile later, at a dilapidated mining cabin, you venture left, away and downhill from the cabin. More ruts than road now exist, and for the next 2 miles simply turn left or east at every intersection on the way. At the end of this excruciating yet fascinating journey you can park and camp at a nice grassy flat beside the clear waters of the Sweetwater River and the tailings of the former Wilson Bar Mine.

Two other paths to this river canyon exist. One is Strawberry Creek Road, which places you near the middle of the canyon. A third access option follows two-track roads from the Hudson/Atlantic City Road east of Diamond Springs, where a two-track leads to an overlook parking area southeast of Lewiston Lakes and opposite of Willow Creek. All roads require a high clearance vehicle. Talk to the Lander BLM folks for up-to-date information and directions on all these roads.

The hike: Sweetwater is the name that dominates central and southwestern Wyoming. Most stories attribute its naming to the fresh water which tasted sweet to trappers and settlers after weeks of drinking alkali water. But there is a story circulating that claims a mule toting a load of sugar fell into the river and hence the name.

This hike is one of those rare gems: unknown, untrammeled, untrailed, and hard to find and access. Sweetwater Canyon forms an unusual scenic prairie canyon of about 11 miles in length. The area is a BLM-recommended wilderness area, awaiting (Republican) congressional approval.

Even if one survives the drive, this is not a hike for everyone. Other than the occasional cattle path, there is no trail to follow. This is extremely rugged cross-country hiking, sometimes through thick brush, across and over dangerously loose rock slopes, and along the shores of the river. You are also as isolated and as far away from everything (including help) as you can get.

The rather bald sage slopes and rocky cliffs that lead to the river are dotted with old mines. The bird life is abundant and varied. And the country is wilderness wandering at its best. Four miles into the canyon a trickle of exceptionally clear water from the north marks the half-way point. East

Sweetwater Canyon

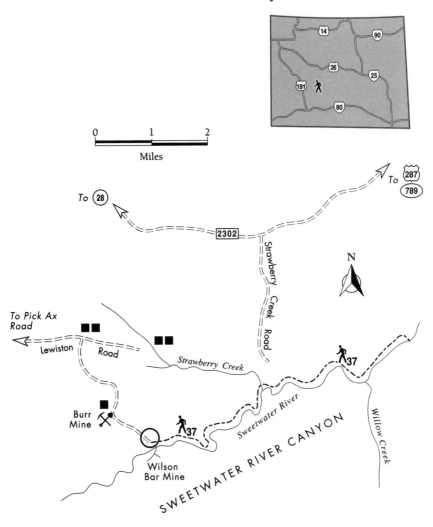

of Strawberry Creek the canyon broadens and the hiking becomes some-what easier. My favorite area was a short distance west of this creek, with its narrower widths and rushing waters. Driving to the canyon via the Straw-berry Creek Road would allow you to day hike both up and down the canyon.

There are lots of ticks, deer flies, and horse flies in the summer. Where the river waters are high and you can't wade them, you must fourth-class scramble some fractured and very crumbly rock cliffs to skirt the river's shore. If you are not well-versed in rock climbing, you should probably try the hike when the water is lower. The BLM and the grazing permittees have built a wire fence to exclude livestock from the river canyon. This is an original area. Tread lightly and leave no trace.

The Eastern Wind Rivers, North

The absolute best trail and topo map of the Wind River Range is published by Earthwalk Press, 5432 La Jolla Hermosa Avenue, LaJolla, CA 92037, 1-800-828-6277. They carry a northern and a southern Wind River Range Hiking Map and Guide Series, each one condensing 15 or more 7.5 minute USGS quadrangles into a single 1:48,000 overview map. Topography is not lost while large overviews of the country are gained. Trails are highlighted, so trip planning is made easier. These maps are available at all sporting goods stores in towns around the range. Again, Falcon Publishing's *Hiking Wyoming's Wind River Range* is also well-mapped.

38 Lake Louise

General description:	A shorter day hike to a pretty, serene, cliff-encompassed lake. Overnight camping is an enjoyable option.
Distance:	6 miles round trip.
Difficulty:	Moderate.
Elevation gain and loss:	1,000 feet.
Key elevation points:	Lake Louise: 8,600 feet.
General location:	14 miles southeast of Dubois, in the northeast section of the Wind River Range.
Special attractions:	Excellent fishing in a deep lake. A hot fire charred the valley above this lake in 1976, and the natural forest regeneration is interesting to witness.
Maps:	Shoshone National Forest south half visitor map; USGS: Torrey Lake, Simpson Lake. Also, Earthwalk Press's Northern Wind River Range.
Manager:	Wind River Ranger District.

Finding the trailhead: The sign 3.8 miles east of downtown Dubois along U.S. Highway 287/26 isn't very big, so watch carefully for it on the southern side of the road. It notes a Wyoming Game and Fish Department fish hatchery location. As you turn off the highway to the south, the road immediately forks. The right or west fork leads to the fish hatchery while the left or southeast branch follows another small sign that points to a conservation camp. Follow this second route toward the camp, and enjoy the ensuing 2.5 miles of washboard gravel road. At the Wyoming Game and Fish Department sheep range sign, the road again forks. The conservation camp sign you want to follow points eastward, and the next 3.5 miles of driving become the worst road in America that a two-wheel-drive rig can still negotiate. The private property owners haven't graded this rock garden of a road since its birth, and it will truly test your driving and your patience.

At the conservation camp, almost 6 miles after leaving the highway, the road forks again. Go right or northwest, following the Glacier Trail sign. Another 2 miles places you in a huge Fitzpatrick Wilderness Trailhead parking area. The Glacier Trail, the Whiskey Mountain Trail, and the Lake Louise Trail begin as one path at the western end of this lot.

The hike: This little hike often serves as a primer to the long Glacier Trail/Gannett Peak hike (Hike 39). It allows folks to test their boots or firm their muscles a bit before undertaking a rather colossal mountain trail. But Lake Louise also affords a great introduction to and escape into the rocky northern-most corner of the Wind Rivers.

Short doesn't necessarily mean easy. The first 0.4 mile of trail switchbacks steeply uphill. Here the Whiskey Mountain Trail branches to the northwest. Continue along the Glacier Trail for another 0.2 mile and a sign will direct you westward toward Lake Louise.

The next 2 miles of trail are easy to follow but somewhat breathy to walk as the trail wanders into, over, and around these impressive waves of rosy-colored granite rock. It weaves into meadowed and forested microenvironments located between the rock-wave troughs. And it passes beside some incredible Torrey Creek cascades. The last several hundred yards of the trail leading to the lake is granite shelf walking.

The deep waters of Lake Louise are completely imprisoned by restricting granite cliffs. One can traverse the lake's distance by either crossing the log jam at the foot of the lake and circumventing the southern shores, or by

Cliff-immured Lake Louise.

Lake Louise

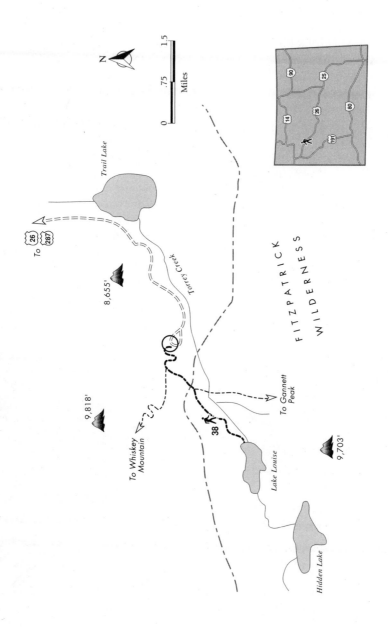

picking a way around the northern cliffs of the lake. Both routes require some scrambling and a little climbing. The southern shore option contains some excellent campsites and is a bit easier.

In 1976 a fire burned the forested area between Lake Louise and its upstream counterpart, Hidden Lake. Rejuvenation has been slow due to the sterile and rugged environment. But a cross-country journey between the lakes and along Torrey Creek is possible, albeit exacting. For the dedicated angler, it may be worth the effort. I've seen Hidden Lake boil like a pot of tea during a hatch-induced feeding frenzy.

39 Glacier Trail

General description:	A rugged, 5 to 8 day (or longer) hike to the largest glacial area and highest peak in Wyoming.
Distance:	Up to 56 miles round trip.
Difficulty:	Strenuous.
Elevation gain or loss:	7,190 feet.
Key elevation points:	Trailhead: 7,600 feet; Burro Flat Pass: 10,895 feet; Double Lake: 9,720 feet; Downs Fork: 9,000 feet; Wilson Meadows: 9,650 feet; End of trail: 10,850 feet.
General location:	15 miles southeast of Dubois, in the northeast section of the Wind River Range.
Special attractions:	The biggest glaciers, the highest peaks, the deepest, cliff-encased valleys, and the most beautiful blue-green glacier-milk creek weaving a channel through it all.
Maps:	Shoshone National Forest southern half visitor map; USGS: Torrey Lake, Inkwells, Fremont Peak North, Gannet Peak, Downs Mountain. Earthwalk Press's Northern Wind River Range hiking map.
Manager:	Wind River Ranger District.

Finding the trailhead: Access via vehicle is exactly the same—including the super rough road—as the Lake Louise Trailhead access (Hike 38). The trailhead is located at the western end of the parking lot.

The hike: The Fitzpatrick Wilderness, 198,838 acres of high-elevation, mountainous rock wonder, was designated in 1976 from what was originally named the Glacier Primitive Area. The area encompasses the northern portion of the Wind Rivers east of the divide. Tom Fitzpatrick was a contemporary of Jim Bridger, and naming agencies decided to place the wilderness appellations of the two trailblazers side by side.

The Glacier Trail forms a 28-mile (one way) adventure. Numerous additional side trails and cross-country explorations are possible in this region, and anyone hiking in for less than a week's time can expect to miss a great deal of adventure and scenery. This is a most popular and sometimes crowded trail. Count on viewing many overused campsites and on encountering many other hikers as you travel. The land, though, still seems large enough to swallow all who enter it.

Older maps will show the trail beginning with a sinuous switchback up the southern sides of Arrow Mountain. In 1976 a massive rockslide wiped out a large section of that mountainside. You can see its scar if you look south-southwest from the parking area. The next year the Forest Service built the current parking facilities and rerouted the trail up the eastern side of East Torrey Creek. This proves to be a less steep, less arid, and less taxing beginning than the old trail. The original route tended to desicate and annihilate first-time and out-of-shape hikers.

A lot of elevation gain accompanies the first 7 or 8 miles of the hike. From a 7,600-foot creek bottom beginning to a 10,895-foot pass above Burro Flat, new trail or not, it's a huffer-and-puffer. Hikers need to be aware that beyond Burro Flat it's 4 more miles to water and tree camping around the Phillips and Dinwoody Lakes area. Above Burro Flat, around what's called Williamson Corrals, water and tree shelter vanish. The open alpine is amazingly beautiful and quite exposed. This second camping area—from Upper Phillips to and including Star Lake—because it forms such a first-day respite after miles of hard hiking, really shows the scars of overuse. Livestock camping and campfires are now prohibited in this area.

From Double Lake southward the trail begins a rugged descent into the Dinwoody Creek drainage. Downs Fork Meadows serves as the

Mountainous country west of Gannett Peak.　PAUL DONHARL PHOTO

Glacier Trail

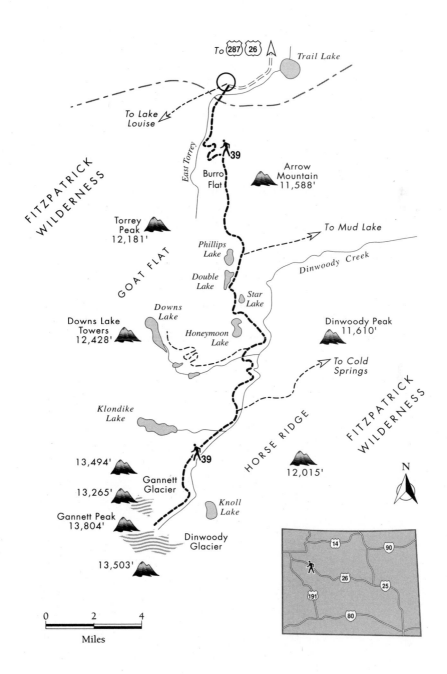

introduction to the exceptionally colored, milky-green creek that will be a companion much of the rest of the journey. Camping is a wherever, whenever choice from now on—as long as you're 100 feet from trails and streams. At Big Meadows, a few miles beyond the Downs Fork Trail intersection, the huge granite monoliths and castles begin to encase the milky-creeked valley. After you pass the Ink Wells Trail intersection, close to 20 miles into the hike, the forests part and the high peaks of Gannett (13,804 feet) and Woodrow Wilson (13,503 feet) begin to rule the western skyline. It all gets bigger and better, more open and more deeply encased, the farther you hike. Even though you're continually loomed over and towered above and tucked in a yawning valley, you still tend to feel you're on top of the world.

The Glacier Trail is well-signed and maintained its entire distance. Some of the side hikes—Inkwells, Downs Fork and Klondike Lake—may not be, although the old Downs Fork bridge was finally replaced in 1996. Good topographic maps are a must on this trip.

Beyond Floyd Wilson Meadows, which contains the last stands of diminishing trees, the trail continues climbing a few miles along the northern banks of a southern branch of Dinwoody Creek. Then it ends as Dinwoody Glacier's moraine becomes too unpredictable to build on. One can continue over Dinwoody Glacier to what's labeled Glacier Pass and drop into the Titcomb Lakes Basin in the Bridger Wilderness. This trek is close to a fourth-class scramble over the most rugged of rocky country and may require an ice axe to safely surmount the huge glacier. Ascending Gannett Peak is also an option, but there are a few technical spots, and it tends to transcend the scope of a hiker's guide.

THE WESTERN WIND RIVERS, SOUTH AND NORTH

In 1931 a large, scenic wildland in the western Wind River Range was set aside as a primitive area. In 1964, that wonderful year of passage of the National Wilderness Act, this acreage became the Bridger Wilderness. In 1984 the area was upped to 428,169 acres. The area's roadless, unspoiled, 99-mile length nestles against a portion of the Continental Divide, whose sheer ruggedness truly personifies the term "backbone of the nation." Approximately 500 miles of intersecting trails leave little of this wilderness inaccessible to hikers, yet cross-country treks to isolated peaks, neighboring creek drainages, and untrailed lakes are easily possible. Please tread lightly across the high-altitude environments if you leave the trail. More than 1,300 lakes (2,300, if you count the unnamed little lakes and ponds) dot the wilderness landscape. Until the 1920s, these lakes supported no fish. Several successful stocking programs have resulted in six trout species, grayling, and/or mountain whitefish inhabiting many of the waterways. Fishing is often superb.

The Pinedale Ranger District has implemented some wilderness-wide rules for the Bridger Wilderness Area. There are no campfires allowed above timberline, and no usage of any Kromnholtz trees for firewood. ("Kromnholtz" means "standing tree"—meaning dead, or alive, or alive with dead branches. In other words, only downed wood can be used for fires.) Groups are limited to 15 people, permits are required for organized groups, and camping is prohibited in a location visible from any lake or trail unless that location is more than 200 feet from that lake or trail. There's also a 16-day stay limit in the wilderness.

40 Little Sandy Lake

General description:	A day hike or easy overnighter to a spectacular lake setting.
Distance:	9 miles round trip.
Difficulty:	Moderate.
Elevation gain and loss:	2,000 feet.
General location:	50 miles northeast of Farson or 60 miles southeast of Pinedale, in the extreme southeastern corner of the Bridger Wilderness.
Special attractions:	One of the shortest hikes granting access to the spectacular peak and lake country of the southern Wind Rivers. Can be used as a jump-off point for longer ventures into the deep wilderness.
Maps:	Bridger-Teton National Forest Pinedale Ranger District map; USGS: Sweetwater Needles, Sweetwater Gap, Temple Peak.
Manager:	Pinedale Ranger District.

Finding the trailhead: About 0.5 mile east of South Pass on Wyoming 28, three signs—a Sweetwater Gap Ranch sign, a Bridger Wilderness Big Sandy Entrance sign, and a county road sign noting the Lander Cutoff Road—direct you onto the Lander Cutoff Road. Drive 15.4 miles northwest along the rolling hills of this graded road. Here, at the first graded road heading northward, a BLM sign points to the Juel Ranch and to Sweetwater Gap. Follow this road north, but don't take the BLM road jutting to the west after 3.5 miles of travel. Continue northward for another 2.5 miles until another BLM sign directs you left or north to the Bridger National Forest. At 8.5 miles along this road a Forest Service sign falsely claims that it's still 6 miles to the Bridger Wilderness. Turn left or west at this road junction, which immediately becomes a jeep road. My little two-wheel-drive truck made it up some serious grades over the road's 2 mile distance, but a lower-clearance vehicle will require you to park and hike these couple of miles. At the road's end, a sign points north to the trail and east to a tiny parking lot.

The hike: In 1988 a massive forest fire swept through several thousand acres of the southeastern corner of the Wind Rivers. The burn generated a heat so intense it actually sterilized the soil, creating a condition of extreme erodibility. The beginnings of this route to Little Sandy Lake and to the Sweetwater Gap area (Hike 41) provide excellent on-site fire ecology lessons. The earth is just now beginning plant successions that will ultimately reforest the area. This particular trail is a much more lightly used pathway to Little Sandy Lake than the popular trail from the Big Sandy access. It's also one of the shortest hiking accesses into the heart of the high peak country.

In but a 0.1 mile distance, beside a wilderness registration sign, the trail

Little Sandy Lake

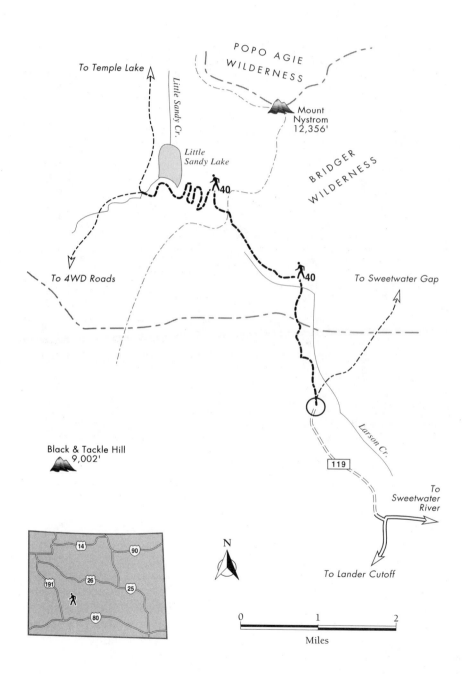

To Temple Lake

Little Sandy Cr.

POPO AGIE
WILDERNESS

Mount
Nystrom
12,356'

Little
Sandy Lake

BRIDGER
WILDERNESS

40

To 4WD Roads

40

To Sweetwater Gap

Larson Cr.

Black & Tackle Hill
9,002'

119

To
Sweetwater
River

N

To Lander Cutoff

14   90

191   26   25

80

0   1   2

Miles

Little Sandy Lake.

forks. There may be no direction sign at this fork, but the Little Sandy Lake Trail heads left while the Sweetwater Gap Trail goes right. After a short downhill ramble into a meadow, the Little Sandy Trail almost vanishes. The trick here is to cut straight northwest across the meadow (sometimes, it's a swamp). A cairn marks the trail's meadow exit, and the track of the trail visibly cuts into the burned forest above the grassy and open area.

The next mile forms an intense experience in fire-transformed landscapes. Near the Bridger Wilderness boundary, the burn stops. One step has you hiking a used-match forest and the next places you beneath a green bower, as if no burn had ever occurred. The trail is gentle for the first 1.5 miles. Then it remembers it has a pass to climb, and the next 2 miles ascend a steep grade. Take time to view the surrounding lodgepole forests. Some amazing burls have formed on these trees. The Continental Divide crossing into the Little Sandy drainage is thickly forested and unspectacular, but the now descending trail's occasional views of the striking walls and cliffs and high pinnacles of the peaks towering over the lake make up for that. A little over a mile of steep downhill switchbacking places you in a Wind River scenic wonderland by the lake.

Camping spots are a bit sparse beside Little Sandy Lake. The trail leading into the high peak heart of this area skirts the southern shores of the lake and crosses Little Sandy Creek before venturing north. If you hike this trip as a day hike, remember the climb and return distance you have yet to cover before day's end.

41 Sweetwater Gap

General description:	A long but quite enjoyable day hike (or a leisurely overnighter) to a high pass that accesses the Popo Agie Wilderness from the south.
Distance:	14 miles round trip.
Difficulty:	Moderate to strenuous.
Elevation gain and loss:	1,620 feet.
Key elevation points:	Sweetwater Gap: 10,420 feet.
General location:	60 miles southeast of Pinedale, in the extreme southeastern corner of the Bridger Wilderness.
Special attractions:	A lightly used trail, wonderful stream fishing, pretty meadow camping and incomparable views.
Maps:	Bridger-Teton National Forest Pinedale Ranger District Bridger Wilderness map; USGS: Sweetwater Needles, Sweetwater Gap.
Manager:	Pinedale Ranger District.

Finding the trailhead: Directions are identical to those in the Little Sandy Lake Trail (Hike 40)

The hike: Sweetwater Gap is a fun adventure into the headwater beginnings of that untamed river. After hiking the initial 0.1 mile from the registration sign, be certain to take the right or east fork at the trail intersection. Like its counterpart to the west, this trail also journeys through the blackened landscape of a recent forest fire. The first 1.3 miles to the Bridger Wilderness boundary is quite a charred-wood experience. Beyond that, green forest dominates the scenery. So do the gentle pools and still pockets of the rapidly forming Sweetwater River. Several peaceful meadows dress the forest and offer ideal camping and stream fishing spots.

The trail wanders gently uphill for more than 5 miles. Then the lodgepole

Sweetwater Gap

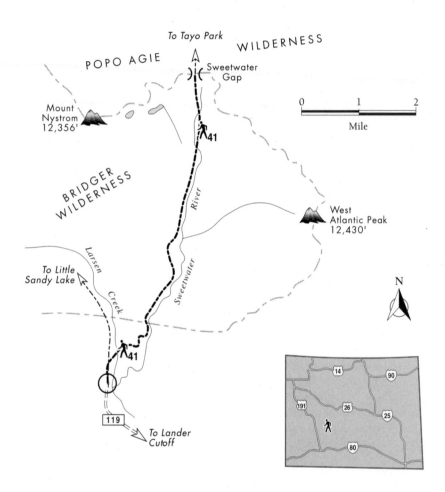

pine turns to limber pine, and the sub-alpine spruce claims hillside dominance. The final 2 miles to Sweetwater Gap become a moderate climb. The pass itself is a large and broad meadow with excellent views northwest toward Wind River Peak.

This trail is a most typical Wind River trail, in that you hike and hike, mostly over rocky path and through obscure lodgepole forests. Occasional glimpses of large peaks present themselves, but the views rarely last more than a moment. Then, near the summit, the mountain world explodes into stunning views. Sweetwater Gap, from this approach, offers a shorter and less-used access into the Tayo Park/Ice Lakes high country of the southern Popo Agie Wilderness (Hike 35). Fine camping spots are available the entire length of the trail, including in and around the open meadows near the pass.

With little hiker usage, both the Sweetwater Gap and the Little Sandy Lake trails are rarely maintained, so you might be climbing over a few logs, especially in the burn areas.

42 Alpine Lakes

General description:	A 6- to 10-day, very rugged trek for experienced hikers into the heart of the Wind River high country.
Distance:	45 miles round trip.
Difficulty:	Strenuous; experts only. Map reading skills essential.
Elevation gain and loss:	4,050 feet.
Key elevation points:	Trailhead: 9,350 feet; Seneca Lake: 10,300 feet; Indian Pass: 12,100 feet; Camp Lake: 9,660 feet; Hay Pass: 10,960 feet; Timico Lake: 10,750 feet; Chain Lakes: 9,980 feet.
General location:	25 miles northeast of Pinedale, in the central part of the Wind River Range.
Special attractions:	High alpine peaks, cross-country glacier walks, and rarely visited terrain.
Maps:	Bridger-Teton National Forest Pinedale Ranger District and Shoshone National Forest south half visitor maps; USGS: Fremont Peak South, Bridger Lakes, Horseshoe Lakes.
Fees:	Trails End Campground: $8 to $10 per night.
Manager:	Pinedale and Washakie Ranger Districts.

Finding the trailhead: The trailhead starts at Elkhart Park, 14 miles northeast of Pinedale. Take Sublette County 134 (prominently signed for Fremont and Half Moon Lakes) east out of Pinedale. The paved road deadends at the Trails End Campground. The trailhead is located at the northeast corner of the parking lot, between the campground and the ranger's station.

The hike: The previous 2 trails (Little Sandy Lake, Hike 40, and Sweetwater Gap, Hike 41) receive almost no usage. Now let's look at an awesome area starting at the highest usage trailhead in the Bridger Wilderness. The parking lot itself is designed to accommodate 120 cars.

This is a rugged 45-mile loop into the central section of the Wind River Range. It crosses the Continental Divide twice and follows a high glacial valley. It is best to allow yourself a minimum of 6 days of travel due to the nature of the terrain and the unpredictability of the weather.

Begin on the Pole Creek Trail, which heads east through the woods following Faler Creek for 1 mile. It then turns northeast and reaches Miller Park after 4 miles. Here a trail to Miller Lake cuts off to the right. Pole Creek Trail re-enters the woods for about a mile and comes out on Photographers

Point, which affords spectacular views of Gorge Lake and the Continental Divide to the east.

Another meadow appears in 0.5 mile where the Sweeney Lake Trail cuts to the right. The main trail rounds a knob and drops down to Eklund Lake. At the north end of the lake, Pole Creek Trail turns right and heads east. The Seneca Lake Trail—your new route—turns left and drops down around the west side of Barbara Lake. This trail then descends several switchbacks and climbs back up to Hobbs Lake.

About 0.5 mile beyond Hobbs Lake the trail crosses Seneca Creek, which must be forded farther upstream during high water in the early part of the season. The trail passes several small lakes in the next mile and drops into a small basin before climbing up to Seneca Lake. You're now about 8 miles from Elkhart Park. Fremont and Jackson Peaks dominate the eastern skyline. With the 200-foot camping limitation, there are very few campsites in this area.

From here the Seneca Lake Trail continues along the shoreline of the western side of the lake. High water early in the season may force a higher route by scrambling over the rocks above the shore. At the north end of the lake the Lost Lake Trail heads left and the Seneca Lake Trail continues to Little Seneca Lake, beyond which it ascends to meet the Highline Trail.

The Highline Trail runs north and south at about timberline for the entire length of the Wind River Range. Follow this trail north up a series of switchbacks to a saddle where the Highline Trail continues north and the Indian Pass Trail—your new route—turns east toward Island Lake.

Alpine splendor at Alpine Lakes. PAUL DONHARL PHOTO

Alpine Lakes

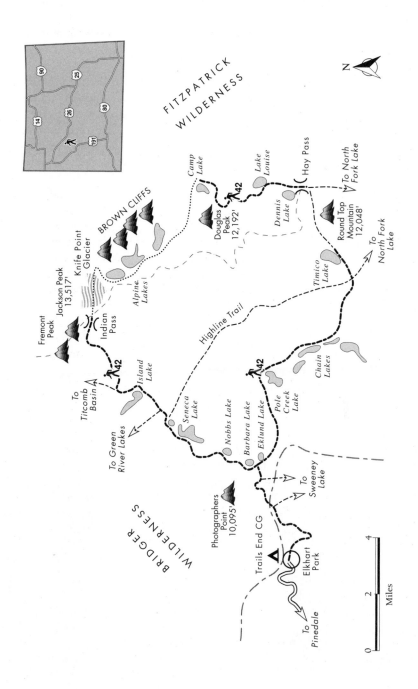

You'll reach Island Lake in about 1.5 miles. This is a most popular area, with many campsites on the southeastern shore. The Indian Pass Trail skirts the southern shore and then starts a gradual climb for 0.75 mile to the cutoff for Titcomb Basin. Titcomb Basin is always overcrowded, with up to 75 camps at a time (way beyond the original wilderness management plan). Indian Pass Trail turns right here, and it's just over 3 miles to the pass (the sign says 6).

Indian Pass Trail climbs about 200 feet in the first mile to Indian Basin. Here there are suitable campsites around the several lakes in the basin. However, the weather is very unpredictable at this elevation, with frequent afternoon showers, lightning, hail, and possibly snow. The trail climbs more than 1,000 feet in the next 2 miles, passing under the bases of Fremont (13,745 feet) and Jackson (13,517 feet) Peaks. At Indian Pass, 12,100 feet, the trail ends.

Beyond Indian Pass, cross-country and wilderness adventure begin. A knowledge of cross-country and glacier travel with appropriate equipment is a prerequisite for this part of the journey. Descend east onto Knife Point Glacier. An ice axe is necessary, and crampons are highly recommended. Journey east past the large rock knobs and then turn southeast toward a looming 12,860-foot unnamed peak. After a mile of glacier crossing, begin a steep ascent to a saddle which lies at 12,120 feet. Maps label this Alpine Pass.

From the top of this saddle it is a fairly steep descent to the highest of the three Alpine Lakes. There is a good area for a campsite at the north end of this lake. The Brown Cliffs rise almost 1,500 vertical feet on the east, as does the Continental Divide on the west.

From the north end of the lake, climb up the western wall to just below the snout of an ice field and stay high above the lake for the next two miles. Be prepared to scramble over some "Volkswagen" sized boulders on the way.

At the north end of the lowest Alpine Lake, some maps show a suggested route which follows the eastern shore. This will result in a 100-foot walk through the lake and in chest-deep water. An alternative is to follow the western shore for about 0.75 mile to the drainage from a lake at the base of Douglas Peak. Go to the lake and turn east, climb about 100 feet to a small saddle, and descend, following the drainage to the three small and unnamed lakes just above Camp Lake.

A real trail appears on the eastern shore of Camp Lake. Follow this trail south and begin a 600-foot climb to 2 small but deep lakes at the southern base of Douglas Peak. Cross the saddle and descend into the Middle Fork of the Bull Lake Creek drainage which contains Upper Golden, Louise, and Golden Lakes respectively. The trail follows the northern shores of these lakes and begins a 700-foot climb to Hay Pass.

At Hay Pass, 10,960 feet, the trail drops into the North Fork of Boulder Creek and eventually meets the cutoff to the Timico Lake Trail. A many-mile-saving alternative to this route is to bushwhack around the northern slopes of Round Top Mountain from Hay Pass. Head southwest from the lake west of Hay Pass to the meadows at 11,000 feet and follow this elevation around to the saddle where you rejoin the trail to Timico Lake. Keep an eye out for bighorn sheep. At Timico Lake there are several good campsites, both at the northern end and also away from the eastern shores.

The trail crosses the Fremont Trail about a mile west of Timico Lake. At the signpost, head almost due west on the Bell Lakes Trail which drops down to Chain Lakes in 3 miles. Continue to Pole Creek Lake where the trail junctions with the aspur trail east to the Highline Trail. Follow the main trail west about 2 miles to the lower ford of Pole Creek. About 0.25 mile past this ford you'll reach the Pole Creek Trail. Eklund Lake lies about 3.5 miles west on this trail, which passes several small lakes, including Mary's Lake. Mary's Lake boasts but a few campsites, but the meadows and ponds east of it supply great camping. Once at Eklund Lake, Elkhart Park is but 6 more miles west.

—Paul Donharl

43 Clear Creek Natural Bridge

General description:	A peaceful day hike to an awesome geological sculpture. A wonderful family hike.
Distance:	10 miles round trip.
Difficulty:	Moderate.
Elevation gain and loss:	250 feet.
Key elevation points:	Clear Creek Natural Bridge: 8,300 feet.
General location:	50 miles north of Pinedale, in the northern section of the Bridger Wilderness.
Maps:	Bridger-Teton National Forest Pinedale Ranger District visitor map and/or USGS: Green River Lakes quad.
Special attractions:	Waterfalls, springs, crystal-clear creeks, a monumental natural bridge, and towering mountain cliffs.
Fees:	Green River Lakes Campground: $8 to $10.
Manager:	Pinedale Ranger District.

Finding the trailhead: From Pinedale drive 6 miles west on U.S. Highway 191 to a Bridger Wilderness Green River access sign that also happens to be Wyoming 352. This road will meander northward for 26.4 miles before the pavement ends and the road transforms into Forest Road 091. Another 20 miles of this long, rutted, and possibly impassible-when-wet road brings you to the Green River Lakes Campground. Just before driving into the fee campground area, a large sign directs hikers to a wilderness/trailhead parking area where a bulletin board explains the various trail options and wilderness regulations.

Water flows from beneath Clear Creek Natural Bridge.

The hike: Anyone who has floated through Dinosaur National Monument or witnessed the amazing confluence of the Green and Colorado Rivers in Canyonlands National Park knows what a mighty body of moving water the Green River becomes. What fun it is to trace that full-grown river to its bubbling spring beginnings amid the flanks of the precipitous Wyoming mountains. The following 3 hikes (Hikes 43, 44, and 45) guide you into the different settings and personalities of the various sources of the Green River. Clear Creek Natural Bridge is the wonderful kind of day hike that allows for easy wandering while permitting you to see a fair amount of incredible scenery. It's also a great first-day, get-the-legs-strengthened hike for the long and rugged journeys one can choose to travel from this location.

By an old cabin near the southwest corner of the hiker's parking lot, a trail sign directs you south into a draw. Soon the trail forks, with the signed

Clear Creek Natural Bridge

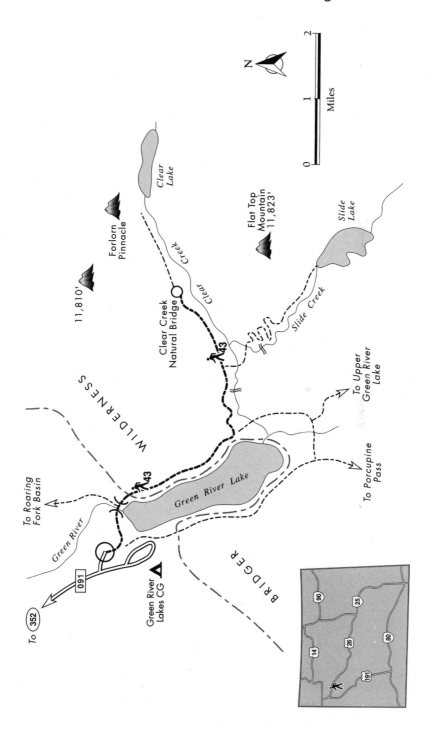

N

Miles
0 1 2

Clear Lake

Forlorn Pinnacle

11,810'

Flat Top Mountain 11,823'

Slide Lake

Clear Creek

Clear Creek Natural Bridge

Slide Creek

43

WILDERNESS

To Upper Green River Lake

To Roaring Fork Basin

43

Green River Lake

To Porcupine Pass

Green River

091

Green River Lakes CG

BRIDGER

To 352

90

25

26

80

14

191

Highline Trail branching left and down that forested draw. Follow this trail east 0.3 mile to a major steel bridge spanning the already huge Green River. Just across the bridge, the trail to Clear Creek Natural Bridge is signed and journeys to the right or southeast.

This trail skirts the south-facing shores of Lower Green River Lake for nearly 2 miles. Southeast of the trailhead 0.1 mile be sure to take the main trail to the right, not the hunting trail to the left. Then enjoy an easygoing stroll in open grassy and sage meadows where the only concern is that there are too many scenic wonders to see.

At 2 miles from the bridge a sign directs the trail eastward and into the Clear Creek drainage. The trail gently switchbacks along a canyon wall that offers great views of cascading Clear Creek Falls. Then it enters into a vast mountain-encompassed meadowland where gentle Clear Creek snakes through the middle of the scenery. Hike 1.3 miles of this and you'll arrive at the Slide Creek Lake Trail intersection. The bridge spanning the Clear Creek was washed out (for the umpteenth time) when I visited and is scheduled for replacement in 1998. On this trail, about 2 long miles of wooded and steep uphill hiking brings you to the large bowl holding aptly named Slide Lake.

Continuing up Clear Creek for another 1.2 miles, you arrive at the natural bridge, a massive, building-sized rectangle of rock that the creek decided to burrow under rather than weave a way around or carve a channel through. Ponderous Flat Top Mountain rules the eastern horizon, and a lofty crag of granite spires named Forlorn Pinnacle grabs all upstream skyline attention. The last mile of hiking to the bridge is through a forest fire burn, but ample camping exists anywhere below that area. Be sure and follow the trail around to the other side of the bridge to see where the water funnels under the rock.

The trail does continue in an unmaintained manner up the creek to Clear Lake, and many adventurers use this area as a step-off into the alpine Bear Basin area.

44 Green River Lakes to Summit Lake

General description:	A multi-day, adventurous backpack into the rocky headwaters of the Green River.
Distance:	32 miles round trip.
Difficulty:	Strenuous.
Elevation gain:	2,230 feet.
Key elevation points:	Trailhead: 8,050 feet; 9.8 mile Green River Crossing: 8,700 feet; Summit Lake: 10,280 feet.
General location:	50 miles north of Pinedale, in the northern section of the Bridger Wilderness.
Special attractions:	This is the breathtaking country that promotional bureaus photograph for their "Visit Wild Wyoming" brochures. Wild vistas of the Gannett Peak area.
Maps:	Bridger-Teton National Forest Pinedale Ranger District visitor map; USGS: Green River Lakes, Squaretop Mountain, Gannett Peak; Earthwalk Press's Northern Wind River Range Hiking and Guide.
Fees:	Green River Lakes Campground: $8 to $10 per night.
Manager:	Pinedale Ranger District.

Finding the trailhead: Road access directions are identical to those in the Clear Creek Natural Bridge hike description (Hike 43).

The hike: So many hiking options exist here, so much outstanding and spectacular beauty abounds, that a week will barely allow you to see and feel the country. Take at least 5 days. Take 10 days. This is not country you want to rush through. The Green River Valley offers awesome views and settings. Summit Lake shouldn't be a final goal but a base camp from which to foray into the surrounding peaks, glaciers and alpine lakes.

You can begin this trail by journeying around Lower Green River Lake via either the southwestern or the northeastern shores. The bridge over Clear Creek has been replaced (but, as mentioned in Hike 43, don't assume it's still there; instead, check with the Pinedale Ranger District for confirmation). The Lakeside Trail is indicated at the hiker's parking lot.

The first 2.5 miles of this level Lakeside Trail skirt the lake's shores, but the forest hides the surrounding views. After you walk across the meadow at the head of Lower Green River Lake, cross the quite large bridge spanning the Green River, and hike a total of 3 miles to Upper Green River Lake. Here the limitless panoramas begin, and they never end. This area is actually one of the most photographed locales in Wyoming. Towering Squaretop Mountain creates a magnificent backdrop to this scenic lake. For 2.5 miles beyond the upper lake, large and open meadows rule the valley bottom.

Green River Lakes to Summit Lake

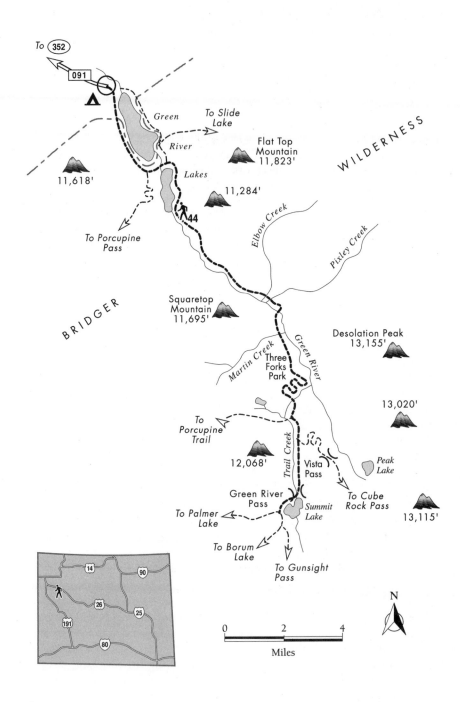

To 352

091

Green

River

To Slide
Lake

Flat Top
Mountain
11,823'

11,618'

Lakes

11,284'

44

To Porcupine
Pass

WILDERNESS

Elbow Creek

Pixley Creek

Squaretop
Mountain
11,695'

BRIDGER

Desolation Peak
13,155'

Martin Creek

Green River

Three
Forks
Park

13,020'

To
Porcupine
Trail

Trail Creek

12,068'

Vista
Pass

Peak
Lake

Green River
Pass

Summit
Lake

To Cube
Rock Pass

13,115'

To Palmer
Lake

To Borum
Lake

To Gunsight
Pass

14   90

26   25

191

80

N

0   2   4

Miles

Squaretop Mountain grows from a distant centerpiece into a looming overhead projection.

After 6 miles of level hiking, the meadows end and the trail becomes typical Wind River valley hiking. Thick forests and rocky trails sneak beneath the sheer and towering granite faces of surrounding cliffs. You must cross the river back to the west side at 9.8 miles. This may be quite a crossing. The Forest Service has removed the wired-together, bobbing-log bridge over the swift waters, and plan to build a more permanent structure in 1998. BUT NOTE: This will be the sixth replacement of the bridge in this area. With the number of wet years increasing, they can't guarantee a bridge will be there when you hike this country. If the bridge is out, one option is to backtrack about 0.3 mile down the trail and ford the river at a stock crossing trail. Use common sense here, and don't chance it if the water seems too deep.

You'll reach Three Forks Park 1.5 miles after the river crossing—a glorious breadth of meadowed country that affords no camping opportunities. Be advised that with the 200-foot camping restriction regulation, it's hard to find suitable camping locations in the first 12 miles of this trail. Up to Three Forks Park, the 11 miles of the trail is mostly level. Beyond Three Forks it begins a steep switchbacking climb for 2 miles. Here you encounter Trail Creek, a too-wide-to-jump gush of crystalline water. No bridge guarantees on this one, either.

About a mile beyond the Trail Creek crossing, a signed intersection offers a route westward to the Porcupine Trail (Hike 45). You've hiked over 13 miles to this point, and the high, jagged, and spectacular country is just beginning. There are now numerous options and decisions to consider. Great camping exists in this Trail Creek Park area. In fact, so many people camp here that you might consider cutting way off the trail to set up a base camp from which to explore. To the south, the 3-mile hike to Green River Pass and Summit Lake is mostly above timberline. At the lake the land is wide, flat, open, and above it all. Along the way, a wild trail jogs eastward to Vista, Cube Rock, and Shannon passes. Every step of this trail places you in the western shadows of the highest Wind River Peaks. In tune with the mode of the country, there can be no guarantee that this trail exists during any given year. The area is highly prone to slides and avalanches, and as often as the Forest Service rebuilds it, the trail gets annihilated.

Be sure and carry a good map for an overview of all the hiking options in this grandest of mountain high country.

45 Porcupine Creek to Porcupine Pass

General description:	A 3-day (or more) hike that is a little-known and less-traveled sister hike to the Green River Trail (Hike 44).
Distance:	18 miles round trip.
Difficulty:	Strenuous.
Elevation gain and loss:	2,650 feet.
Key elevation points:	Porcupine Creek Falls: 8,320 feet; Porcupine Pass: 10,700 feet.
General location:	50 miles north of Pinedale, in the northern section of the Bridger Wilderness.
Special attractions:	Many additional routes branch off from this trail.
Maps:	Bridger-Teton National Forest Pinedale Ranger District; USGS: Green River Lakes, Squaretop Mountain.
Manager:	Pinedale Ranger District.
Fees:	Green River Campground: $8 to $10.

Finding the trailhead: Same as Hike 43.

The hike: The Continental Divide backbone of the Wind Rivers forms a most spectacular, jagged, and awesome line of mountainous crags. No less captivating are the unique peaks and cirques, flats, and drainages within the range that lie outside the immediate sphere of these high granite steeples. In fact, much of the range's wildlife lives within these encircling boundaries. The mountains surrounding Porcupine Creek project a more rounded and flat-topped look than the high neighbors to the east. The cliffs overlooking the drainage emanate an untamed, almost ferocious beauty.

Trace the first 2.3 miles of the Lakeside Trail along the beginning of the Green River Lakes hike (Hike 44). At this point, near the head of Lower Green River Lake, a sign will direct you southward and onto the Porcupine Trail.

After 0.2 mile of level meadow skirting, you meet the first crossing of Porcupine Creek. Look upstream, as there MAY be some hefty spruce trees spanning the waters and facilitating an easier crossing. The next 1.5 miles switchback quite steeply through a basic no-view lodgepole forest. Finishing this ascent, it's time to again cross the creek in a probable wade. Immediately beyond this ford, the Twin Lakes Trail breaks away to the west and will, in a bit more than 1 mile's steep uphill distance, take you into a small mountain bowl hiding 4 reclusive lakes.

The main trail continues southward and now begins breaking into various meadows. Beyond the Twin Lakes intersection at 0.3 mile, count on again wading the creek. But also know that your hiking efforts are about to be rewarded. The meadows become vast and open, and the towering

Porcupine Creek to Porcupine Pass

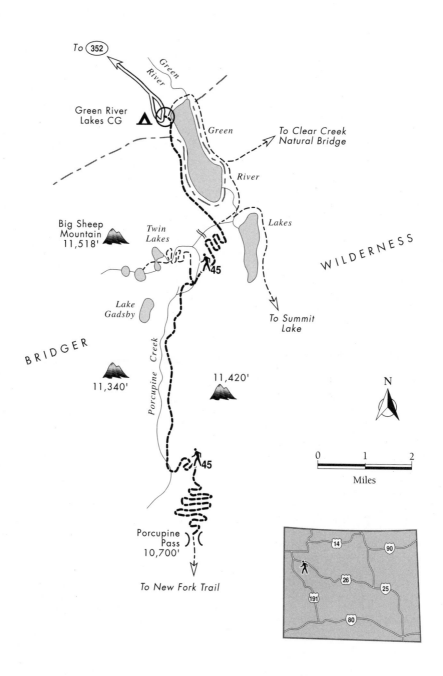

To (352)

Green River

Green River
Lakes CG

Green

To Clear Creek
Natural Bridge

River

Big Sheep
Mountain
11,518'

Twin
Lakes

Lakes

WILDERNESS

45

Lake
Gadsby

To Summit
Lake

BRIDGER

11,420'

Porcupine Creek

11,340'

N

45

0   1   2

Miles

Porcupine
Pass
10,700'

To New Fork Trail

14

90

26

25

191

80

mountains stand tall and beautiful around them. The next 2 miles distance has the hiker walking a gentle to moderate slope through deepening forests and into many slide areas where the trees have been obliterated by winter avalanches.

Another east-to-west creek crossing occurs almost 5 miles after the beginning of Porcupine Trail. Here you start to penetrate the subalpine country. The trail recrosses the creek 0.2 mile later for the last time and then jogs east and begins a steep switchbacking ascent toward Porcupine Pass. The last section of this journey forms a phenomenal zigzag that climbs 0.2 mile of mountain in 1.5 miles of switchbacks. Porcupine Pass, at 10,700 feet, is small in area and offers no available liquid, so water needs to be carried if you feel the urge to camp near (200 feet or more from the trail) the summit. Good camping does exist further southward and down from the pass.

The trail continues south of the pass, providing access to the New Fork Lakes area and loop access to numerous lakes, canyons and peaks in the Bridger Wilderness. Following the New Fork Trail east past the Lozier Lakes, over Greely Point, and into Trail Creek Park not only offers a nice loop hike back to the Green River Lakes (Hike 44), it also provides excellent views of the western faces of the high mountains. Good maps are essential to show you all the possibilities.

SALT RIVER RANGE

Not all of Wyoming's many mountain ranges are granite cored. A softer and more subtle beauty distinguishes high mountains composed of sedimentary sea remnants. In the southwestern sector of Wyoming, two exceptional parallel mountain chains offer remote and unpublished hiking opportunities amid the crumpled and steeply tilted rock layers of the Salt River and Wyoming Ranges. Divided by the Greys River, these two north-south ranges of the Overthrust Belt are actually part of an identical structural mountain-chain formation.

Geologists are not certain where these mountain ranges originated. Thick sections of thrust-deformed sedimentary rocks, later to be named the Salt River and Wyoming Ranges, slid into Wyoming and piled against the Gros Ventre and Teton Ranges. But from whence they slid still remains a mystery.

The Overthrust Belt tells a sad story for many Wyoming conservationists. Nearly 700,000 acres of wilderness were identified in this area during the RARE studies. This wasn't just quality wilderness; this was quiet, isolated, and untrodden wilderness. But a 1984 USGS study claimed the Overthrust area "to be highly favorable for the occurrence of gas and oil." The Wyoming congressional delegation proposed but one-fifth of the acreage for wilderness study. These mountain ranges are now blanketed with oil, gas, and mineral leases.

The Bridger-Teton National Forest map for this area is the Big Piney, Greys River, and Kemmerer Ranger Districts map. The Big Piney District is located in Big Piney, the Greys River District in Afton, and the Kemmerer District in Kemmerer. The Forest Service map is excellent in contour detail, but wisdom dictates checking with these districts when planning a new and undocumented hike into these ranges. Trails very often have been converted into roads that lead to new drillholes. Also, ATVs have claimed many of the former hiking trails as motorized domain, and the map doesn't note the occurrence. This section of the state—and these two ranges in particular—feature the friable kind of soil mentioned in the introduction to this book. Cattle, sheep, and horses can completely alter the trails in a summer.

On the other hand, this section of Wyoming still offers a kind of exploration rarely found these days. The country is very big, people are rare, and hikers can create trips that are not defined by the thousands who tread before them.

46 Poker Creek Trail to Lake Alice

General description: A 2- to 3-day, long and rugged journey into one of the few natural lakes in the Commissary Ridge/Salt River Range area.

Distance: 15 miles round trip.

Difficulty: Moderate to strenuous.

Elevation gain and loss: 2,670 feet.

Key elevation points: Trailhead: 8,550 feet; Commissary Ridge Pass: 9,600 feet; Lake Alice: 7,980 feet.

General location: 40 miles west of Big Piney, in the Bridger-Teton National Forest.

Special attractions: Scenic hiking on a little-used trail. A beautiful and large lake to play in, at, or on.

Maps: Bridger-Teton National Forest Big Piney, Greys River and Kemmerer Districts map; USGS: Graham Peak.

Manager: Kemmerer Ranger District.

Finding the trailhead: When driving roads to trailheads in this sector of the forest, it's highly recommended that you have the forest visitor map in your lap and trace every mile of the journey, especially marking off all the road intersections. Road junction sign-thieves create havoc for newcomers in this area by stealing or vandalizing the forest road markers.

There are 4 ways to access the Poker Creek Trailhead: 1) The Greys River/La Barge Creek Road (Forest Road 10138), which leaves U.S. Highway 189 about 1 mile south of the town of La Barge; 2) The Smiths Fork Road (Forest Road 10072), which exits U.S. Highway 89 about 6 miles south of the town of Smoot; 3) The Greys River/La Barge Creek Road (Forest Road 10138), which also leaves U.S. Highway 89 at the town of Alpine; and 4) from the town of Big Piney, which is kind of complicated and described below:

From Big Piney turn west on Wyoming 350. It's paved for nearly 11 miles. Then Sublette County 142 begins as you follow the signs left or south toward Snyder Basin. La Barge Meadows is your final goal, so any sign with this name is a direction sign. The county road ends after 4.4 miles, and a 1-mile section of private road with some gruesome speed bumps follows. After this section you cross a cattle guard and come upon an unsigned intersection. Turn left or south, continuing beside South Piney Creek. Forest Service land begins 5.5 miles later, and Forest Service Road 10128 is a welcome relief after the bumps of the preceeding BLM road. Follow this road past the Snyder Guard Station. Turn right 6.1 miles after the forest boundary and 1.4 miles later turn right again, into the Kemmerer Ranger District and over what is labeled Witherspoon Pass. Three miles later the road T's into Forest Road 10138. Another right or west turn and 6.5 miles of driving places you at a huge, commemorative "La Barge Meadows" sign. Near the south end of the La Barge Meadows, about 1 mile south of the junction of the Greys River/La Barge Road (Forest Road 10138) and the Smiths Fork

The glorious and unknown Mt. Isabel in Commissary Ridge.

Road (Forest Road 10072), a road parallels the east side of Little Corral Creek. Any two-wheel-drive vehicle can handle this rough road for the few tenths of a mile to the trailhead if you are good at straddling ruts.

Another, easier access route (if you happen to be journeying from Jackson), is to drive 16 miles south of Afton on U.S. Highway 89. Just beyond the forest boundary turn east onto Forest Road 10072, the Smiths Fork Road. This graded and graveled road weaves throughout the mountains for 24 miles to the Tri Basin Divide intersection. Turn southward and drive toward La Barge Meadows (on Forest Road 10138) for a bit over 1 mile. Little Corral Creek is signed, and the road leading to the trail is just east of the creek.

The hike: Hiking the more southern portions of the massive Bridger-Teton Forest requires arduous drives over military roads. Consequently, few

Poker Creek Trail to Lake Alice

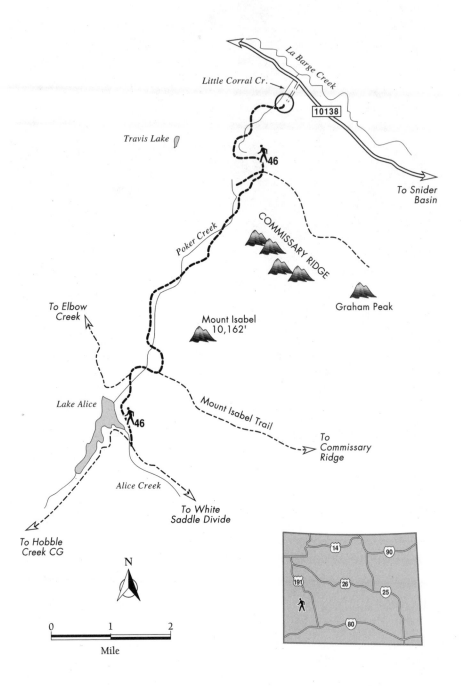

La Barge Creek

Little Corral Cr.

10138

Travis Lake

46

To Snider Basin

COMMISSARY RIDGE

Poker Creek

Graham Peak

To Elbow Creek

Mount Isabel 10,162'

Lake Alice

46

Mount Isabel Trail

To Commissary Ridge

Alice Creek

To White Saddle Divide

To Hobble Creek CG

N

0   1   2

Mile

14

90

191

26

25

80

casual explorers venture here. Commissary Ridge, named after the commissary or supply wagons hauled into this country by the stockmen who grazed sheep here in the 1880s, is a many-mile crest of 9,000- to 10,000-foot ridge elevations and open forests that extends from La Barge Meadows south to Fossil Butte (Hike 22). Not an official wilderness area, this unique roadless area's edges are being encroached upon by piecemeal development. Lake Alice is the largest natural lake in the Wyoming division of the Bridger-Teton National Forest. It was formed thousands of years ago when a huge section of Lake Mountain slid into the valley below. It gained its name in memory of a small child who drowned in its waters in the early 1900s. Renowned for its scenic grandeur and fishing, it contains the only pure Lacustrine strain of Bonneville Cutthroat Trout in the world.

The trail begins along the eastern shores of Little Corral Creek, and passes beneath a towering forest of monstrous spruces—trees so huge three people holding hands couldn't hug them. There are several creek crossings in the 2 miles to the top of Commissary Ridge, but they are simple hops. No ridge walking is required after this first steepish climb, as the trail immediately and steeply descends into incredible, ravine-like Poker Canyon. This gorge is awesome in depth while shy in width, and offers animated scenery to match its ruggedness. It's over 5 miles of bold downhill to Lake Alice. A mile before the lake, the trail crosses to the south side of the stream in a wade, and then a half mile later, by a permanent hunting camp, it re-crosses. This second crossing, in July, is a watery and willowed jungle that is almost impossible to negotiate. I had to backtrack and re-cross Poker Creek upstream. On the return hike I easily avoided both creek crossings by staying on and cross-countrying the western shore of the creek.

The best camping occurs in the meadows near Poker Creek's inlet into the lake. Being a reservoir (albeit a natural one), the sides of the lake extend up the steep and forested hillsides and camping is non-existent around the edge of the lake. Also note that around the first of July, due to high runoff, the trails around both sides of the lake may be under water in places. This situation corrects itself as summer wears on.

A second trail to the outlet of Lake Alice is but a few miles hike from the Hobble Creek Campground west of the lake. But it's a much more spectacular and isolated journey to touch the clear, deep, and blue waters of Lake Alice via the back entrance.

The soil in this country is a bizarre kind of clay that turns to pure goosh when it's wet and concrete when it dries. It can be really rough walking if horse and game hooves have cratered the wet ground and the soil later dries in that shape. Also, stinging nettles occasionally line the trail. Be wary if you have a particularly strong reaction to their touch. Numerous other hiking trails can be found in this area, including another route to Lake Alice over Mount Isabel.

47 Lander Cutoff or The Way Trail

General description:	An enjoyable day hike along an historic Oregon Trail route.
Distance:	Up to 12 miles round trip.
Difficulty:	Easy.
Elevation gain and loss:	1,400 feet (in several ups and downs).
Key elevation points:	Trailhead: 8,500 feet; Wagner Pass: 8,700 feet.
General location:	45 miles west of Big Piney, near the southern end of the Salt River Range and northern beginning of Commissary Ridge, in the Bridger-Teton National Forest.
Special attractions:	A little-known hike along the famous covered-wagon route of the mid-1800s.
Maps:	Bridger-Teton National Forest Big Piney, Greys River and Kemmerer Districts visitor map; USGS: Poison Meadows.
Manager:	Kemmerer Ranger District.

Finding the trailhead: If you come from the east and Big Piney, follow the directions to Little Corral Creek/Poker Creek as given in Hike 46. Continue west 1 more mile to a major road intersection, Tri Basin Divide. Turn west onto the Smiths Fork Road and travel 0.6 mile to the well-signed and visible La Barge Meadows Guard Station. Turning south on this road and parking near the station places you by the signed "Old Lander Trail."

If you drive from Afton, again follow the second set of directions in Hike 46, turning onto the Smiths Fork Road and driving approximately 23.5 miles to the same La Barge Guard Station sign.

The hike: The Oregon Trail is certainly the most famous of the many wagon routes to and through the West. From 1834 to 1868, more than 30,000 travelers a year strained a passage through the inhospitable country that later became the state of Wyoming. In 1858, General F.W. Lander directed construction of an Oregon Trail shortcut route that both shortened the journey's distance by 200 miles and stayed closer to the welcome wood and water of the southern Wind River and Wyoming Ranges. Only a tiny portion of the Lander Cutoff isn't part of or quite close to a modern-day roadway. The Old Lander Trail affords an unequaled opportunity to retrace a portion of that history. This section of the Lander Trail, from the La Barge Guard Station to the Smiths Fork Road has been described as the best preserved emigrants' road in the United States.

This trail is as much a journey into your mind as it is a pleasant physical walk. The more you read and know about the Oregon Trail and its trials and hardships, the more you'll be able to imagine the creaking wagons and the hope behind the incredibly arduous journey you're reliving. After an uphill

Lander Cutoff or The Way Trail

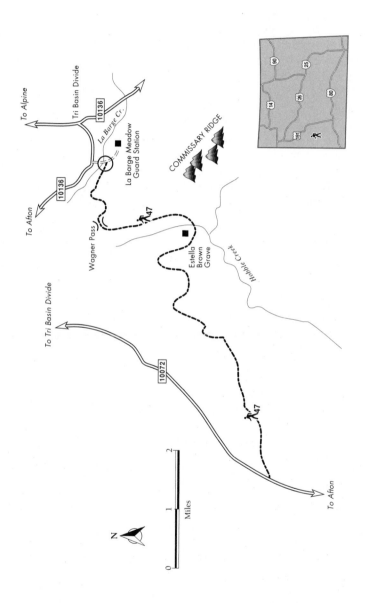

mile to Commissary Ridge at Wagner Pass, and another mile down into the Hobble Creek drainage, you too will be in awe of what these pioneers managed to do and where they managed to go. All the while, there is also the bonus of exceptionally beautiful and peaceful mountains with great valley views and huge trees.

In l996, the Kemmerer Ranger District began maintaining the trail again, and outfitters also help keep it open. Perhaps you'll be lucky enough to spot the square stone noting: "Estella Brown, layed [sic] two [sic] rest, July 29, 1891." This is a splendid and enjoyable hike, both physically and mentally. A lot of history endures along that trail.

A point of interest for anyone focused on emigrant trails is the grave of Elizabeth Paul, which is located just off the La Barge Creek Road about a mile south of Clear Creek. Mrs. Paul died in childbirth in 1862. In 1990 the Forest Service dedicated a sign at her grave which provided some information about her and her family, including her baby, who died a week later and is buried near Grays Lake in Idaho. The Kemmerer Ranger District has videos available about both this event and the Lander Cutoff Trail, which are free for the viewing if you're in Kemmerer and visit the district office.

48 Crow Creek

General description:	An enjoyable and not-too-steep day hike into a lovely high mountain setting. Great camping if an overnight is desired.
Distance:	10 miles round trip.
Difficulty:	Moderate.
Elevation gain and loss:	920 feet.
Key elevation points:	Trailhead: 7,480 feet.
General location:	45 miles southeast of Alpine Junction along the Greys River Road, in the central section of the Salt River Range.
Special attractions:	Impressive views of Mount Fitzpatrick.
Maps:	Bridger-Teton National Forest, Big Piney, Greys River and Kemmerer Districts visitor map; USGS: Box Canyon, Red Top Mountain.
Manager:	Greys River Ranger District.

Finding the trailhead: Driving west from Alpine Junction on the Greys River Road, travel 41 miles southward and upstream. All of the perpendicular creek crossings along this road are well-signed, and the "Crow Creek" sign sits across from mile marker 41. The map shows the trail beginning a mile to the north of Crow Creek. That is actually an old and forgotten road that is accessed by an older bridge that doesn't appear too driveable. One mile north of this unmarked road and bridge is a small parking area on the west side of the road, by the "Crow Creek" sign. Another and newer foot

Mellow meadow walking above Crow Creek.

bridge that spans the Greys River is visible to the southwest. This is the hiking trailhead.

The hike: The problem with coming upon a topographical name like "Crow Creek" is that in this country you don't really know if it commemorates a subtribe of Native Americans or a flock of birds. A more leisurely hike through easygoing mountain country landscape does not exist.

Once across the river, you need to wander cross-country and southwest for a few tenths of a mile, toward the mouth of Crow Creek Canyon. Here the trail becomes visible as it follows the north side of the creek. About 0.7 mile from the bridge, the trail crosses Crow Creek, and a few tenths of a mile later it re-crosses back to the north side. It is possible to avoid these two wades by skirting the north bank of the creek, but one wall of

Crow Creek

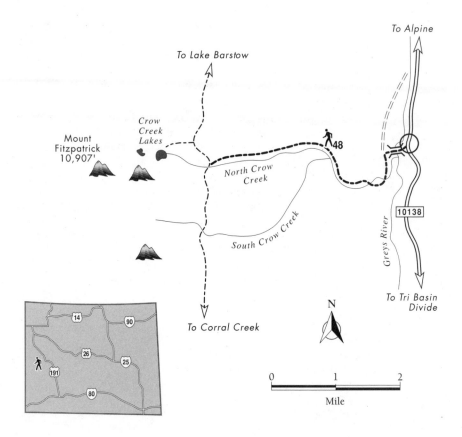

conglomerate dirt and rock slopes toward the creek at 70 degrees and is quite tricky to cross wearing a backpack. The remaining 4 miles of this not-too-used trail form a wonderful, unhurried, gentle climbing walk through quiet forests. High country meadows create great camping spots below the foot of the impressive cliffs of Mount Fitzpatrick. Since this trail is but 5.5 miles north of the Wyoming Range's Box Creek Trailhead (Hike 51), these two-day hikes—one the epitome of rushing waters and towering cliffs, the other filled with almost inert beauty—make interesting mountain range comparison hikes.

The abundance of wildlife in this drainage is everywhere visible. The meadows below Mount Fitzpatrick make an excellent base from which to experience a fairly rugged yet not too difficult cross-country peak climb (see Hike 49).

49 Mount Fitzpatrick (false summit)

General description:	A wonderful example of Wyoming cross-country hiking and peak climbing.
Distance:	5 miles round trip from Crow Creek Meadows (Hike 48).
Difficulty:	Strenuous.
Elevation gain:	2,096 feet.
Key elevation points:	Meadow below Mount Fitzpatrick: 8,400 feet; false summit: 10,496 feet.
General location:	5 miles west of the Crow Creek Trailhead, in the central Salt River Range.
Special attractions:	A hard-earned and breathtaking view of the mountainous Wyoming world from more than 10,000 feet.
Maps:	Bridger-Teton National Forest Big Piney, Greys River, and Kemmerer Ranger Districts map and/or USGS: Box Canyon Creek and Red Top Mountain quads.
Manager:	Greys River Ranger District.

Finding the trailhead: Same as Hike 48.

The hike: This is a somewhat rugged journey, yet easy to complete in a day from the meadows along North Crow Creek (Hike 48).

When I first began hiking 30-some years ago, I joined a mountaineer club whose members were gung-ho about hiking to the tops of peaks. Every week we climbed a different mountain summit. The untrailed, difficult, and unforgiving alpine terrain imparted in us beginners a kind of special confidence in and verve for the wilderness.

Realizing that a very large portion of the Wyoming landscape is composed of peak tops, I've endeavored to include a few examples of this form of hiking in this guidebook. This hike is geared for the kind of people who love challenging cross-country adventures. While this particular hike is quite suitable for beginners, it is advised that rookies do travel with someone more experienced. Cross-country uphill, especially at above-timberline elevations, can at any moment produce situations that can catch anyone off guard.

Follow the directions for the Crow Creek Trail (Hike 48) and begin at the meadows at the foot of Mount Fitzpatrick. The maps show the trail forming a T here, and the trails were maintained as of 1997. But there may be no intersection signs, and there are so many game trails crossing the faded main trail that it's hard to distinguish the intersection. If so, continue along the main-ish trail westward until you notice it climbing uphill and venturing to the north. Here look south and downhill to North Crow Creek, and

Mount Fitzpatrick (false summit)

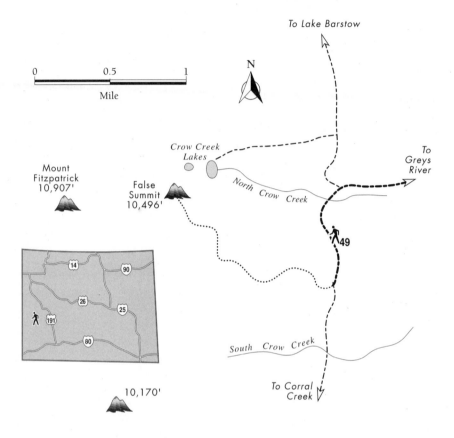

you'll see a quite visible trail crossing that creek. Head south to that trail, cross the creek, and angle southwest toward the mountain for 20 yards to again watch the trail reappear where it journeys southward and into the forest. The next mile's distance is very steep, and a lot of fallen trees can impede this section of the hike.

At the ridge top, .5 mile south of North Crow Creek, the landscape levels out. Here the main-ish trail continues to the south, but you want to turn west and follow this ridge through the forest. A short distance later the landscape tilts steeply upward, and a short but tricky almost-fourth-class scramble places you onto a level, forested plateau. Continue wandering westward to another steepish climb. This will put you on the ridge that journeys northwest and all the way to the false summit of the mountain. BE SURE you have the ability to gauge landmarks so you can find your way back through the forested plateau to the fourth-class scramble. All other land surrounding this one spot is cliff, and the potential for getting up there

Cross-country ridge hiking up Mount Fitzpatrick.

and not being able to find a way down does exist.

Along this main ridge, which consists of steep stair stepping and scree slope walking, you'll have to decide if you're dizzy from the elevation or from the awesome views spreading out before you. Crow Creek drainage and the Wyoming Range to the east create spectacular vistas. Along this ridge at 0.6 mile a rocky cliff obstructs the way. This makes for a fifth-class climb and is not recommended as a course. By veering left and staying beneath the base of the rocks, you'll soon find a climbable break in the cliffs that again places you on the ridge. Tiny Crow Creek Lakes are now about 1,000 feet straight down and to the north. You'll also discover that the view of Mount Fitzpatrick from the Crow Creek Trail reveals but a fourth of the mountain. It's another 0.5 mile scree-slope plod to the false summit of the peak.

To keep this adventure in the realm of a hiker's guide, this first summit is as far as I go. One view of the knifelike edges and intense rockslide slopes of the ridge to the real summit explains why. But the vistas from this point—the Wyoming Range, the Gros Ventres, even the Tetons—and the exhilarating feeling of accomplishment leave you feeling like you're in the Himalayas.

Common sense precautions such as appropriate weather gear, being in shape and properly acclimatized to the altitude, and making sure every step is a safe step, apply in triple strength on these adventuresome peak explorations.

50 Middle Ridge Trail/Greys Peak

General description:	A long, rugged trail that offers a gamut of hiking opportunities.
Distance:	12 miles round trip to Greys Peak, or 18 miles one way to shuttle.
Difficulty:	Strenuous.
Elevation gain:	2,850 feet.
Key elevation points:	Trailhead: 6,050 feet; Greys Azimuth Peak: 8,500 feet; Greys Peak: 8,900 feet; Deadman Creek: 6,520 feet.
General location:	9 miles east of Alpine, on a long ridge located between the northern ends of the Salt River and Wyoming Ranges.
Special attractions:	A little-used trail requiring exceptional navigating skills; lots of wildlife.
Maps:	Bridger-Teton National Forest Big Piney, Greys River and Kemmerer Ranger Districts visitor map; USGS: Pine Creek, Deer Creek, Man Peak.
Manager:	Greys River Ranger District.

Finding the trailhead: Twelve miles south of Jackson lies Hoback Junction, and another 23 miles from Hoback, along U.S. Highway 26/89, sits Alpine Junction. South from here and across the Snake River, in the tiny tourist town of Alpine, the Greys River Road—often unsigned—heads east from town and toward the Bridger-Teton National Forest. The pavement on this road lasts about 1 mile to the forest boundary where it becomes Forest Road 10138. Follow this well-maintained road to milepost 8, 0.2 mile beyond the Little Greys River Road intersection. Here a sign notes the Middle Ridge Trail and that it is an 18-mile walk to Deadman Creek. Supposedly, an early trapper was setting a heavy bear trap when it sprang shut and caught him instead. The creek was named after his body was found.

The hike: This trip can be a fairly long 12-mile round-trip day hike to a scenic peak top. It can also be an exceptionally long but exceedingly beauti-

Middle Ridge Trail/Greys Peak

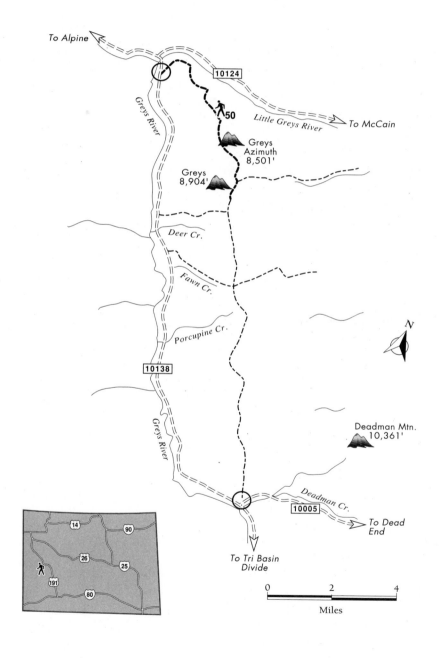

To Alpine

10124

Greys River

Little Greys River

To McCain

50

Greys Azimuth 8,501'

Greys 8,904'

Deer Cr.

Fawn Cr.

Porcupine Cr.

N

10138

Greys River

Deadman Mtn. 10,361'

Deadman Cr.

10005

To Dead End

To Tri Basin Divide

14

90

26

25

191

80

0   2   4
Miles

Ridge walking at its finest in the Salt River Range, on the way to Greys Peak.

ful ridge hike (18 miles). Finally, it can be a high-ridge camping overnighter if one carries lots of water or is willing to lose hard-earned elevation and hike down to creeks to get water. Also, except during hunting season, there is virtually no human traffic here.

After traveling north for 0.5 mile the narrow and sloping trail immediately begins its steep ascent. This narrow and angled hiking eases a bit as the trail gradually curves south and penetrates open woodlands. Being well blazed, the trail is fairly easy to follow, but be advised that dozens of side hunting/horsepacking trails jot off from the main arm, whose major trait is that it travels south and uphill. After 1.5 miles, and for much of the rest of the journey, this hike is the essence of ridgetop walking. Soon the Little Greys River valley to the east comes into view, and the scenery on both sides carries you along the many troughs and humps and bumps that comprise normal ridgetop walking. After 3.5 miles you find yourself atop a hump where the view of the world in every direction makes all the huffing and puffing worth the effort.

Now the work begins. It's 4.7 and 5.0 miles respectively to Greys Azimuth Peak and Greys Peak, the latter being a 9,000-foot high, long and stony ridge that is hard to hike on. Beyond these peaks, the trail really becomes confusing, mainly because the mountainside crawls with several herds of sheep, and the pitter-patter of their hooves obliterates real trails and leaves false paths everywhere. Although the map shows the forest trail skirting the west side of Greys Peak, in reality it goes down and around the east side and then back up to open alpine meadows. Here the hiker is left to guess (again due to sheep) where the trail continues its traverse along the ridge. I traveled no farther south than here, but maps and hearsay describe the remaining 13 miles as a gentle ridgetop descent into the Greys River/ Deadman Creek drainages, and there is a trail sign at the Deadman intersection.

Some notes: Maps show a couple of side trails leaving the river bottom and intersecting this Middle Ridge Trail. They may or may not be signed; they are probably not maintained. Also, numerous private (i.e., made by horse hoof) trails come and go all the time. I followed one such track down the mountainside to Greys River bottomland, and "adventure" is a nondescript but adequate word to portray that part of the hike. The soil here is a powder clay that works great if it's dry and becomes slicker than slime if it rains. Water is not available on the ridgetop.

The Wyoming Range

Wyoming Territory was created in 1868, and this long and wild eastern segment of the Overthrust Belt—originally called the Bear River Range— was renamed after the newfound land. The Wyoming Range towers between the Green River to the east and the Greys River to the west, and is an absolute treasure of lightly traveled hiking opportunities and pure mountain splendor.

From the Bryan Flat Ranger Station 20 miles south of Jackson, to the Snider Basin Ranger Station 25 miles west of Big Piney, a barely-known, 70 mile-long Wyoming Range National Recreation Trail traverses the entire length of the Wyoming Range. The trail is the pride of the Big Piney Ranger District and offers a vast variety of terrain, scenery and challenge for the hiker. Wide and green alpine meadows give way to 10,000-foot, knife-like ridges. Wildlife abounds, especially in the many east and west drainages dropping from the main north/south crest. Many hiking loops are possible along the trail. The Big Piney district ranger notes that their trail crew is in constant process of upgrading the Wyoming Range National Recreation Trail, but that some portions are still in a primitive state and not easy to discern. He recommends that hikers purchase topographical maps before venturing into the range. Further information is available from the Big Piney Ranger District, P.O. Box 218, Big Piney, WY, 83113, 307-276-3375.

51 Box Canyon Creek and Pass

General description:	An unforgettable day hike into a unique box canyon.
Distance:	8 miles round trip.
Difficulty:	Moderate to strenuous.
Elevation gain:	1,900 feet.
Key elevation points:	Trailhead: 7,750 feet; Box Canyon Falls: 8,100 feet; Box Canyon Creek Pass: 9,650 feet.
General location:	Approximately 52 miles southeast of Alpine Junction along the Greys River Road, in the central section of the Wyoming Range.
Special attractions:	Steep canyon walls, a rushing creek, impressive waterfalls, and stunning views.
Maps:	Bridger-Teton National Forest Big Piney, Greys River and Kemmerer Ranger Districts map; USGS: Box Canyon Creek, Mount Schidler.
Manager:	Greys River Ranger District and Big Piney Ranger District.

Finding the trailhead: Three miles from the Idaho border and on U.S. Highway 89, the only paved road in the tiny tourist town of Alpine that journeys eastward is the Greys River Road. Although the pavement ends after 1 mile, this 63-mile artery of mostly uncontrolled dust opens endless doors to both the Salt River and Wyoming Ranges. Almost all the creeks intersecting this road are labeled with brown signs noting their names. Drive 51.5 miles along this road, until you see a "Box Creek Trail" sign (Dick Creek is directly west of this creek and is also labeled). A two-track road turns east at the Box Creek sign and in 0.2 mile it deadends at a campfire ring.

The hike: A not-so-recent forest fire, a salvaging clearcut, and a bulldozer's attempt at land reclamation make this trailhead both unappealing and hard to locate. Do not skirt the creek bank upstream in this first distance. Instead, cut up the hillside just to the north of the creek. Place yourself atop this little hill and above the stream and then head upcanyon. After 0.3 mile the fire and clearcut end while blaze marks and a viable trail reveal themselves.

A rousing feeling of adventure permeates this canyon: the trail is little used (and may need maintenance), the fire wiped out the south side of the creek yet spared the north (trailed) side, and as you hike, the absolute wall of a mountain begins to loom ahead, a wall you know must somehow be surmounted to exit the canyon.

After about a mile, in a large and open meadow, the trail disappears. Here you need to head slightly north or uphill, toward the middle of a massive rock slide. About 75 yards above the creek, the trail cuts directly across the rock slide slope.

Box Canyon Creek and Pass

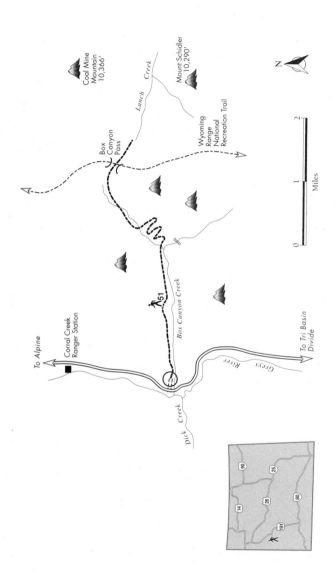

After an easy amble beneath amazing cliff structures of stratified rock, another hard-to-follow section manifests. Here you see the impressive Box Creek Falls to the south. The trail now crosses the main stream and veers away (to the left) from the falls to follow the north branch of the creek. Shake hands with the 1,000-foot wall that has dominated this entire trip. I can't begin to describe the views that accompany one up this next very steep 1-mile section of the hike. The trail does level out though, and by continuing eastward you discover that the crest of the Wyoming Range does not resemble the steep and rocky face that the last 4 miles have presented. Huge, open meadows and gently rolling alpine hills now rule the landscape. Lunch Creek Meadows is a perfect alpine setting to take such a break.

It's easy to spend a leisurely day atop this pass. Several mountaintops are within easy hiking distance, and trails wander off in all directions. You are situated in the heart of the Wyoming Range. Camping is possible in these meadows, as the nearby streams begin their flow not too far down the slopes.

52 Cliff Creek Pass

General description:	A 2- or 3-day camping trip into lofty highlands with multiple opportunities to explore various intersecting trails.
Distance:	16 miles round trip.
Difficulty:	Moderate to strenuous.
Elevation gain and loss:	1,900 feet.
Key elevation points:	Roosevelt Meadows: 8,100 feet; Cliff Creek Pass: 9,100 feet.
General location:	25 miles east of Alpine, in the northern section of the Wyoming Range.
Special attractions:	A horsepacker's trail few hikers ever experience.
Maps:	Bridger-Teton National Forest Big Piney, Greys River and Kemmerer Ranger Districts map; USGS: Pickle Pass, Hoback Peak.
Manager:	Greys River Ranger District.

Finding the trailhead: From the town of Alpine, the 1 paved road that travels east is the Greys River Road (pavement ends where the national forest begins, 1 mile later). At 7.8 miles along this nice gravel road, the well-marked Little Greys Road (10047) intersects. Follow this road northeast for 12.5 miles to the Telephone Pass Trail sign and here turn right or south. In a small parking lot 2 miles later, a sign marks the Cliff Creek Trailhead.

The hike: The Greys River was not named for the dense gray sedimentary rocks that constitute much of the surrounding mountains. John Grey, a fur trapper, stabbed a fellow trapper and trader who had insulted his daughter.

Cliff Creek Pass

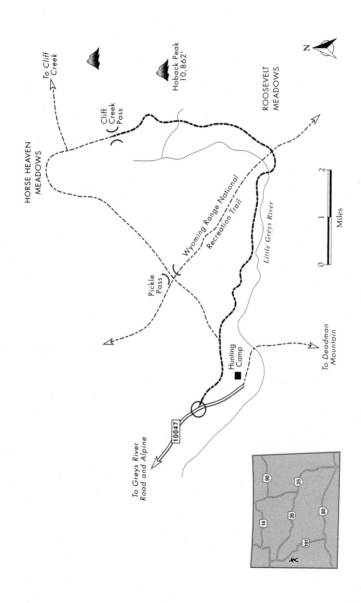

To Cliff Creek

Hoback Peak
10,862'

Cliff Creek Pass

HORSE HEAVEN MEADOWS

ROOSEVELT MEADOWS

Wyoming Range National Recreation Trail

Pickle Pass

Little Greys River

Hunting Camp

To Deadman Mountain

10047

To Greys River Road and Alpine

N

0   1   2
Miles

90
25
14
26
80
191

This act somehow placed his name into the chronicles of topography. The clear and playful branch named the Little Greys River is a popular, unimproved camping area for RVs and auto campers. But few venture to the road's end and enjoy the headwaters of this unique little stream.

Except during hunting season, this sweet trail is basically deserted. The first 1.5 miles offer a hefty climb into the forested hills far above the river. An unsigned intersection greets you after this distance, the right fork being the main way to Cliff Creek Pass. Then the trail does what Wyoming trails love to do. It loses almost all of that hard-earned elevation gain in a steep descent. But over the next couple of miles you'll regain that height and more. The trail never really skirts the Little Greys River, but opts to stay high on the slopes, so if fishing is your bent, you'll have to cut south through the thick forest to its shores. The first nice camping meadows appear about 3.5 miles into the hike. Now the ascents and descents become more gentle, and the forest opens into inviting views of the high mountains ahead. In July, the hillsides were literally blanketed with multicolored flowers.

After 5 miles of hiking, the trail crosses the Little Greys River, which is now a small stream. Beyond this crossing lie the massive and lush Roosevelt Meadows. Here the trail can play a vanishing game, but keep heading east. It's a bit confusing, because the Wyoming Range National Recreation Trail intersects just before the Cliff Creek Trail veers to the north and ascends the open alpine slopes to the east of the Little Greys River. Nothing was signed when I hiked the country, and most of these trails were faded or overgrown. But the Greys River Ranger District recently revamped this section of trail. The trick is to look carefully to the north and see the Cliff Creek Trail reappear as it climbs some steep slopes toward the pass. Hiking 3 more miles of open alpine beauty will bring you to another confusing sector, the pass area itself. You actually have to descend a bit to be atop Cliff Creek Pass where the waters part company. The camping opportunities from Roosevelt Meadows to the pass area are unlimited.

The map shows a trail making a loop through what's called Horse Heaven Meadows, along a high and broad ridge, to a pass named Pickle Pass. Supposedly a trail descends from Pickle Pass and intersects the Cliff Creek Pass trail at that first intersection 1.5 miles from the trailhead. I couldn't find the trail beyond Pickle Pass, but the Greys River Ranger District notes that this area has been re-maintained, which means that the trail does actually exist. If you have an adventuresome spirit and have a sense of direction that permits such wandering, the views are exceptionally grand, and trying to complete the loop would be a worthwhile journey.

53 Little Cliff Creek/Monument Ridge Lookout Tower

General description:	A long day hike or an easy overnighter into the rarely explored country lying between the Wyoming and the Gros Ventre Ranges.
Distance:	9 miles round trip.
Difficulty:	Moderate.
Elevation gain and loss:	1,457 feet.
Key elevation points:	Lookout tower: 8,257 feet.
General location:	17 miles east of Hoback Junction, or approximately 50 miles northwest of Pinedale, in the very northern fringes of the Wyoming Range, just south of the Gros Ventre Range, in western Wyoming.
Special attractions:	Open vista walking in small, hidden valleys, endless ridge walking, wildlife galore, and an abandoned fire lookout tower.
Maps:	Bridger-Teton National Forest Buffalo and Jackson Ranger Districts forest map; the Bridger-Teton National Forest Big Piney, Greys River and Kemmerer Districts forest map; USGS: Bondurant, Noble Basin.
Manager:	Big Piney Ranger District.

Finding the trailhead: East of Hoback Junction 15 miles on U.S. Highway 189/191, Cliff Creek Road (Forest Road 30530) jogs to the south. This road is unmarked from the west, but it's the first main gravel road to take off south once you pass the Granite Creek sign along the Hoback River. Go south 2.25 miles on this road to where a tiny sign denotes a "Little Cliff Creek" streamlet crossing the road. A primitive camping and parking area sits on the north side of this creek, and the trail (unsigned) begins to the east where an old road cuts up the mountainside and into the forest.

The hike: The old road's beginning lasts but 0.5 mile before it funnels into a normal and narrow trail that hangs high on the south-facing slopes above the creek bottom. After 1.3 miles the path descends to the valley bottom and through a cattle gate (please close) and then heads east into some fascinating country. About 0.5 mile past the gate, to the south, stands an aging concrete obelisk marking the grave of "Mr. Tom Poole, died August 31, 1893." One's imagination can have some fun here.

Abundant wildlife call this country home, but cattle are the dominant species here. This creates a couple of situations: one is that the water, although plentiful, needs to be filtered; another is that trails can head off in all directions at any time; and third—and this actually happened to me—is that you can be ambling along and suddenly find yourself face-to-face with

Little Cliff Creek/Monument Ridge Lookout Tower

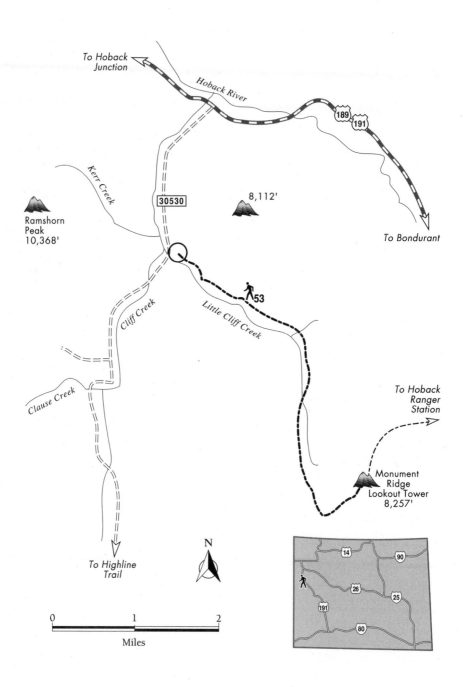

To Hoback
Junction

Hoback River

189
191

Kerr Creek

30530

8,112'

Ramshorn
Peak
10,368'

To Bondurant

53

Cliff Creek

Little Cliff Creek

To Hoback
Ranger
Station

Clause Creek

Monument
Ridge
Lookout Tower
8,257'

N

To Highline
Trail

0   1   2
Miles

14

90

26

25

191

80

The open, sage-covered Little Creek valley, on the way to Monument Ridge.

the resident 2,000-pound Hereford bull, who will probably claim trail right-of-way privileges.

After 2.0 miles the cattle trails tend to head east, but you want to turn south and stay in the main creek drainage, first on the east side of the drainage and then at 2.7 miles crossing the creek and following its western contours. Blazes do signify that there is an official trail here. Views of the Gros Ventres to the north are awe-inspiring.

At 3.6 miles the trail re-crosses the now tiny creek, and after this point the cattle paths take over and it's anyone's guess which trail is the designated one. That open ridgeline to the east is Monument Ridge, and any of the 3 ridgelines leading from the valley floor and up to it offer a great cross-country workout. Nothing is technical about this climb, and the views from the top are astounding. You can sit beside a piece of history—the abandoned, 4-sided lookout tower (not locked)—and face the entire Gros Ventre Range to the north, the entire eastern front of the Wyoming Range to the west, and the vast Hoback Valley spreading below for many miles. Far to the east, the jagged granite needles of the Wind River Range rise up.

Another, shorter trail ascends Monument Ridge from the east and the Hoback Ranger Station. But visiting via the back door—Little Cliff Creek—is definitely the more adventurous and worthwhile journey.

Western Wyoming

THE GROS VENTRE RANGE

The Gros Ventre Range may be a bit lower in elevation and not as sharply defined as its Teton Range neighbor, but this colorful, glacier-carved upheaval of stratified rock is no less magnificent and is certainly a delightfully unique area to hike. The 287,000-acre Gros Ventre Wilderness Area lies within the Greater Yellowstone ecosystem, an area internationally known for its wildlands, wildlife, geological features, and scenic beauty. This wilderness includes more than 30 percent of the Greater Yellowstone Ecosystem. The highest peak in the area is Doubletop (11,682 feet) although spectacular views of the Teton Range and the surrounding countryside can be seen from virtually any high point. These mountains can be a collage of rock colors. Snow-capped peaks in one setting can tower over the polychromatic badland cliffs of another. Wildlife is abundant and varied, and you may very well espy a large elk herd or catch sight of a grizzly bear track.

The Gros Ventre (GROW-vont) Indians were a Blackfoot sub-clan (some references swear they were Nez Perce) who frequented the area. The word means "big bellies," in reference to their sign language origins—they had a tendency to communicate by rubbing their bellies, and white folks interpreted this to mean that they were always hungry.

Simple and common sense regulations for the wilderness area include: no camping within 200 feet of a lakeshore; group size limits of 15 people; a 16-day maximum stay at any campsite; no soap in or near water; human waste must be buried at least 200 feet from water; and pack out everything you pack in.

The following trail descriptions explore the rugged southern section of the wilderness. The entire wilderness area has twenty peaks over 10,000 feet high, with several of these exceeding the 11,000-foot mark.

54 Granite Highline Trail

General description:	A rugged, variable-length day hike, or a 2-day hike featuring access to several high peaks.
Distance:	Up to 28 miles round trip.
Difficulty:	Strenuous.
Elevation gain and loss:	2,400 feet.
Key elevation points:	Trailhead: 6,800 feet; Little Granite Creek intersection: 8,000 feet; Turquoise Lake Trail intersection: 9,200 feet.
General location:	35 miles east and slightly south of Jackson, in the southwestern sector of the Gros Ventre Wilderness.
Special attractions:	Awesome timberline country, an adventuresome trail, and nearby hot springs.
Maps:	Bridger-Teton National Forest Jackson and Buffalo Ranger Districts map; USGS: Granite Falls, Bull Creek, Turquoise Lake, Cache Creek.
Manager:	Jackson Ranger District.
Fees:	Campground fees range from $7 to $9 dollars per night. Granite Hot Springs rates: $5.50 per adult, $3.50 per child.

Finding the trailhead: South of Jackson 13 miles on U.S. Highway 191/89/26 lies a major highway intersection named Hoback Junction. Here Highway 189/191 traces the Hoback River east toward Bondurant and Pinedale. At 12 miles east of Hoback Junction a large sign indicates the Granite Recreation Area, and gravel Granite Creek Road (Forest Road 30500) cuts north for 10 miles to end at the Granite Hot Springs pool and picnic area. This is a Forest Service-owned hot springs that is leased and operated by a private concessionaire. A large pool structure, up to 8 feet deep, captures some of the hot water pouring out of the hillside. In the summer the pool is open from 10 A.M. to 7 P.M.

At the Swift Creek Road intersection (Hike 56), 2 miles before these springs, a sign on the west side of the main road marks the Granite Highline Trail. There is no parking by the trailhead. The best parking is found by turning right or east on the Swift Creek Road and parking in the large meadow west and south of the nearby concrete bridge that crosses Granite Creek. Another nearby place to park and camp is located 1 mile north of the trailhead, on the main Granite Creek Road at a Forest Service fee campground.

The hike: I can only offer an introduction to this wonderful trail. An early-season snowstorm caught me off guard and chased everything without a natural fur coat off the mountain. But it's a marvelous adventure into absolutely unique country. Hunting season is about the only time the trail sees more than a few people.

If one survives the first very steep 1.5 miles of uphill forest hiking, one

Granite Highline Trail

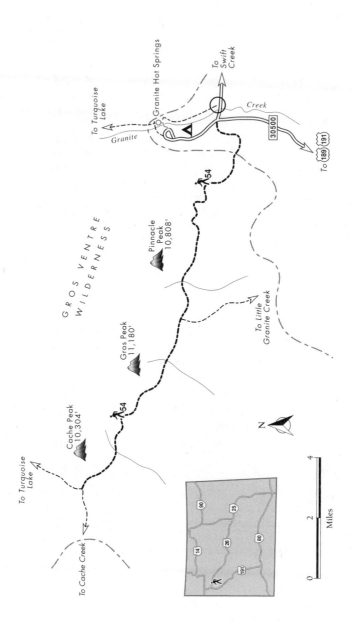

Endless open terrain on the Granite Highline Trail.

then enters into a fascinating high-country world. The trail more or less levels out and cuts a path into various open alpine meadows. The trees thin out as the path traverses these mighty mountainsides near or above timberline. What the hiker experiences is miles of alpine colored meadows—flowers in the summer, autumn reds and yellows in the early fall. Awesome views expand toward the Hoback Valley to the south while vistas of 11,000-foot peaks open to the north.

The somewhat level trail dips into gullies and ravines and then swings out to the many ridges. The land is quite dry for 4 miles to where a first small creek trickles down as part of the headwaters of Little Granite Creek. The surrounding area offers some excellent camping spots which can serve as base camp for further explorations west or for a climb to the summit of impressive Pinnacle Peak. West and beyond this mark, the country can become quite confusing. Both the Forest Service and the USGS topo maps show an intricate braid of trails throughout this area. The maps grossly understate the situation. The soil of this country is so delicate that any large pack train of horses taking off cross-country can create a new trail. Hunting trails wander in every direction, and many of them appear more mainstream than the official trail. Hiking becomes a matter of moving in a westward traversing course and choosing by inner guidance the trail that "feels" right. (A topo map really gives the intuition a boost.)

If you only make it to the first creek crossing at 4 miles, you will have experienced an exceptionally splendid hike. The hunters I questioned as we raced off the mountain in the blizzard declared 2 things: the country and views only get better the farther west one travels, and nothing is signed. So good topographic maps are essential for exploring this area.

Also know that even though the word "Granite" pervades maps of this country, the mountain slopes are composed of silts and clays that transform into soft gum when wet. Most of the plant life in these beautiful meadows grow waist-high, so a rain storm will also really soak anyone hiking through the area.

The entire trail covers 14 miles to Cache Creek. From there, another 17-mile hiking loop down Granite Creek (Hike 55) will place you at the hot springs pool.

55 Turquoise Lake

General description:	A rugged and long, 3- to 5-day (or more) backpack into the heart of the Gros Ventre mountain range.
Distance:	27 miles round trip.
Difficulty:	Strenuous.
Elevation gain and loss:	2,580 feet.
Key elevation points:	Box Lake: 8,600 feet; Turquoise Lake: 9,480 feet.
General location:	35 miles east and slightly south of Jackson, in the southwestern sector of the Gros Ventre Wilderness.
Special attractions:	Spectacular scenery culminating in a deep blue-green lake nestled beneath the base of 11,190-foot Gros Ventre Peak.
Maps:	Bridger-Teton National Forest Jackson and Buffalo Ranger Districts forest map; USGS: Granite Falls, Crystal Peak, Turquoise Lake, Cache Creek.
Manager:	Jackson Ranger District.
Fees:	Developed campground fees range from $7 to $9 per night. Granite Hot Springs pool charges $5.50 per adult, $3.50 per kid.

Finding the trailhead: Follow the directions to the Hike 54 trailhead. Here turn right onto a gravel road that cuts east, and cross large Granite Creek atop a new-looking concrete bridge. Just north of this crossing, the road leads to a parking circle.

If you are treating this trail as a day hike, and if you promise to be back to your car before 7 P.M., you can drive to the Granite Hot Springs parking lot and cut 2 miles off the trip. If you're saddled with 40 to 60 extra pounds of gear and going in for multi-night adventures, the Forest Service requires you to plod those additional 2 miles by making the trailhead parking lot mandatory. The parking area near the hot springs will be gated and locked after the pool closes.

The trail begins at an unsigned, chained road at the northwest corner of the parking lot. Take the trail immediately to your left, just beyond the

Turquoise Lake

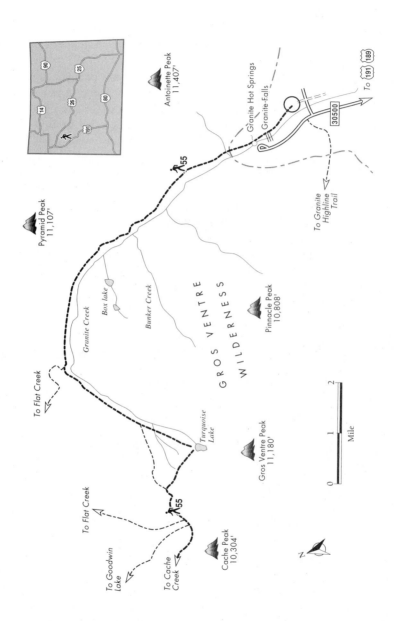

Antoinette Peak
11,407'

Granite Hot Springs

Granite Falls

30500

To 191 189

To Granite Highline Trail

55

Pyramid Peak
11,107'

Box lake

Granite Creek

Bunker Creek

G R O S   V E N T R E
W I L D E R N E S S

Pinnacle Peak
10,808'

To Flat Creek

Turquoise Lake

Gros Ventre Peak
11,180'

To Flat Creek

55

Cache Peak
10,304'

To Goodwin Lake

To Cache Creek

0   1   2

Mile

N

chain. The road continuing to the right leads to a Girl Scout Camp and is not an exciting hike.

The hike: This monumental hike into the heart of the Gros Ventre Wilderness really needs 3 days minimum for one to fully experience the country's grandeur. It's 5 miles of really hard hiking before you can again walk beside Granite Creek, and 2 more miles to where the country begins to show itself off.

The first 2 miles hiking to the hot springs takes you past the astounding roar of Granite Falls and the narrow, rocky canyon that funnels Granite Creek into some amazingly complex hydraulics. Then, for the next 3 miles, the trail does everything it can to stay high on the flanks of the hillsides and away from the creek. The walking here is extremely rugged, with stair-stepping boulder gardens and huge spruce tree roots creating a sort of obstacle course.

It's 5 miles of hiking until the first good camping meadow, upstream and uphill from the first place to get creek water. A couple more miles of varied hiking and the country begins to acquire its "big-time" feel, as meadows open up into breathtaking views of the surrounding peaks. Campsites become more frequent, and fishing holes more accessible. This is a VERY cold creek, even in August.

At 7.8 miles the trail splits, with the left fork looking like the easiest and main trail. But this fork leads to a creek wade, an outfitter's camp, and tiny Box Lake. The official trail cuts upward and to the right along the rocky hillsides.

Now the broadening valley begins a westward swing, revealing more open meadows, lots of camping opportunities, and views of the surrounding mountainsides. The broken piles of spruce trees near the valley bottom provide evidence of the tremendous avalanches that must cascade off the mountains' flanks in the winter. At 9 miles an unsigned trail wanders to the right and up into these mountains. At 10.75 miles an old and broken Forest Service sign noting the Flat Creek Trail Cuttoff lies beside the trail. At this location there was no sign of an existing intersecting trail, so explore with your map in hand and a good sense of adventure.

Every mile hiked reveals greater beauty. As the trail angles southward (after 11.5 miles), 11,000-foot Gros Ventre Peak and its flanking 10,500-foot companions dominate the scenery. Another mile of gradual climbing and a short descent takes you to the base of these spectacular mountains and the shores of blue-green Turquoise Lake. Lots of camping options exist here, along with evidence of horse use.

From Turquoise Lake, it's 2 more miles of climbing to Cache Pass, where several trail options present themselves, including a circular return to the parking lot via the Granite Highline Trail (Hike 54). Have your topo maps ready, as this is a hard trail to follow.

56 Swift Creek to Shoal Lake

General description:	A rugged, steep, 2- to 3-day hike into the high alpine country of the Gros Ventre Wilderness. An excellent loop hike.
Distance:	12 miles round trip.
Difficulty:	Strenuous.
Elevation gain and loss:	3,350 feet.
Key elevation points:	Trailhead: 6,900 feet; Pass before Crystal Creek: 10,250 feet; Shoal Lake: 9,600 feet; Shoal Falls: 8,800 feet.
General location:	35 miles southeast of Jackson off U.S. Highway 189/191.
Special attractions:	A seldom-used trail leading to flower-covered meadows and wonderful vistas of the Tetons.
Maps:	Bridger-Teton National Forest Jackson and Buffalo Ranger Districts map; USGS: Granite Falls, Crystal Peak.
Manager:	Jackson Ranger District.

Finding the trailhead: Follow the directions for Hike 55. Beyond the chained road at the northwest corner of this lot, hike just a short distance and note a trail jotting to the right or east. There may be a sign here marking the trail as closed, but this refers only to horse travel, as the trail is exceptionally rocky.

The hike: Leaving the Granite Recreation Area where the sign notes the Swift Creek Trail, the trail begins its steep ascent through the forests, never far from earshot of the cold rushing waters of Swift Creek. There is no scarcity of water on the trail, and level campsites, while not plentiful, are not hard to locate. For more than 3 miles this trail is one continuous climb.

Eventually the trail leaves the creek, beginning its ascent toward the talus and boulder fields flanking 11,407-foot Antoinette Peak. Don't be fooled by appearances into thinking Antoinette Peak is an easy scramble. Careful route finding by experienced mountaineers is recommended on this peak.

Above timberline and replete with views, the trail heads eastward from the base of Antoinette Peak and winds through flower-covered meadows offering vistas of the snow-capped Tetons and the Wyoming Range. Antoinette Peak, Palmer Peak, Triangle Peak, and Doubletop Peak form the graceful line of gentle mountains that define the spine of the Gros Ventre range.

Travel 3 more miles to a trail intersection where the Shoal Lake/Creek/Falls Trail drops to the right. Time to lose all that hard-earned elevation as the trail heads to Shoal Falls on a route that criss-crosses back and forth across Shoal Creek. Shoal Falls is a 5-minute hike off the main trail and well worth the diversion. The falls area offers some scenic campsites.

The trail continues westward now for a gentle up and down 6 miles back

Swift Creek to Shoal Lake

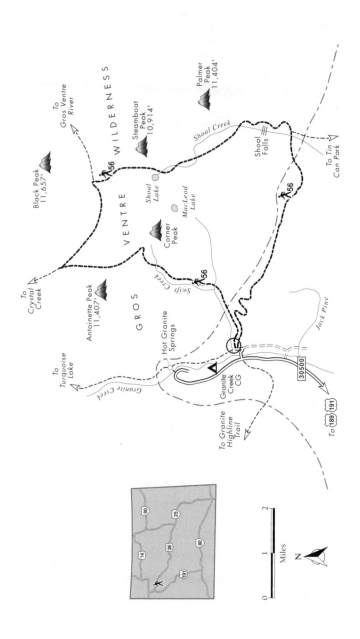

to the Granite Creek Trailhead. A good early season hike in this area is this Shoal Falls trail, climbing over Deer Ridge and connecting with Shoal Creek.
  —Laurie Muth

THE MOUNT LEIDY HIGHLANDS

A marvelous and fairly vast section of critical grizzly bear habitat and major elk migration and calving ground lies directly north of the Gros Ventre Wilderness. The Mount Leidy Highlands, surrounded by the more notable Grand Teton, Yellowstone, and Gros Ventre areas, is a little-known piece of unclassified wilderness. Actually, several capitalistic concerns are well aware of this area's presence, and road building, logging, and gas and oil exploration continue to increase in the area. The Jackson Hole area residents, whose entire economy depends on wildlife habitat and undissected peaks and forests, are actively protesting the development in this unique mosaic of aspen forests, grasslands, and alpine meadows. I caught it at a rare time when no one else was around. It proved to be some of the most peaceful country in all of Wyoming.

57 Slate Creek to Mount Leidy

General description:	A peaceful, leisurely day hike or overnighter into the gentle forests and creek drainages of a little-used mountain area.
Distance:	13 miles round trip.
Difficulty:	Moderate.
Elevation gain:	950 feet.
Key elevation points:	Trailhead: 7,100 feet; Dallas Fork of Slate Creek: 7,500 feet; Carmichael Fork: 8,050 feet; Mount Leidy: 10,326 feet.
General location:	30 miles northeast of Jackson, north of the Gros Ventre River in the southern section of the Mount Leidy Highlands.
Special attractions:	Fine family hiking through huge meadowed bowls beneath pretty mountains.
Maps:	Bridger-Teton National Forest Jackson and Buffalo Ranger Districts map; USGS: Mount Leidy.
Manager:	Jackson Ranger District.

Finding the trailhead: On U.S. Highway 26/89/191, 7 miles north of Jackson and 2 miles north of Grand Teton National Park's southern boundary, a well-signed Gros Ventre Junction sends a paved road eastward toward the tiny burg of Kelly. Driving the 7 miles to Kelly and another mile along the

The broad, open and reclusive Mount Leidy Highlands.

road as it swings north puts you at the junction of the paved Gros Ventre Road. Follow this road (30400) east, into the Bridger-Teton National Forest, for 13.5 miles (1.2 miles past the Crystal Creek Campground). Here the graveled road forks, and you want to go left, toward Slate Creek, as a sign indicates. Then, 0.1 mile after this fork, Forest Road 30380 jogs to the left or north. Follow this dirt two-track 0.6 mile, take the fork to the right or east, drive past the hunting camp, and park on the banks overlooking the Gros Ventre River.

The unmarked trailhead begins with a 20-yard ford of this large river. In late August the clear waters were never more than mid-calf depth. It is illegal to drive across this ford.

Should you wish to enter this country in mid-June when the river is high, an alternate entrance route exists 4.9 miles after the Gros Ventre Road pavement ends. A short distance before the Red Hill Campground, the road crosses

Slate Creek to Mount Leidy

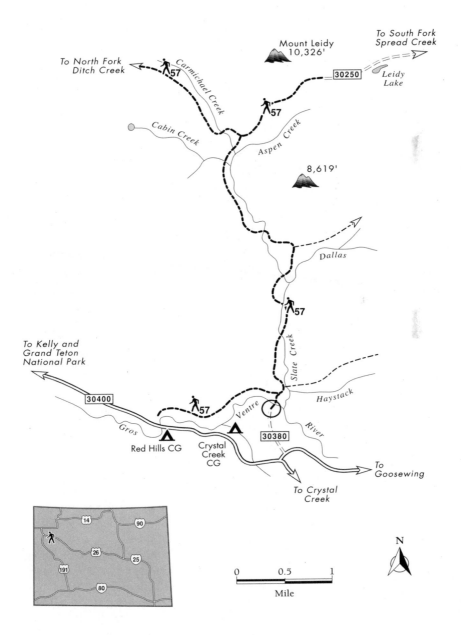

Mount Leidy
10,326'

To South Fork
Spread Creek

30250

Leidy
Lake

To North Fork
Ditch Creek

57

Carmichael Creek

57

Cabin Creek

Aspen Creek

8,619'

Dallas

57

To Kelly and
Grand Teton
National Park

Slate Creek

30400

57

Haystack

Ventre

Gros

River

30380

Red Hills CG

Crystal
Creek
CG

To Crystal
Creek

To
Goosewing

14

90

26

25

191

80

N

0   0.5   1

Mile

the Gros Ventre River via a major bridge. On the west side of this bridge, a jeep road follows the north shore of the river for 3 miles to this same ford.

The hike: Northwest Wyoming became known through a series of explorations and surveys conducted by government and private enterprises. Three of the more renowned and revealing USGS expeditions were led in the 1870s by Dr. Ferdinand Hayden, who studied the geology and zoology of the area while mapping many of its peaks and drainages. Mount Leidy which is 10,326 feet high, and the Leidy Highlands were named for Professor Joseph Leidy, an anatomist on the Hayden surveys. Like that forgotten researcher, these mountains claim little notoriety but are indispensable to the ecology of the area.

Hike western and northwestern Wyoming long enough and you're going to yearn to break free of lodgepole forests. The open sage and meadow country of the Leidy Highland foothills offers a welcome tract of free and easy country to explore. Once across the Gros Ventre River and a few hundred yards up the trail, you'll notice two things. First, an old sign directs you north onto the Slate Creek Trail. And second, lack of protection has turned this area into an ATV playground. The trail becomes a wide track that accommodates but does not restrict these mega-wheeled creatures. I can only say that this particular area constitutes some of the most unique and soothingly beautiful landscape in Wyoming, and the threat of machines does not mean you shouldn't hike, explore, and enjoy it. Early in the morning on weekdays is the best time to find yourself alone here.

For 1.5 miles the trail traverses rolling, open hills, ridges, and valleys that offer endless opportunities for cross-country hiking access. Views of the Gros Ventre Mountains to the south are incomparable. Then the path descends to Slate Creek and into a meadowed valley. Three creek fords and another 1.5 miles lead you to a vast bowl encompassing many square miles of open grasslands. To journey toward Mount Leidy, follow the Carmichael Creek Fork to the left or northwest. A topo map will be handy here, as nothing is signed. This massive basin is used by hikers, horse packers, elk, cattle, and ATVs, and a lot of trails wander off in all directions.

One mile later, the official trail crosses Carmichael Creek and heads west into the forests. Here the ATV signs are left behind, and after another mile's distance the trail breaks into a second vast and meadowed bowl, this one sitting beneath the gentle slopes of Mount Leidy. Such a peaceful setting exists only in fairy tales or in Wyoming. Hike another mile to Cabin Creek and enjoy the enchantment of this gentle land. When setting up a camp in this area, one feels like one is accepting a natural invitation to peaceful living.

Beyond Cabin Creek 0.3 mile the trail again crosses Carmichael Creek and forks. To the east you journey toward Mount Leidy and eventually onto the Leidy Lake Road. To the west you can follow Carmichael Creek into several other drainages that help create this unique country.

For a first-time backpacking experience, or for gentle family hiking, this is the place. Never have I felt a country seemingly extend such an open welcome to hikers.

58 Grizzly Lake

General description:	A peaceful day hike that could easily convert into a leisurely overnighter.
Distance:	7 miles round trip.
Difficulty:	Easy to moderate.
Elevation gain and loss:	1,200 feet. (Mostly in short ups and downs)
Key elevation points:	Grizzly Lake: 7,184 feet.
General location:	28 miles northeast of Jackson, south of the Gros Ventre River and north of the Gros Ventre Mountains.
Special attractions:	Breathtaking views of the Teton Range and a small chance of seeing grizzly bears.
Maps:	Bridger-Teton National Forest Jackson and Buffalo Ranger Districts map; USGS: Grizzly Lake, Blue Miner Lake; Earthwalk Press's Grand Teton National Park Recreation Map.
Manager:	Jackson Ranger District.

Finding the trailhead: Follow the Hike 57 directions to the Gros Ventre Road and drive into the Bridger-Teton National Forest for 6 miles beyond where the pavement ends, right to the entrance of the Red Hills Campground, about 0.5 mile east of the Gros Ventre River bridge crossing. The trailhead sign and a small parking area sit on the north side of the road. Please NOTE that both the Bridger-Teton forest map and the Earthwalk Press recreation map show a road before (west of) the campground jotting south and to the trail. This road is on private land and may not be accessible. The trailhead across from the campground offers public access while skirting the private land.

The hike: Another map clarification needs to be made here. Both of the above-mentioned maps show a shorter trail route to Grizzly Lake via a supposed trailhead 2.5 miles west of or before the Red Hills Campground trailhead. However, there's no sign, no parking, and one exceptionally steep embankment to descend to get to the Gros Ventre River just before the upper reaches of Lower Slide Lake. Once there you had better have a long-legged horse with you, because this crossing puts you into a big river. The trailhead by the campground provides by far the better route.

The first 0.3 mile of the trail is nothing but ruts. Then a small sign leads you to the right or west and into the open sage country that dominates this hike. Another signed trail intersection at 0.5 mile again points you to the

Grizzly Lake

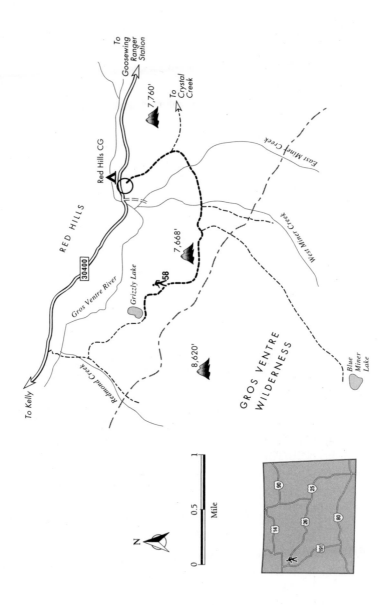

right or west. For the next mile, just wander across the sage prairie, beholding the resplendent views of the Tetons looming on the western horizon and over the river valley.

The only tricky spot is where the trail crosses East Miner Creek (1.2 miles) via a couple of slippery logs that may or may not still be there. Here it jogs south, following the west side of the creek. Soon, though, the path cuts sharply uphill, beginning a westward traverse of ridge and valley. The next 2.5 miles are continuously up and down, with the trail slicing into every little valley and careening over every minor ridge. It's really an amazing and enjoyable hike, as every valley presents a different perspective on the environment and every ridgetop offers its own unique perspective of the Gros Ventre River valley.

Just beyond the 2.4 mile intersection with the trail that heads south or left to Blue Miner Lake (on the sign it's spelled "Minor"), a small creek empties into a fascinating swamp and pothole area. A pair of nesting swans might occupy the largest water body—please stay on the trail and don't disturb these enthralling creatures.

The last mile to the lake descends through a wooded valley and to a fair-sized pond. It's an incredibly peaceful spot with lots of good camping, but do note that Grizzly Lake isn't a stream-in/stream-out body of water. It's a depression in the landscape, a pothole that has filled up. The water isn't particularly potable.

59 Red Hills/Lavender Hills

General description:	A half-day, little-known hike that offers excellent views of the Tetons and Gros Ventres.
Distance:	3 to 4.5 miles round trip.
Difficulty:	Moderate.
Elevation gain and loss:	Between 950 feet and 2,050 feet.
Key elevation points:	Trailhead: 7,100 feet; first ridge: 8,350 feet; second ridge: 9,150 feet.
General location:	25 miles northeast of Jackson, north of the Gros Ventre River and the Gros Ventre Mountains.
Special attractions:	Some of the oddest and most striking land formations in Wyoming.
Maps:	Bridger-Teton National Forest Jackson and Buffalo Ranger Districts map; USGS: Mount Leidy, Grizzly Lake.
Manager:	Jackson Ranger District.

Finding the trailhead: Driving directions to the Gros Ventre Road are the same as for Hike 57. After you leave the pavement on the Gros Ventre Road, drive another 4.2 miles to just past the large "Red Hills Ranch" sign on the southern side of the road. Land to the south is private ranch property, but those towering, red, crumbly, striated, and foreboding hills to the north are on Forest Service land and open to exploration. Though unmarked and un-

Entrancing hiking in the Red Hills.

Red Hills/Lavender Hills

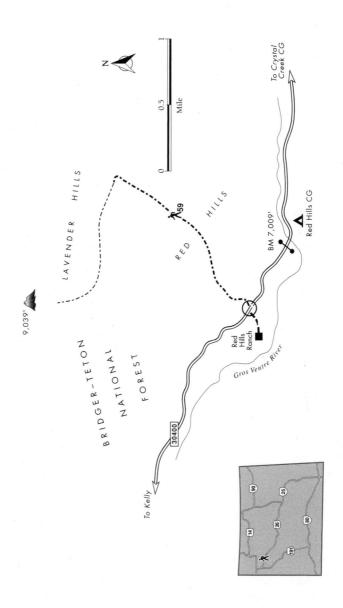

noticeable from the road, a good trail begins about 100 yards east and across the road from that Red Hills Ranch gateway. If you miss the starting point, drive east to the bridge crossing the Gros Ventre River, then backtrack 0.5 mile until you see the first larger canyon cutting northeast and into those red hills. There is room for parking on the south edges of the road.

The hike: Outward appearances can leave one thinking that this is a colorful but desolate and barren landscape. Hiking just a short distance into these hills reveals more life and beauty amid the slopes than can be imagined.

The first 1.5 miles climb a steep grade to an open ridgetop. To the north stand the striated Lavender Hills, which are the kaleidoscopic backbone of the Red Hills.

This ridgetop feels climactic in itself, but if you travel west and climb hills twice again as steep for another 0.7 mile to a second, higher ridgetop, you encounter what is perhaps the earth's most secluded and glorious view of the Tetons. Here those mighty mountains rise above the red-colored cliffs and slopes of the Red Hills. A faint, hard-to-follow trail does lead to this second ridgetop. If you cut a bit to the left or south after you lose the trail above the first ridgetop, you'll see signs of it barely touching the steep land.

As with most of Wyoming's quirky badland landscapes, this area will make for hot and hard hiking on a July afternoon. It seems like a hike meant for early or late season and/or early morning or late afternoon. Bring water. A second unmarked trail also probes the Red Hills 0.8 mile to the east. But the first trail is the longer and more spectacular of the two.

THE GANNETT HILLS

---

60 The Gannett Hills

General description:	An unmaintained trail and cross-country hike through lower elevation sage and aspen covered hills.
Distance:	20 miles round trip.
Difficulty:	Moderate to strenuous.
Elevation gain and loss:	2,732 feet.
General location:	23 miles south of Afton in the unheralded Gannett Hills, along the Idaho border of Wyoming.
Special attractions:	Scenic country that very few people explore. Lots of big game and other wildlife.
Maps:	USGS: Salt Flat (Wyoming), Giraffe (Idaho). Also, for exploration into the northern Gannett Hills, USGS Smoot (Wyoming) and Elk Valley (Idaho). Also, the Bridger-Teton National Forest Big Piney, Greys River and Kemmerer Districts map.
Manager:	Greys River Ranger District and Kemmerer Ranger District.

Finding the trailhead: U.S. Highway 89 (not Wyoming 89 in the same area) divides the westernmost portion of Wyoming in a north/south direction. Traveling south on U.S. Highway 89 from Afton, the road climbs for 18 miles to Salt River Pass. Then it descends exactly 5 more miles to an unmarked road that veers off to the right or north. This path is directly north of Forest Road 10328, heading downhill and to a corral to the south. Turn north and drive 0.2 mile back up what looks like an old highway to an unmarked dead end and the beginning of two possible hiking options. On Forest Service maps, the first hike I'm describing is listed as trail number 026.

The hike: This off-the-beaten-track area also offers a moderate trail hike and a 2- to 4-day backpacking exploration combination.

Other than during hunting season, the secluded and open Gannett Hills receive little attention. Situated on the western fringe of the massive Bridger-Teton National Forest, the land is a fantastic, untraveled hiking playground. Since the south-facing hillsides are relatively open, it's the kind of country that invites a hiker to explore in any direction. Scenic ridgetop hiking is always an option.

Although maps show that a Forest Service Trail 026, heads from the highway up an unnamed valley and into the Gannett Hills, this is not correct. There once *was* a trail up this fairly steep, knee-deep-in-sage gulley. Now springs and seeps, barricaded by active beaver dams, often supercede the

The Gannett Hills

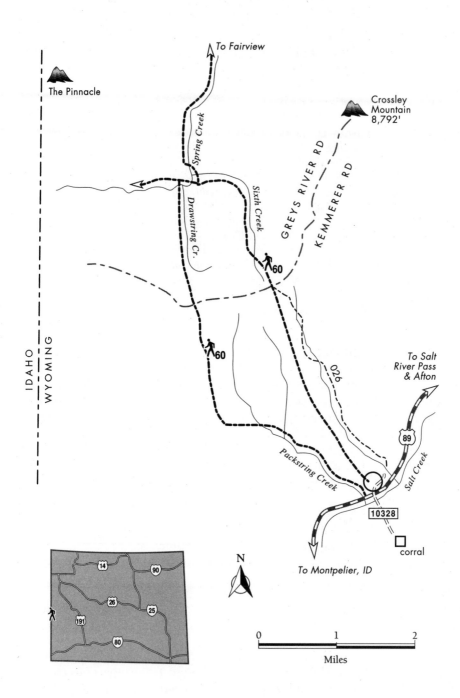

To Fairview

The Pinnacle

Crossley Mountain 8,792'

Spring Creek

Sixth Creek

Drawstring Cr.

GREYS RIVER RD

KEMMERER RD

026

60

60

To Salt River Pass & Afton

89

Salt Creek

Packstring Creek

10328

corral

IDAHO

WYOMING

N

To Montpelier, ID

14

90

26

25

191

80

0   1   2

Miles

Overview of the beautiful but unheralded Gannett Hills country.

barely distinguishable 3 miles of this nonmaintained hunting trail. It's a fun cross-country adventure, though. As the last 0.5 mile of this particular canyon becomes more thickly forested, the path of least resistance leads one up and west to the ridgetop separating this drainage and the Packstring Creek drainage. Here, on the ridge, one encounters a great trail carved by pack strings. This "real" trail actually begins 0.25 mile west of the Trail 026 drainage, climbing and following that ridgetop north to the east/west ridge that forms the backbone of the Gannett Hills. If you're backpacking into this country, this is the more logical path.

Atop this east/west divide, amidst a phenomenal overview of the hilly country, you can choose your own hiking directions. You can cross-country westward toward Packstring Creek and descend into a smaller, aspen-filled gully that constitutes a captivating 10-mile loop back to the car. One can easily continue northward on the pack trail and descend into a 12-mile long area called Spring Creek. You can also journey eastward along this dividing ridgetop and stand atop 8,792 foot Crossley Mountain, the highest point in these hills.

Although unsigned, Packstring Creek boasts a well-maintained and alluring trail that follows its course. This opens more hiking and loop options in this unique country.

THE SNAKE RIVER RANGE

61 Cabin Creek/Wolf Mountain

General description:	A day hike or easy overnighter across varied forests and open meadows.
Distance:	10 miles round trip.
Difficulty:	Moderate.
Elevation gain and loss:	3,423 feet.
Key elevation points:	Wolf Mountain: 9,483 feet.
General location:	20 miles south of Jackson, in the southern end of the Snake River Range, in northwestern Wyoming.
Special attractions:	Lightly used forest trails in peaceful country. Except for climbing Wolf Mountain, this is a great family hiking area.
Maps:	Bridger-Teton National Forest Buffalo and Jackson Ranger Districts forest map. USGS: quads Munger Mountain and Pine Creek.
Fees:	Nearby campgrounds cost $8 to $10.
Manager:	Jackson Ranger District. This area is actually part of the Targhee National Forest, but it is administered by the Bridger-Teton National Forest.

Finding the trailhead: From Hoback Junction 12 miles south of Jackson, turn southwest on U.S. Highway 26/89. After 8 miles you'll pass the Cabin Creek Campground, and about 0.2 mile beyond that a small sign noting the Cabin Creek Road points west. This rocky and rutty, 0.75 mile excursion is on a very rugged, one-lane road. If you've got a low-clearance vehicle, you'd better park off the highway by the road sign or at the campground. The unsigned trailhead is easy to find, as it cuts up a hillside on the north side of the road's end.

The hike: The Snake River Range forms the northern extension of the larger Salt River Range. Gentle foothills mask the range's rugged limestone-shale-sandstone crests. This introductory hike into the range will allow you to sample both aspects of these varied and dynamic mountains.

The Cabin Creek area is defined by pleasant hiking opportunities. For 3.2 miles, other than a few dips into the creek bottom in the first mile, the trail hangs above the canyon floor, alternating between forests and open meadows. Occasional views of the high mountains ahead augment the sweet scenery. At 3.2 miles, a trail junction sign bolted to a tree indicates that the Dog Creek drainage lies to the right and Cabin Creek/Wolf Mountain are to the west.

Another 0.6 mile of level walking brings you to a second (not on the

Cabin Creek/Wolf Mountain

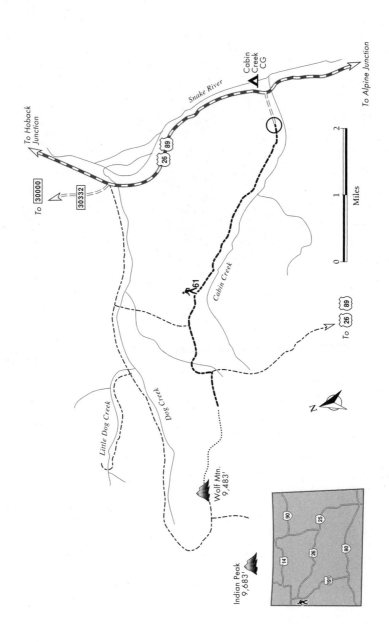

To Hoback Junction

To 30000

30332

26 89

Snake River

Cabin Creek CG

To Alpine Junction

61

Cabin Creek

To 26 89

N

Little Dog Creek

Dog Creek

Wolf Mtn. 9,483'

Indian Peak 9,683'

0   1   2
Miles

90

25

14

26

90

191

Wolf Mountain rising above the meadows of the Cabin Creek drainage.

maps) intersection and an old elk-chewed sign pointing to the south and a 6-mile trail leading to Highway 26. The sign also notes that it's 3 miles west to Wolf Mountain. But here both the level hiking and the trail maintenance end. It's uphill, rugged, and obscure in several places—if a horse packtrain doesn't travel through soon, there will no longer be a trail. (At 4.8 miles from the trailhead, I lost the trail altogether, and climbing Wolf Mountain became a cross-country effort.) The flanks of this huge mountain are covered with brush and so laced with confusing game trails that I ran out of daylight before I could complete the ascent. You could wander north and onto the ridge flank right after that second trail sign, or journey into Dog Creek and approach the mountain from its western flanks.

The lower parts of this trail along Cabin Creek offer great family hiking opportunities and lots of meadow camping.

Northwestern Wyoming

The northwest corner of Wyoming boasts 10,000 square miles of mountainous country (6 different mountain ranges) and a large portion of it is protected as either wilderness or national park. In this rarest of modern-day occurrences, an entire ecosystem, the Yellowstone, is viably surviving in this country.

If the 1984 Wyoming delegation's Wilderness Bill had included the 100,000 acres of important winter range for big game that is found on the eastern drainages outside the Absaroka and Washakie Wildernesses, these incredible biosystems would be self-contained. But even this classic wilderness proposal, which protects glaciers and rocks and high mountain pinnacles while opening lower meadows and forests to development, still leaves enough land for a lifetime of hiking.

This extensive land (save for the Tetons, whose peaks belong to an entirely different volcanic time period) is of Tertiary volcanic origin. Yellowstone is a still-active representation of this activity. The Washakie and Absaroka Ranges are the visible results of ancient lava surges and volcanic ash debris buildups. It's interesting to note that destructive volcanic eruptions and explosions have occurred in this Yellowstone country for the last several million years at about 600,000-year intervals. Even more interesting is the fact that the last major blow-up happened 600,000 years ago.

Just a reminder: northwest Wyoming is the pre-eminent habitat of bears and big game. If you are really aware and cautious, you have a good chance of seeing a grizzly or two.

THE WASHAKIE RANGE

The Washakie Mountains are located on the Teton Wilderness border but are not included in any of the Washakie Wilderness. The Washakie Wilderness lies in the southern half of the Absaroka Range.

In the 1930s, a Wyoming geologist discovered that buried beneath the southwestern sector of the Absaroka Range are a second series of mountains of completely different geologic orgin. Their resemblance to the Absarokas stems from the bottom range—the Washakies—being covered by the geologic formation materials of the southern Absarokas.

The Teton Wilderness, an unspoiled 585,468-acre parcel of land, borders the southern boundary of Yellowstone National Park and the eastern border of Grand Teton National Park. It preserves valuable habitat for the kind of large mammals that require lots of elbow room. Nearly every large, indigenous mammal still survives in this part of the country. The headwaters for both the Yellowstone and the Snake Rivers lie within the boundaries of the

Teton Wilderness. The Bridger-Teton National Forest Buffalo Ranger District, located east of Moran, administrates this area.

62 Pilgrim Creek/Wildcat Peak

General description:	A 3- to 5-day backpack into wild country, traversing everything from creek bottoms to open ridgetops.
Distance:	20 miles round trip.
Difficulty:	Strenuous.
Elevation gain:	2,343 feet.
Key elevation points:	Trailhead: 7,350 feet; Bobcat Ridge Trail intersection: 7,620 feet; Rodent Creek Trail intersection: 8,700 feet; Wildcat Peak: 9,693 feet.
General location:	11 miles north of Moran Junction (Moran is 33 miles north of Jackson), in the western sections of the Teton Wilderness.
Special attractions:	One of the most difficult and wild hikes presented in this book and abundant wildlife.
Maps:	Bridger-Teton National Forest Jackson and Buffalo Ranger District map and/or USGS: Two Ocean Lake and Huckleberry Mountain quads.
Manager:	Buffalo Ranger District, Blackrock Ranger Station.

Finding the trailhead: On U.S. Highway 89/287, inside Grand Teton National Park, 2 miles south of Colter Bay Village or 3.5 miles north or Jackson Lake Junction, the well-signed Pilgrim Creek Road splits off the paved highway and journeys northeast for 2.5 miles. The trailhead at the end of this road is unsigned, but a visible trail beyond the buck-and-pole fence heads directly north. Plan on arriving at this location with a few hours of daylight left. The Park Service classifies this as a "day use only" area, and you'll need to hike 0.5 mile to reach Forest Service land where camping is legal. (Believe me, the park rangers drive by both late at night and early in the morning to enforce this regulation.)

The hike: Every hiking guide needs to present at least one trail and area like this. The wilderness here is of large, untouched proportions, and sometimes that kind of wilderness doesn't necessarily welcome strangers into its heart. In fact, it seems to derive pleasure in testing one's abilities, resolve, and patience to the maximum. Even the personnel at the Blackrock Ranger Station, the overseers of this area, call it their "primitive area within a wilderness," and few know very much about what's back there.

The first 3 miles, although level walking, finds the trail crossing the creek—the creek you can't jump but have to wade, even in late August—15 times. When not splashing in the water, you're often slipping off of a muddy path that weaves a seemingly unplanned route through the willowy jungles that

Pilgrim Creek/Wildcat Peak

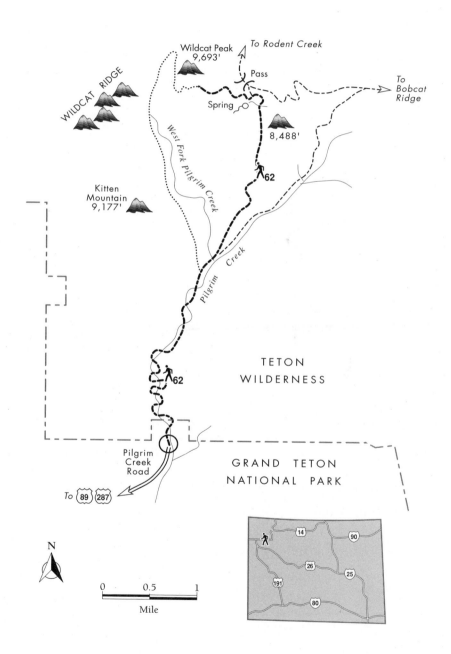

Wildcat Peak
9,693'

To Rodent Creek

WILDCAT RIDGE

Pass

To Bobcat
Ridge

Spring

8,488'

West Fork Pilgrim Creek

62

Kitten
Mountain
9,177'

Pilgrim Creek

TETON
WILDERNESS

62

Pilgrim
Creek
Road

GRAND   TETON
NATIONAL   PARK

To 89 287

N

0   0.5   1
Mile

14   90

26

191   25

80

surround the creek. Finally the trail leaves the watercourse via a steep hillside, and for 0.5 mile it allows you a level walk before again descending to the water and willows.

Now you're in a massive and most striking valley. It's huge beyond comparison and, due to the preamble required to reach it, feels like an especially hidden and wild place. It's a trick to keep going when fresh bear tracks adorn the trail as you vanish into neck-high, view-strangling willows. For 2.5 miles the trail wanders through this valley. When you reach the first creek you can cross without wading, travel 0.3 mile farther east, into the forest. Here the trail forks, and an old sign, if it's still there, points north to Wildcat Peak and east to Bobcat Ridge.

The steep trail toward Wildcat Peak is almost overgrown and forgotten. It's tough to follow as it passes through alternating forests and meadows.

A steep elevation gain over the next 3.5 miles brings you to a divide. Where once a sign existed, all that remains now is a bare post. The Rodent Creek drainage stretches to the north. Maps show a trail heading west toward Wildcat Peak, but the first 100 yards west and into the forest must be walked on faith. The trail does reappear, only to struggle against the downed timber and spot-fire scars that are working to obliterate it. Not quite 1 mile later it vanishes again, and the last 0.5 mile to Wildcat Peak and Ridge is a rugged and steep cross-country climb.

On top of this promontory, the glorious views of the Tetons and the lakes nestled in their shadows take away what little breath one has remaining.

All maps show a loop trail descending from Wildcat Ridge and down the West Fork of Pilgrim Creek. They lie. There was a trail, but it is now a 5-mile, wild, cross-country adventure. With the many forest fire burns in that area, that trek is only going to become more adventurous over the years.

The recreational forester of the Buffalo District recently remarked that, due to horrific budget cuts, it's unlikely a regular maintenance crew will tackle this trail. She does plan to assign a volunteer crew to the area, but how much and how good a job they'll do is always up for grabs. She also notes that even if some new signs get placed in the area, bears usually rub them down within a short time.

This is a hike for experienced wilderness lovers only. Know and respect the area for its potential dangers. Map and compass navigation are essential, and rescues in such wild country are difficult, so be careful.

63 Box Creek Trail

General description:	A day hike or 2- to 3-day backpack that offers great access to the heart of the Teton Wilderness.
Distance:	18 miles round trip.
Difficulty:	Strenuous.
Elevation gain and loss:	1,720 feet.
Key elevation points:	Lava Creek Trail intersection: 8,350 feet; Enos Lake: 8,820 feet.
General location:	40 miles northwest of Jackson, in the south-central Teton Wilderness.
Special attractions:	Awesome after effects of the Teton Tornado.
Maps:	Bridger-Teton National Forest Buffalo and Jackson Ranger District map; USGS: Joy Peak, Two Ocean Pass, Gravel Mountain.
Manager:	Buffalo Ranger District, Blackrock Ranger Station.

Finding the trailhead: You can reach the Box Creek Trailhead by driving approximately 3.5 miles east of Moran Junction on U.S. Highway 26/287. Here, well-signed Buffalo Valley Road, or Forest Road 30050, jogs northeast toward Turpin Meadows. Follow this paved road approximately 9.5 miles east to the Box Creek Trailhead sign. Turpin Meadows is located 2 miles further down the road, where 2 other trailheads are also located.

The hike: In 1987 a tornado ripped through the Box Creek area, toppling trees and leaving trunks and debris stacked 10- to 15-feet high in places. It also left a 14,000-acre swath of destruction behind. Never before had a tornado been recorded at such a high elevation.

Since the blowdown, Forest Service, American Hiking Society, Sierra Club, and Student Conservation crews, as well as commercial outfitters, have worked to reopen the closed trails using—as required by the area's classification as wilderness—only crosscut saws and other primitive tools. The Box Creek Trail is once again open to hikers and horse travel.

The beginning 4 miles of this easy-to-follow trail are a fairly strenuous uphill climb. The trail then levels out as it traces the western flanks of Gravel Ridge. Be sure to carry some water for these first 5 miles. Lava Creeek is the first sure source of water.

Here you intersect the Lava Creek Trail, jogging to the west. It, too, offers Teton Tornado views. The Enos Lake Trail continues northeast for approximately 4 miles to a large lake. The forest here offers many camping opportunities. From here you can venture any number of directions deeper into the wilderness and toward Yellowstone. A suggested loop hike would be to return to Turpin Meadows via the Clear Creek Trail. A 2-mile road walk back to the Box Creek Trailhead would conclude such a loop.

As you travel through the blowdown area, consider the changes that have

Box Creek Trail

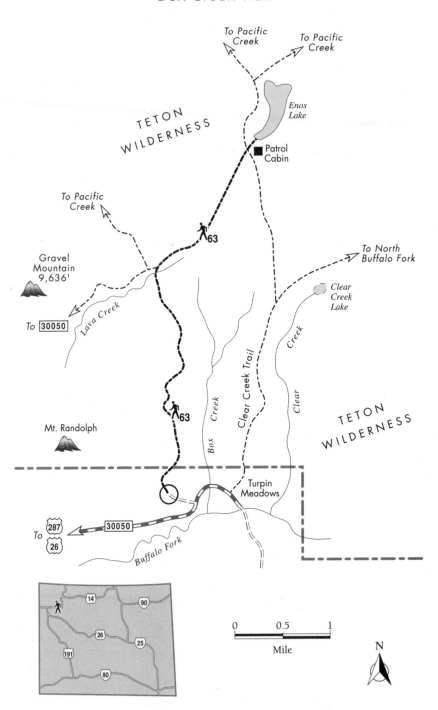

occurred. Wilderness provides an opportunity to see natural forces at work and to observe how plants and animals adapt to these changes. The Teton Wilderness is also home to the grizzly bear. Stop in at the Blackrock Ranger Station for information on the special rules that apply to hiking in bear country and updates on recent sightings.

—Rebecca Fitzwilliams

64 Holmes Cave

General description:	A beautiful day hike or a leisurely overnighter into the pinnacled terrain of the Teton/Washakie Wilderness Areas.
Distance:	9.2 miles round trip.
Difficulty:	Easy to moderate.
Elevation gain:	2,000 feet.
Key elevation points:	Teton Wilderness Boundary: 10,300 feet; Holmes Cave: 9,650 feet.
General location:	6 miles west of Togwotee Pass, which is west of Dubois and east of Moran Junction, in the very southeastern corner of the Teton Wilderness.
Special attractions:	Awesome wildflowers and alpine country on the way to an interesting cave entrance.
Maps:	The Bridger-Teton National Forest Buffalo and Jackson Ranger Districts visitor map; USGS: Togwotee Pass, Angle Mountain.
Manager:	Buffalo Ranger District, Blackrock Ranger Station.

Finding the trailhead: From Moran Junction, travel approximately 21 miles east; or, from Dubois, drive about 35 miles west (it's U.S. Highway 26/287 either way) to an unsigned, little rut of a road that jogs due north. This road begins near a cautionary yellow curve symbol highway warning sign, but this landmark could be wiped out by a snowplow. Just keep in mind that, once you've traveled the prescribed number of miles, it will be the only road in the area that heads north. It only travels 0.25 mile before a sign indicates trailhead parking.

The hike: Beyond the parking area the road ruts continue north for another 0.25 mile, ending at an active cow-camp cabin. Park at the trailhead parking sign and not in these folks' driveway. A small sign north of the cabin notes both the trail's beginning and the fact that you are entering grizzly bear habitat.

For 0.5 mile the trail primes your lungs and legs as it steeply gains elevation, before it drops into an open vale. Here begins a journey into exquisite scenery that only gets better with each passing mile. A small creek crossing at the bottom of this valley occurs before the trail gently curves to the east

Holmes Cave

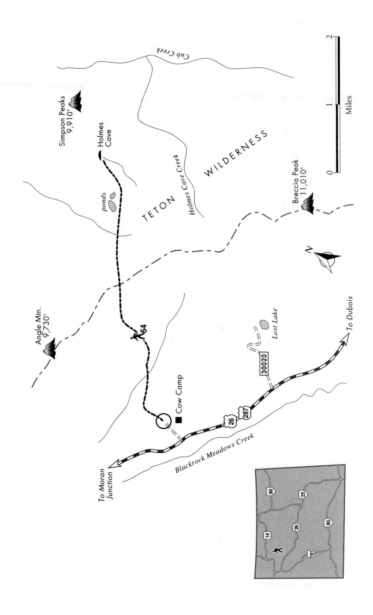

and begins heading uphill toward fabulous, striated volcanic cliffs. After 2.5 miles the trail again veers north and ascends a steep hillside; the top marks the Teton Wilderness boundary. If you only travel the 3.1 miles to this spot, you will have fulfilled your Recommended Daily Allowance for Wildland Beauty (RDAWB).

Unless you bushwhack toward some of the surrounding peaks, it's now time to lose that hard-earned elevation. The trail becomes indistinguishable as it descends toward the east. Look for cairns, and be sure to head more to the right or east than you think you should. After about 0.25 mile, the trail reappears on the south side of a small creek dropping into a gorgeous alpine valley. At the bottom, still continuing eastward, again climb to a second ridgetop, past a small lake and a smaller pond. At 4.6 miles the trail divides, with Holmes Cave lying downhill and to the left. Again the trail becomes grassed-over, but look downhill at the stream course and follow it to a rocky outcropping in the meadow. Where the creek vanishes into the earth marks the beginning of Holmes Cave.

Outwardly, this cave is really just a tiny hole in the ground, exciting only because of the amazing adventure required to reach it. Inwardly, the cavern extends over 4,000 feet underground and boasts 3 large chambers. Speleology is beyond the scope of this guide, but to me—cold from the wind and with no rope, wet suit, or other caving equipment—the idea of crawling into that moss-covered rocky hole with an icy mountain creek in its center held no appeal. But outside was a fun place to enjoy lunch and let my imagination follow the water into the volcanic bowels of the earth.

THE ABSAROKA RANGE

The Crow Indians in Wyoming and Montana country were sometimes referred to as the Absarokas, a name meaning "people of the great winged bird." There are 3 different pronunciations for this word, the local favorite being Ab-Sor-Kees. The proper diction of Ab-sar-O-kas holds second place, while Ab-ZORKS occasionally slips into the conversation of the lazy-tongued.

Tremendous piles of volcanic ash and lava have layered themselves onto this country. The high ridges and mountaintops display a plateau-like crest, and this crest reveals a vast, horizontal bed of lava. Massive forces of erosion sculpted these rock layers into extremely steep slopes and spectacular pinnacles. The multicolored and banded cliffs rise to 11,000- and 12,000-foot elevations, often above astonishingly large, level, grassy meadows. Lakes are few in this erosion-prone country, while narrow canyons and large creek drainages charge through the crumbly rock with a vengeance.

Little is written about this range and its wildernesses because it is, compared to other areas, little explored. It is an area where a hiker can still discover a remnant tepee ring or an old pile of stones that may have served as a dwelling for members of the ancient Sheepeater tribe called Tukuarika. It's an even more exciting land because here an explorer can leave the trail any time, snoop into a small side canyon or hike across the broad alpine upland, and feel as if he is the first person to walk this section.

65 Jade Lakes

General description:	A short hike to two pretty, high-country lakes.
Distance:	5 miles round trip.
Difficulty:	Easy.
Elevation gain and loss:	490 feet.
Key elevation points:	Upper Jake Lake: 9,620 feet; Lower Jade Lake: 9,500 feet.
General location:	27 miles northwest of Dubois, in the northwestern corner of the Shoshone National Forest.
Special attractions:	Beautiful lakes set beneath towering cliffs, good fishing.
Maps:	Shoshone National Forest north half visitor map; USGS: Togwotee Pass, Dundee Meadows.
Manager:	Wind River Ranger District.
Fees:	No user fees, but please register at trailhead. Nearby Brooks Lake Campground costs $7 to $8 per night.

Finding the trailhead: Approximately 27 miles west of Dubois on U.S. Highway 287/26, or 7.8 miles east of the Togwotee (toe-GUH-tee) Pass, Brooks Lake Road jogs north. This graveled main road is easy to follow for the 5.2 miles to the Brooks Lake Campground. Just before Brooks Lake Lodge, turn north at the campground sign, but don't enter the camping area. Stay west and drive the short distance to the signed trailhead near the southern shores of Brooks Lake.

The hike: U.S. Highway 287 west of Dubois climbs into an absolutely enticing section of southern Absaroka high country. While driving, one notices that these somewhat wild and unusual stratified layers of volcanic cliff keep bobbing into view. Upper and Lower Jade Lakes offer an easy 2.5-mile (one way) hike that places you both directly under those naked cliffs and beside emerald lakes that reflect the majesty of the surrounding country. Jade, by the way, is Wyoming's official state stone.

The first 0.5 mile of trail follows the Yellowstone Trail, Trail 823 (Hike 66). Here a sign points northwest to Jade Lakes. A new, relocated section of trail lets you avoid what used to be 5 or more eroded paths cutting up a steep hillside. Follow this uphill for a bit more than 0.5 mile. Then the walk mellows, and for the final 1.5 miles the path wanders through a gentle and more open forest.

The tiny, stagnant pond at 1.5 miles, although green in color, is not one of the Jade Lakes. Continue along the trail for another 0.5 mile and descend

Jade Lakes

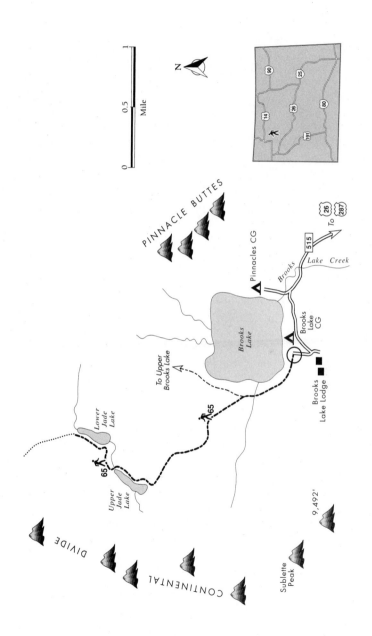

Mile

0 0.5 1

N

90 25

14 26 80

191

PINNACLE BUTTES

Pinnacles CG

515

To 26 287

Brooks Lake Creek

Brooks Lake

Brooks Lake CG

To Upper Brooks Lake

Brooks Lake Lodge

65

Lower Jade Lake

65

Upper Jade Lake

9,492'

CONTINENTAL DIVIDE

Sublette Peak

Absaroka beauty at Upper Jade Lake.

into a depression holding the beautiful, deep waters of Upper Jade Lake. Here, those layered Absaroka cliffs tower over and reflect off the lake's waters. Excellent camping is found near the lake's southwestern shore and at its northern shore by the creek outlet (100-feet-from-shore rule applies).

Lower Jade Lake lies downhill 0.5 mile farther along the trail. It forms the big cousin of Upper Jade, but doesn't offer the cliff reflections or as many camping opportunities. Both lakes contain fish.

At the extreme northwest corner of the lower lake, a hunting trail cuts to the north. It appears to be an ancient Forest Service trail that they are trying to forget, and my advice is to help the Forest Service and don't follow it. I did walk the route, and it was a fun adventure until several miles later when I lost both the path and my sense of direction. I staggered back to Brooks Lake 12 hours later, having somehow traversed the untrailed Clear Creek Drainage of the Teton Wilderness, an entire drainage away. This was a most humbling lesson on how even an experienced hiker can get confused and turn a simple hike into a lost-and-found situation.

66 Upper Brooks Lake/ Bear Cub Pass

General description:	A level and open hike to a scenic alpine lake.
Distance:	7 miles round trip.
Difficulty:	Easy.
Elevation gain and loss:	150 feet.
Key elevation points:	Upper Brooks Lake: 9,350 feet; Cub Pass: 9,400 feet.
General location:	27 miles northwest of Dubois, in the northwestern corner of the Shoshone National Forest.
Special attractions:	A gentle trail surrounded by spectacular stratified cliffs, great fishing in lovely lake settings.
Maps:	Shoshone National Forest north half visitor map; USGS: Togwotee Pass, Dundee Meadows.
Manager:	Wind River Ranger District.
Fees:	Brooks Lake Campground costs $7 to $8 per night.

Finding the trailhead: Same as for Hike 65.

The hike: The Jade Lakes Trail (Hike 65), Trail 823-1A, introduced you to the forested settings of the Togwotee area. Neighboring Yellowstone Trail, Trail 823 to Upper Brooks Lake, affords a completely different experience in this spectacular country. It contains some of the most relaxing meadow walking imaginable. Brooks Lake and Creek were both named after Bryant B. Brooks, the cowboy governor of Wyoming from 1905 to 1911.

All access directions are identical to the Jade Lakes Trail (Hike 64) access descriptions, up to and including the first 0.5 mile of hiking. At this intersection journey right or northeast, continuing the trek through the flowered meadows and around the western shores of lower Brooks Lake.

A small climb at the north end of the lake constitutes one of the few uphill slopes on this hike. Above this hill, the trail follows a mini ridgetop that runs between 2 small valleys that sit below the cliffs that rule this area. After 2.0 miles of short-grass meadow walking, the trail fords Brooks Creek from west to east and climbs a short distance into the forest. Here it intersects the Bonnieville Pass Trail, Trail 808, the long-journey access to the mostly secret Dunoir area. (The Shoshone Forest Service map depicts this trail intersection as being close to Lower Brooks Lake, when actually it's nearer to Upper Brooks Lake.)

After 0.5 mile, Upper Brooks Lake comes into view. This beautiful lake sits in a gentle, high-country environment. Camping spots exist all around, but easiest access to them comes via following the trail almost to Bear Cub Pass and then hiking around the northern shores of the lake.

Bear Cub Pass isn't much more than a wooded hilltop that divides the Shoshone National Forest from the Teton Wilderness. But it does serve as an excellent passageway to this Bridger-Teton wildland. Beyond the pass the

Upper Brooks Lake/Bear Cub Pass

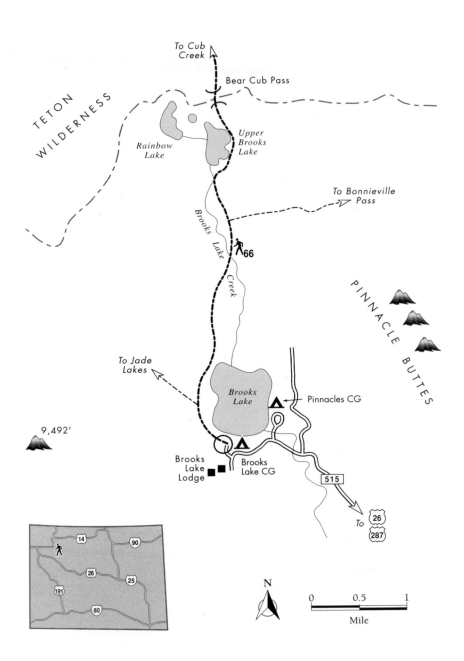

trail drops for 2 miles into the Cub Creek Drainage, a very pretty and private piece of open valley country.

The Yellowstone Trail is an ideal hike for families or for anyone wanting a scenic, leisurely hike.

THE WASHAKIE WILDERNESS

Wyoming claims several firsts in the field of national treasures. The first national park, the first national monument—and here, the nation's first national forest was established when the Yellowstone Park Timberland Reserve of 1891 became the Shoshone National Forest in 1902. The northern half of the Shoshone National Forest hosts a wonderful abundance of wildlife, including deer—both white-tailed and mule—elk, bighorn sheep, antelopes, mountain goats, mountain lions, coyotes, moose, and black and grizzly bears. Watch for the numerous eagles, both golden and bald, circling in the sky. The reintroduction of the wolf into its historic Yellowstone ecosystem range has been accomplished, although this move still faces strong opposition from hunters, livestock owners, and legislators.

Chief Washakie of the Shoshone Indians is in second place for the number of geographic features in Wyoming named after him; he has 11 place names, behind Jim Bridger who has 22. Washakie was sometimes called the best Indian ally the whites ever had. A noted warrior, he nevertheless tirelessly pursued peaceful settlements with the intruders. In 1900, he was buried with full military honors by the United States Army, the only Native American (at that time) ever so honored. It seems fitting that such a beautiful wilderness be named after such a visionary and peaceful man.

67 Frontier Creek

General description:	A 2- to 3-day, exceptionally scenic backpack into a sheltered canyon.
Distance:	18 miles round trip.
Difficulty:	Moderate to strenuous.
Elevation gain and loss:	1,800 feet.
Key elevation points:	Cougar Creek intersection: 9,200 feet; end of trail: 9,750 feet; Green Lake: 10,600 feet.
General location:	30 miles north of Dubois, in the south-central section of the Washakie Wilderness.
Special attractions:	Ancient petrified forest remnants are still visible in this drainage.
Maps:	Shoshone National Forest north half map; USGS: Snow Lake, Emerald Lake.
Fees:	Double Cabin Campground costs $7 to $8 per night
Manager:	Wind River Ranger District.

Finding the trailhead: From downtown Dubois, turn north and leave town on paved Horse Creek Road. The road isn't especially well marked. It begins just west of the 1 bridge on the main street of Dubois, directly across from Welty's General Store. The pavement ends after 5 miles, and Forest Service Road 285 begins in another 5 miles. For the next 20 miles this road is your guide into the ever-increasing beauty of the southern Absarokas. Double Cabin Campground is your goal, so follow any intersection signs pointing to it. Don't drive into the campground but continue north for a few hundred yards to the large wilderness trailhead sign sitting in a meadow. The "parking lot" is that meadow, south of the sign.

The hike: When a geologically recent Yellowstone volcanic eruption added yet another layer of ash on top of this land, the large forests in the southern Absarokas were instantly buried under thick and powdery rock debris. Time and pressure mineralized the encased wood; water and erosion then excavated the large drainages named Wiggins Fork and Frontier Creek. Huge, petrified stumps adorn the higher cliffs surrounding the waterways. Smaller pieces of the mineralized wood lie in the riverbed. Every summer, after high runoff, new samples of this colorful rock are unearthed.

In the past, the petrified wood has been carried out by visitors and by commercial entrepreneurs. Entire rock trees have been dynamited and toted out of the wilderness via mule pack train. While a petrified wood fireplace may be an impressive addition to someone's ranch house, it doesn't do a thing for the future generations who will hike this wild country unable to sample its unique qualities. Leave the wood where you find it. It's the proper course of action, and it's the law.

The Frontier Creek Trail sign notes that the trail begins directly north of the wilderness sign. It's an easy path to make out as it journeys north across

Frontier Creek

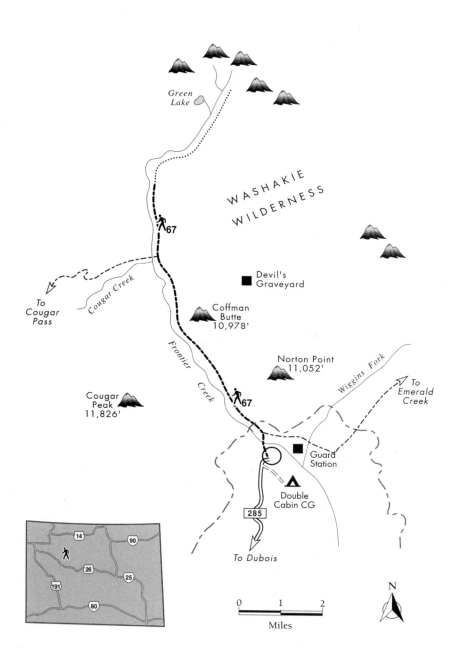

Green Lake

WASHAKIE WILDERNESS

67

To Cougar Pass

Cougar Creek

Devil's Graveyard

Coffman Butte 10,978'

Norton Point 11,052'

Wiggins Fork

Frontier Creek

67

To Emerald Creek

Cougar Peak 11,826'

Guard Station

Double Cabin CG

285

To Dubois

14

90

26

25

191

80

0   1   2
Miles

N

the meadow and toward Frontier Creek Canyon. After 0.5 mile, the trail crosses Frontier Creek. This can be a cold, swift, and slippery wade. It can also be low in the morning and raging in the afternoon, due to snowmelt.

The first 6.5 miles of this trail traverse easier, mostly level terrain through forested lands. Lodgepole dominates the land at first, but by the time you reach the Cougar Pass intersection at 6.7 miles, fir and spruce have claimed control. But forest doesn't necessarily dominate the hike; those somber, gray, conglomerate volcanic cliffs on both sides of the canyon are a powerful presence too. From 4 miles on, several nice camping meadows appear.

One suggestion for a trip is to camp above or just below the Cougar Pass Trail intersection (the meadow right at this intersection is closed to camping) and day hike to Cougar Pass one day and upper Frontier Creek the next.

Older maps show a trail exiting the main trail to the east and climbing to what's labeled Devil's Graveyard. This supposedly is a hidden alpine bench where a field of flat stones lie perpendicular to the ground and form a sort of natural tombstone cemetery setting. In 4 attempts over the years to locate this spot, I never have found the right trail or the graveyard. But some amazing campfire ghost stories are generated around this anomaly.

Above the Cougar Pass Trail intersection, the Frontier Creek Trail continues upstream for a bit more than 2 miles. Then it drops to the creek and ends. Here is where you want to scan the cliffs to the west. Large stumps of petrified wood, some of them more than 8 feet in diameter, occasionally dot the gray rock. Here also you can see in the cliffs the hundreds of feet of volcanic debris that at one time covered this land.

It is a somewhat rugged journey to continue upstream and cross-country to Green Lake. This puddle of colored water resides in the middle of a broad and glorious basin surrounded by towering peaks.

68 Wiggins Fork to Emerald Lake

General description:	A multi-day hike into a wild, volcanic canyon that ends in an enchanting alpine lake setting.
Distance:	28 miles round trip.
Difficulty:	Strenuous.
Elevation gain:	2,250 feet.
Key elevation points:	Wiggins Fork: 8,600 feet; Burwell Creek: 8,700 feet; Emerald Lake: 10,850 feet.
General location:	30 miles north of Dubois, in the south-central section of the Washakie Wilderness.
Special attractions:	Petrified wood, plus lovely creek and woodland settings climaxing in a gem of a lake.
Maps:	Shoshone National Forest north half map; USGS: Snow Lake, Emerald Lake.
Manager:	Wind River Ranger District.
Fees:	Double Creek Campground: $7 to $8 per night.

Finding the trailhead: Same as for Hike 67.

The hike: The long and winding Wiggins Fork/Emerald Creek Trail accesses some mighty wild Washakie Wilderness country. Jack Wiggins, a nearby homesteader, enjoyed the country so much that when he packed surveyors into its boundaries in 1900, he gave them a quarter of beef to name the creek after him.

At the wilderness trailhead, a sign points east to the Wiggins Fork Trail. Be sure and bring a pair of tennis shoes and a walking stick on this trip, as there are several river crossings and not one of them is easy.

Immediately you wade Frontier Creek. After following the trail 0.5 mile around the north side of the Forest Service guard station, you wade the many channels of Wiggins Fork and cross to the east side of the riverbed. Before wading, look across the channel to the southeast for the fencepost marker indicating where the trail continues. After walking less than 0.5 mile in the wrong direction, i.e., south and away from Wiggins Canyon, you'll intersect the Indian Point Trail. In these open meadows, at a signed intersection, the Wiggins Fork Trail begins its northerly journey.

The next 4.5 miles of trail contain 2 river crossings, the marks of a 1,250-acre human-caused fire that razed the land in 1952, extraordinary views of the towering and jagged volcanic cliffs that surround Wiggins Fork, and lots of wonderful and fairly easy forest hiking. A bit more than 5 miles after its beginning, the trail crosses Wiggins Fork. Here the Emerald Creek Trail continues northward and the Wiggins Fork Trail branches to the west.

Don't let the first mile of this Emerald Creek Trail fool you. With its gentle walking, excellent campsites and vibrant scenery, the trail portends easy hiking. But you must cross large Emerald Creek to the west after 1

Wiggins Fork to Emerald Lake

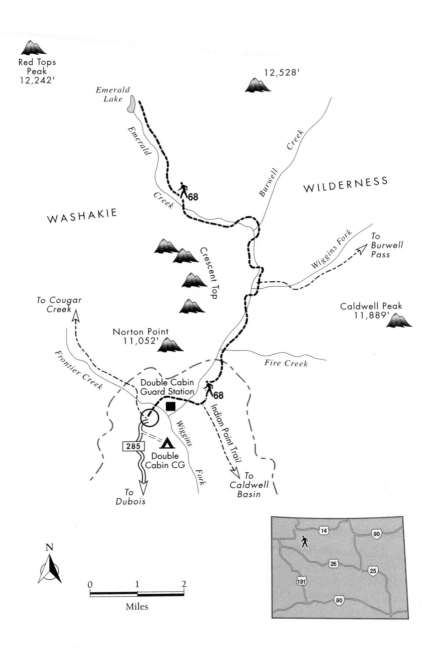

Red Tops Peak 12,242'

12,528'

Emerald Lake

Emerald Creek

Burwell Creek

WILDERNESS

68

WASHAKIE

Crescent Top

Wiggins Fork

To Burwell Pass

Caldwell Peak 11,889'

To Cougar Creek

Norton Point 11,052'

Fire Creek

Frontier Creek

Double Cabin Guard Station

68

Indian Point Trail

285

Wiggins Fork

Double Cabin CG

To Caldwell Basin

To Dubois

N

0   1   2
Miles

14

90

26

25

191

80

Looking into the Emerald Creek drainage.

mile, go back to the east after another 0.8 mile, then cross a large side waterway—Burwell Creek—in 0.3 mile, and again wander back to the west side of the river in another 0.2 mile. Trying to stay on one side of the river to avoid wading doesn't work. The trail's crisscross antics serve the purpose of avoiding the steep cliffs that drop into the creek waters. After each crossing, the country seems to acquire a more wild and remote feel.

The next 2.5 miles are dry and travel through a thickly wooded north-facing hillside. After a final creek crossing to the north, the trail becomes fairly rugged walking as it seriously begins to gain elevation. This next 1.5 miles sport a most unique limber pine forest.

About 11.5 miles from trail beginning, the forest starts to thin and become interspersed with alpine meadows. High and impressive peaks surround the country. The final mile to the lake leaves the hiker in totally open country and picking one's way up long and taxing slopes. The trail vanishes in the grass, but by remaining on the eastern side of the now small creek and mucking out the steep climb, you reach the jewel of the trip, Emerald Lake. The flowered grassland and cliff-encompassed setting of this long and shallow lake surpasses any words a guidebook author can find. It's about 14 miles from trail beginning to the lake's end.

A word needs to be said about probable potential trail changes in this country. These mountains are steep and extremely friable. A single major rainstorm or a heavy winter runoff can modify the land by creating new gullies that the trail suddenly disappears into. Also, the creek bottoms that this trail so frequently crosses are wide, and every year the water changes course and wipes out some of the trail. On any of the many crossings you may have to search for signs of where the trail again enters into the forest across the riverbed.

Be also aware that this is prime grizzly habitat. In this drainage I came upon the biggest track I've ever seen.

69 East Fork Wind River

General description:	A multi-day backpack into gentle, vast, open and rolling alpine high country.
Distance:	23 miles round trip.
Difficulty:	Moderate to strenuous.
Elevation gain:	2,430 feet.
Key elevation points:	East Fork Trailhead: 8,620 feet; East Fork of East Fork intersection: 9,150 feet; Coal Chute Pass Trail intersection: 10,500 feet; East Fork Pass: 11,050 feet; Bear Creek Pass: 11,100 feet.
General location:	40 miles northeast of Dubois, in the southeastern section of the Washakie Wilderness.
Special attractions:	Country that exemplifies the gently rolling mountaintops of the eastern Absarokas. Great moose, bear, and elk habitat.
Maps:	Shoshone National Forest north half map; USGS: East Fork Basin, Dunrud Peak. Add Castle Rock and Wiggins Peak quads if planning on making this a loop that joins Bear Creek.
Manager:	Wind River Ranger District.

Finding the trailhead: Leave Dubois and drive east on U.S. Highway 287/ 26 for 10.8 miles. A tiny, green East Fork Road sign and a huge "Thunderhead Ranch Registered Simmentals" sign direct you north onto a good gravel road. This is one long and scenic byway. Several cigarette commercials were filmed in this area, and if you thought the country looked impressive on television, you ought to experience it in person and without herds of horses being chased by white-hatted cowboys with little puffs of carcinogenic smoke trailing behind them.

After 10 miles of gravel-road driving you come to a major fork. Follow the main road to the east. After 15.5 miles the road descends into a huge valley. Pass under the Bitter Root Ranch sign, but 1.2 miles later DON'T drive down to the Bitter Root Ranch, as the sign points; instead, turn left at this fork and head north and up a long hill. You'll pass through a Wyoming Game and Fish Department elk fence, enter the Shoshone National Forest and, via Forest Road 500, ascend to the top of a pass. The road's fork at this point should be signed. Left or west leads you toward Bear Creek while

East Fork Wind River

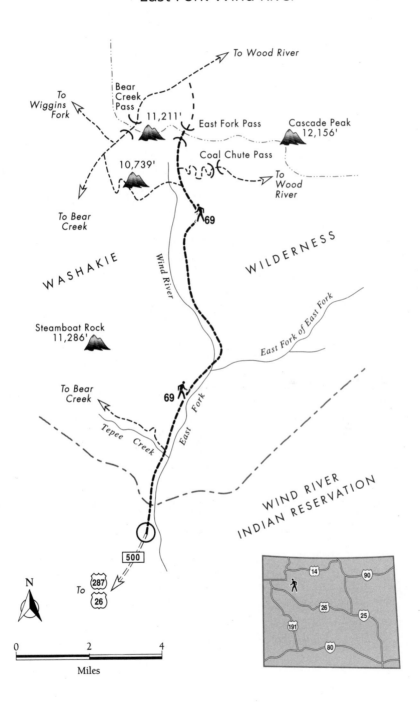

To Wood River

Bear Creek Pass

To Wiggins Fork

11,211'

East Fork Pass

Cascade Peak 12,156'

Coal Chute Pass

10,739'

To Wood River

To Bear Creek

69

WASHAKIE

Wind River

WILDERNESS

Steamboat Rock 11,286'

East Fork of East Fork

To Bear Creek

69

East Fork

Tepee Creek

WIND RIVER INDIAN RESERVATION

500

N

To 287 26

0   2   4

Miles

14   90

26

25

191

80

straight or north descends into the East Fork Drainage. NOTE: if a major rainstorm catches you beyond this pass, the hill will require four-wheel-drive to reclimb. Beyond the pass 2.7 miles, the main road ends at a Washakie Wilderness/East Fork Trailhead sign.

The hike: The Absaroka Mountains and the Washakie Wilderness have many different faces. Hike 67 and Hike 68 reveal a rougher, wilder, more spectacular aspect of these vast mountains. The East Fork of the Wind River displays a completely different wilderness personality. Here the mountaintops reach 12,000-foot elevations, and tundra-like meadows create favorable habitat for an abundance of wildflowers and wildlife. Except during hunting season, this area sees little use.

After 1.3 miles of gentle hiking you come to the Tepee Creek Trail intersection. The sign here notes that it's 5 miles to Bear Creek. What it doesn't say is that in that 5 miles you go from 8,600 feet in elevation to 11,500 feet in elevation and back down again.

One west-side-to-east-side river crossing comes almost 4 miles up the trail. This is usually an easy wade until August, when it becomes a hard jump. From here the trail gradually climbs and the trees thin out as the country opens into expansive alpine meadows. Approximately 7.5 miles up the drainage, the Nine Mile Trail jogs to the west and into some alluring mountains. This trail was maintained as recently as 1997, but you still may have to look for rock cairns directing the way.

The joy of the East Fork Trail is the access it affords to many alpine passes. Beyond Nine Mile Trail 1.5 miles, the Coal Chute Pass Trail banks steeply off to the east. If you continue northward on the main trail, 1 mile of steep climbing places you atop East Fork Pass, which overlooks a grand view of the Wood River Valley. Several loop routes can take you around to the headwaters of the Bear Creek drainage. Highly recommended is a hike up the East Fork, a circle around any of the trails leading into upper Bear Creek, a pretty journey down Bear Creek and finally crossing back to the East Fork via steep Tepee Creek and Pass.

The only cautionary note for this trail is that you carry a good topography map on the journey. The trail often disappears in the alpine meadows. It's then nice to be able to determine the route from the map.

70 Jack Creek

General description:	A wild 2- or 3-day trip following a little-known and even less-traveled creek drainage.
Distance:	15 miles or more round trip.
Difficulty:	Strenuous.
Elevation gain and loss:	3,070 feet.
Key elevation points:	Haymaker Pass trail junction: 9,100 feet; Haymaker Pass: 10,820 feet; Jacks Peak: 11,202 feet.
General location:	30 miles directly west of Meeteetse, just outside the northwestern border of the Washakie Wilderness. Meeteetse is 25 miles south of Cody.
Special attractions:	A little-used trail that culminates in a wide valley beneath an 11,000-foot peak.
Maps:	Shoshone National Forest north half map; USGS: Phelps Mountain, Francs Peak, Irish Rock.
Fees:	The Greybull District has donation boxes at its trailheads.
Manager:	Greybull Ranger District.

Finding the trailhead: South of Cody 25 miles, or 52 miles north of Thermopolis, on Wyoming 120, sits the most scenic town in the world: Meeteetse, Wyoming. The name literally translates as "measured distance near and far." From the center of town, Wyoming 290 heads due west and remains paved for 11.6 miles. At pavement's end, turn right and head for Pitchfork. Drive this road 0.2 mile and turn left onto the Pitchfork Ranch Road. Don't go right and across the bridge at this intersection.

Too many intersections exist along the next 18 miles to describe. Simply abide by one rule: always follow the signs that say Jack Creek. All the road intersections are well signed. The last 5 or 6 miles form a narrow, one-lane gravel road where you can hope you don't meet an oncoming horse trailer. Follow the signs left and through the campground, uphill to the Jack Creek Trailhead.

The hike: In response to my queries, the Greybull District ranger wrote the following: "The Greybull District offers opportunities for the hiker who is interested in solitude, scenery, wildlife, and who does not necessarily need to rely on well-marked trails to navigate in the wilderness." She also mentioned that the trails cross streams and rivers a number of times, and that high-water conditions (pre-Fourth of July) can make these crossings dangerous, if not impossible. When she noted that hikers often travel 10 days and have limited or no contact with other people, I knew I had to explore this area.

Jack Creek is a swiftly tumbling tributary in a large and long drainage. The trail climbs steeply above the creek's eastern hillsides and for more

Jack Creek

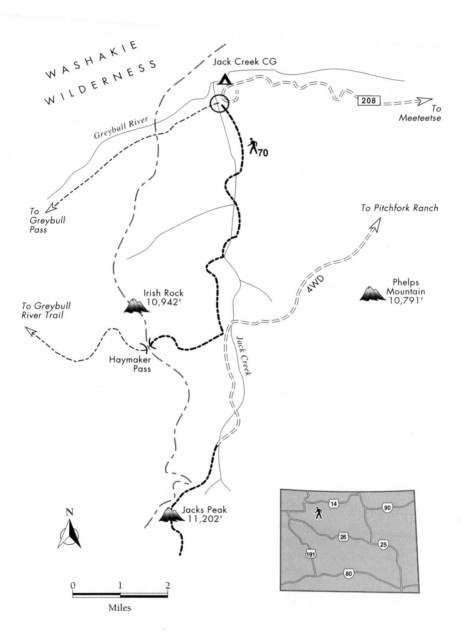

WASHAKIE WILDERNESS

Jack Creek CG

208

To Meeteetse

Greybull River

🚶70

To Greybull Pass

To Pitchfork Ranch

4WD

To Greybull River Trail

Irish Rock 10,942'

Phelps Mountain 10,791'

Jack Creek

Haymaker Pass

Jacks Peak 11,202'

N

14

90

26

25

191

80

0   1   2
Miles

than 1 mile cuts through the meadows that surround the canyon's lower end. By 1.6 miles and the first creek crossing (a large log may or may not be spanning the waters), the forest has claimed the hillsides and stream bottom. In fact, because the creek channel is such a timbered or rocky maze, the trail generally stays high, dropping twice to the creek only where it recrosses the waters. These crossings make for fun, chilly wades.

Lots of steep climbing dominates the first 3.5 miles of the trail. But then you find out what all the work is for. The trail enters the most treasured feature of the Absaroka Mountains and Washakie Wilderness, the vast and rolling plains of high alpine country with awesome views. After about 2 more miles the trail crosses some meadows and is somewhat hard to follow. Look for the green steel fence posts, cairns, and tree blazes that mark the trail's path.

At nearly 6 miles the trail again descends to the creek and joins an old road. According to the maps, the road is open to vehicles, but there are few signs of motorized usage on that road. Here you get to choose directions. You can wander for several miles up the road (it does return to trailed walking) and to the canyon's most beautiful beginnings. You might even climb the northwest ridge of 11,202-foot Jacks Peak. (In early July, it was solid snow and ice.) Or you can follow the road for a few hundred yards, cut uphill to the right or west and intersect the unsigned Haymaker Trail. Just 2 miles of uphill on this trail places you atop a high pass that overlooks the massive, serene, and verdant upper Greybull River Valley. Excellent opportunities exist here to explore the open alpine fields that create the high mountains, including 10,942-foot Irish Rock to the north of Haymaker Pass.

This is not an easy trail. There's a lot of uphill hiking. And this is prime bear habitat; when I hiked this trail, a huge set of fresh tracks kept me company.

At least 2 "Jack Creeks" flow in Wyoming. As best I can tell, this particular one was named for an early trapper and not for a villainous desperado.

71 Greybull River

General description:	A week (or longer) trek into a spectacular and important river drainage in the western section of the Washakie Wilderness.
Distance:	40 miles round trip.
Difficulty:	Strenuous.
Elevation gain:	3,450 feet.
Key elevation points:	Trailhead: 7,750 feet; Anderson Creek: 8,280 feet; Venus Creek: 8,520 feet; Bonne Creek: 9,000 feet; Greybull Pass: 11,200 feet.
General location:	30 miles west of Meeteetse.
Special attractions:	One of the largest sections of untrammeled wilderness in the state.
Maps:	Shoshone National Forest visitor map (north half); USGS: Phelps Mountain, Irish Rock, Francs Peak, Mount Burwell.
Manager:	Greybull Ranger District.
Fees:	The Greybull District puts donation boxes at its trailheads.

Finding the trailhead: Same as Hike 70.

The hike: The Greybull Ranger District out of Meeteetse notes that this is their most popular trail. I never saw a soul my entire time there. Perhaps some of the original medicine still lives along the Greybull River. It was named by and remains sacred to Indians because of an albino bull buffalo that once roamed the land.

The Forest Service did a neat thing here in recognizing the difference in leg length between horses and backpackers. At the west end of the parking lot a sign reads "Greybull River high flood water and backpacking trail." The original horse trail starts directly west of the campground with an immediate neck-deep (for humans) river ford. On this high trail, you too must begin with a ford, but wading Jack Creek is possible. The Greybull River can be big-time water.

This is a delightful trail. The first 0.2 mile places you high above the river and offers exceptional views of the valley. The horse trail on the other side of the river appears to suffer all kinds of ups and downs, but for several miles the hiking trail is so gentle you can actually look around while walking. After 3 miles of traversing diverse and lusher north-slope vegetation, the trail dips down to river level. Here the horse trail again crosses the river, joining the hiker's path. For 2 miles it now parallels a wild and white river that cuts through a thick forest and between cliffs. There really is no suitable camping for the first 5 miles. A wilderness rule here states: "No camping within 50 feet of the trail," and for the initial 5 miles, level spots away

Greybull River

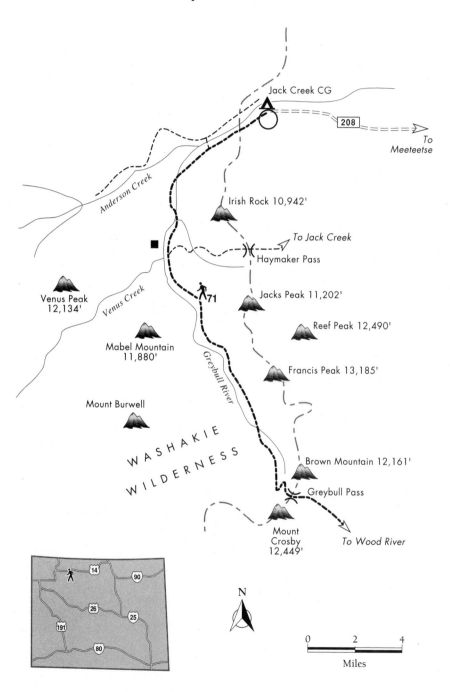

Jack Creek CG

208

To Meeteetse

Anderson Creek

Irish Rock 10,942'

To Jack Creek

Haymaker Pass

Venus Peak
12,134'

Venus Creek

🚶71

Jacks Peak 11,202'

Reef Peak 12,490'

Mabel Mountain
11,880'

Greybull River

Francis Peak 13,185'

Mount Burwell

W A S H A K I E

W I L D E R N E S S

Brown Mountain 12,161'

Greybull Pass

Mount
Crosby
12,449'

To Wood River

14

90

26

25

191

80

N

0   2   4

Miles

from the trail are nonexistent.

Just beyond those first good camping sites (at 5 miles), the trail crosses to the west side of the river. About 0.8 mile later it crosses back. Be aware that the water at these two fords, especially the second one, is a bit deeper, a lot swifter, and much colder than it looks. Around July 1 I found it to be hip-deep, and I'm a long-legged person. Tennis shoes and a hiking stick are necessities. Although the water will have less volume later in the year, rain upstream or a hot day of melting snow could leave you stranded on one side or the other. On the return journey I stayed on the east side of the river, attempting to avoid both crossings. Stay with the trail and fords. That sure path, even with the crossings, takes a lot less time and effort, and is the easier and safer of the two.

Now the Greybull Basin really broadens its scope. The valley is wide and open, and huge peaks line its boundaries. The river braids into several courses through its rocky bottom. At 7 miles the trail intersects the Haymaker Creek Trail (to the east), and a few-tenths of a mile later it meets the Venus Creek Fork (west). In fact, in the more than 20 miles from the trailhead to the top of Greybull Pass, numerous trail intersections are encountered. Some of these trails are maintained; many are old stock driveways that get listed as trails but are tough to find and follow. Trail intersection signs may or may not survive in this country. The Greybull Ranger District indicated that the Greybull River, Anderson Creek, Venus Creek, and Wiggins Fork trails receive the most use and maintenance. Check with the district if you have questions. The farther up the river one travels, the wilder and more spectacular the country becomes.

Numerous possibilities in this country present themselves for even longer hikes. One can venture south toward Dubois and the Wind River Indian Reservation; one can head west via some lengthy journeys into the Teton Wilderness; or one can return east in a circle back toward the Greybull River Road. All are reasonable options from the Greybull River Trail.

72 Four Bear Trail

General Description:	An intriguing day hike into convoluted, lower-elevation, badlands-type country.
Distance:	10 miles round trip.
Difficulty:	Moderate to strenuous.
Elevation gain	1,902 feet.
Key elevation points:	Trailhead: 5,700 feet; Four Bears Mountain: 7,602 feet.
General Location:	18 miles west of Cody or 25 miles east of the Yellowstone National Park east entrance, south of the Rattlesnake Mountains, northwest of Buffalo Bill Reservoir on the North Fork of the Shoshone River, and near the southeast corner of the North Absaroka Wilderness Area.
Special attractions:	Untrailed country, lowland flora and fauna, and one of the few areas on earth where you can simultaneously encounter a grizzly bear and a rattlesnake.
Maps:	This is a brand new trail and it does not appear on any maps. The visitor map for the Shoshone National Forest's north half shows the ownership patterns (lots of private land here). USGS: Jim Mountain, Logan Mountain. The Cody BLM resource office can produce a copy of where the trail sits on the map.
Manager:	Cody BLM Resource Area.

Finding the trailhead: A simple 18-mile drive west from Cody along U.S. Highway 14/16/20 places you at a brand new BLM sign indicating the Four Bear Trailhead. This location sits 0.75 mile before the highway crosses from the north side to the south side of the North Fork of the Shoshone River. Turn north and drive into a huge and new parking facility. The trailhead begins at the northeast corner of this lot.

The hike: Note: This area can serve as an entrance into the hard-to-access country near the southeast corner of the North Absaroka Wilderness area.

This little trip is one of those rare bonuses hiking guidebook authors just relish: a brand new, unmapped, and unknown trailhead, spontaneously happened upon. Maps are meaningless, and what the trail holds is revealed only through step by step exploration. As you can guess, the Four Bear area gets its name because an 1880s adventurer (one Colonel Pickett) bagged 4 bears in one morning at a nearby creek.

The Cody BLM, with the help of horsepackers and the Forest Service, constructed this great access and exploration trail in 1995. Private land owners get ever stickier about letting the public cross their domains for access into public lands. Keeping this access trail on BLM land meant weaving it up impossible mountainsides of twisted conglomerate rock. Lots of work and even some blasting made the impossible possible here, and allows us to enjoy a fascinating journey into Wyoming's badlands country. The Cody BLM is to be congratulated and thanked for creating such a trail, especially in this day of recreation budget cutbacks.

The trail begins as an old road, and stays that way for about 1 mile. Just 0.2 mile beyond the trailhead there is an unsigned intersection with a path jutting to the north, but this eventually peters out. The first official trail intersection occurs after about a mile, by a gate (please close) where the Jim Mountain Trail wanders left, an unmarked trail heads north, and Four Bear Trail continues to the east or right. (The BLM notes that the Jim Mountain Trail leads into a subdivision and private land.)

After about 1.7 miles the trail enters a dry draw and heads north toward the wild, sandstone rock cliffs of towering Four Bear Mountain. At about 2 miles this well-marked trail (flagged by brown, flexible, fiberglass highway stakes) crosses the draw to the east side and begins climbing the jagged and rocky hills. Uptrail 2.5 miles another gate needs to be closed after you pass through it. Here the trail splits, with the right or east course being the official direction.

At 3 miles, after dropping into and climbing out of the little canyon, the trail enters conifer country, and here the CLIMB to the top begins. The trail dizzily weaves across the tortured landscape with at least a trillion (I made a special note to say "trillion" and not "billion" here) switchbacks up and across badland clay hillsides and washes. It's a good huff-and-puff here, but what's so amazing is how the trail does such a good job on not being TOO uphill in a landscape that is nothing BUT uphill. Check out the views of the North Fork Shoshone River as you climb.

It's 4.5 miles to a ridgetop cairn that stands between Four Bear Mountain to the east and a series of ridges to the west. At this point more spectacular country to the north comes into view. From here one could accomplish a trail-less climb to the top of Four Bear Mountain, and/or continue northwest along the now diminished trail for 1.5 miles to the Forest Service boundary, where it ties into a series of trails in that sector. I asked the BLM recreation ranger how far one could wander from there, and he offered an answer often given in this neck of the woods: "As far as you want to."

From May through September, this country can blister under the heat of the sun. I did the hike late one August afternoon and evening and it was perfect. But if you're hiking midday, carry lots of water and sunscreen.

Four Bear Trail

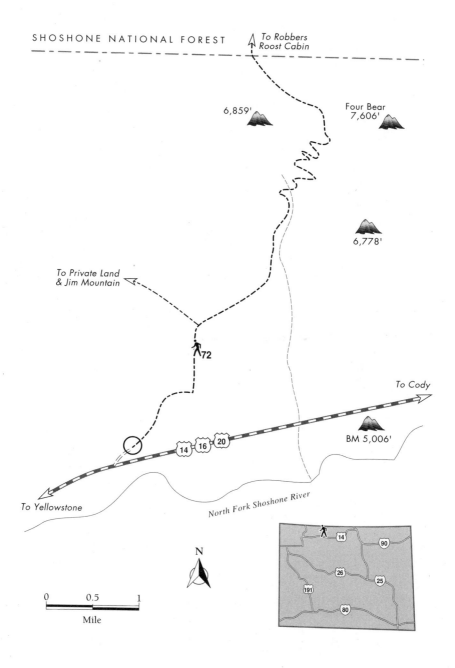

SHOSHONE NATIONAL FOREST

To Robbers
Roost Cabin

6,859'

Four Bear
7,606'

6,778'

To Private Land
& Jim Mountain

72

To Cody

BM 5,006'

14 16 20

To Yellowstone

North Fork Shoshone River

N

0   0.5   1
Mile

14

90

26

25

191

80

73 Blackwater Fire Memorial

General description:	An enjoyable day hike through a 55-year-old forest fire scar.
Distance:	8 miles round trip.
Difficulty:	Moderate.
Elevation gain and loss:	1,890 feet.
Key elevation points:	Blackwater Fire Memorial: 8,990 feet.
General location:	40 miles due west of Cody, outside the northern boundaries of the Washakie Wilderness.
Special attractions:	A moving memorial to firefighters who lost their lives at their work.
Maps:	Shoshone National Forest north half; USGS: Clayton Mountain, Chimney Rock.
Manager:	Wapiti Ranger District.

Finding the trailhead: Driving west from Cody on scenic U.S. Highway 14/16/20, travel 24.3 miles through remarkable Shoshone Canyon to the Shoshone National Forest boundary. Add 12.7 miles to this westward trip and you come to the first firefighters' memorial and a large sign marking the Blackwater Creek Ranch. Leave the highway here and travel south across the river atop an older steel bridge, across another wooden bridge spanning Blackwater Creek, through a pole gate, and up to a large sign south of some corrals marking the trailhead. Actually, this trail is open to vehicles for another 2 miles beyond this sign, but this is four-wheel-drive stuff, and even jeepsters are going to be unhappy if they meet a vehicle coming from the opposite direction on this narrow path. At the road/trail's end, beside the waters of Blackwater Creek, there is a sweet little camping spot. This camp area makes a great headquarters for a hike up to the memorial one day, and another hike to the Blackwater Natural Bridge (Hike 74) the next.

The hike: Between August 20 and August 24, 1937, an intense fire consumed much more than the 1,254 acres of forest it blackened. A sudden gale-force wind on August 21 whipped the fire into a roaring inferno. Fifteen men died and 39 more were injured as the blaze raced up the mountainside on which they were working. A stone and brass memorial now stands high on the northern slopes of 10,219-foot Clayton Mountain to honor those men.

From the trailhead camp, your first dozen steps wade Blackwater Creek. Then it's a gentle journey through an intricate forest that contains every conifer imaginable, including juniper and Colorado blue spruce. Just over 1 mile later the trail forks. Someone has shredded most of the signs on this trail, but journeying left or southeast and across the Blackwater Creek's east fork (a rock hop at this point) sends you moderately upward for a couple of miles to the fire's point of origin.

Blackwater Fire Memorial

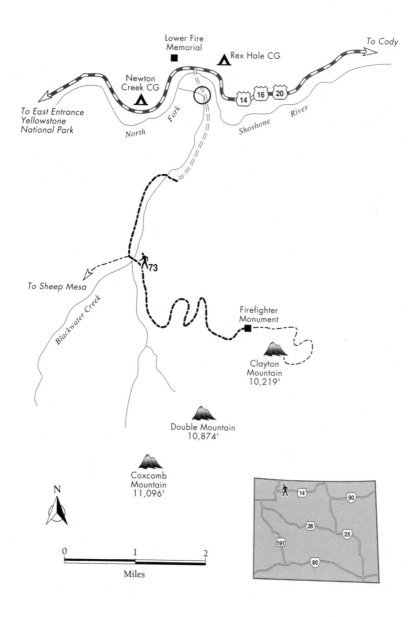

To Cody

Lower Fire
Memorial

Rex Hale CG

Newton
Creek CG

14 16 20

To East Entrance
Yellowstone
National Park

North   Fork

Shoshone   River

To Sheep Mesa

73

Blackwater Creek

Firefighter
Monument

Clayton
Mountain
10,219'

Double Mountain
10,874'

Coxcomb
Mountain
11,096'

N

14

90

26

25

191

80

0   1   2

Miles

Blackwater Fire Memorial overlooking Yellowstone country.

After hiking so many areas in this sector of Wyoming that were crisped by the 1988 fires, it's refreshing to touch a forest where the new-growth trees are 30-plus feet high, demonstrating first-hand that the land does heal itself. For 2 miles the trail switchbacks up a steeper hill and to a ridgetop. The views of high peaks to the south and of the valley below spreading northwest toward Yellowstone become more magnificent with every step of elevation gain.

At 4 miles beyond that first crossing of Blackwater Creek you will come upon the main memorial. It's a beautiful work of rock art that overlooks the entire valley. From here you can easily trace the broad path of the fire, see the rocky gully in which the men tried to escape its heat, and read their names on the brass marker. "They gave their last full measure of devotion," is part of the epitaph, and it's natural to become overwhelmed emotionally in this meditative setting.

A trail does continue beyond the memorial and to the top of Clayton Mountain. Due to budget cutbacks and bear activity (this is prime grizzly habitat), the Forest Service has ceased maintaining this part of the trail. There will be some washouts to cross in attempting this climb.

The trail to the memorial has a few steep grades, but it's remarkably rockless and quite easy to walk. Bring some water, as the gullies of Clayton Mountain are a bit stingy in that regard.

74 Blackwater Natural Bridge Trail

General description:	A long day hike or enjoyable overnighter to exquisite alpine meadows and great views of a spectacular natural rock arch.
Distance:	14 miles round trip.
Difficulty:	Strenuous.
Elevation gain and loss:	3,900 feet.
Key elevation points:	Sheep Mesa: 11,000 feet.
General location:	40 miles due west of Cody, outside the northern boundaries of the Washakie Wilderness.
Special attractions:	Hard hiking rewarded by views of a large, natural rock bridge high on a ridgetop.
Maps:	Shoshone National Forest north half; USGS: Clayton Mountain, Chimney Rock, Sheep Mesa.
Manager:	Wapiti Ranger District.

Finding the trailhead: Same as Hike 73.

The hike: It's always amazing how neighboring trails so often lead to totally different hiking and scenic experiences. This trail presents a lot of rugged, uphill work, but the many rewards at trail's end more than compensate for the efforts.

Cross Blackwater Creek and follow the trail the first 1.1 miles to the fork where the stream divides into east and west branches. There probably is no sign here, but you want to head westward or right. A couple of hunting/horse trails also intersect at this point, so be sure and stick with the main trail that follows the west shores of the creek. This is also a good place to tank up with water, for the next couple of miles make for steep, rocky, and rugged hiking, with the trail keeping high above the creek waters.

Washakie Wilderness country is composed of extremely friable soils, and many of the small side canyons and ravines intersecting the trails tend to be washed out, creating irregular and broken hiking. For almost 5 uphill miles the trail traverses a rock-strewn landscape beneath fir, lodgepole, and finally spruce forests. Then, after it crosses to the east side of the creek, the real uphill switchbacks begin. After 0.75 mile of pure huff-and-puff, the trail breaks into gorgeous alpine meadows. Straight-faced cliffs of striated volcanic rock surround the high fields. As the trail continues to climb, the meadows become more glorious and the forests are reduced to sporadic and isolated clumps of trees. About 6 arduous miles after the first creek crossing, the trail disappears, the trees simply stop, and a vast, tundra-like valley stretches before you.

These luxuriant meadows afford for wonderful camping. Several horse camps are located here, but more than enough room exists for everybody. The meadows are waterless, but a steady and crystal-pure creek flows about 0.25 mile to the east.

Blackwater Natural Bridge Trail

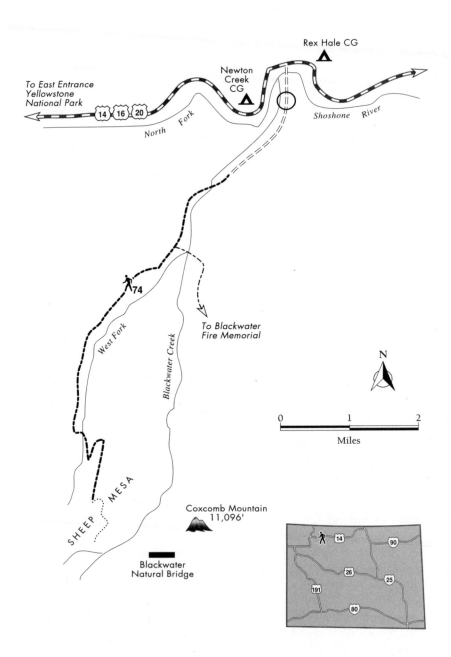

To East Entrance
Yellowstone
National Park

14 16 20

North Fork

Newton
Creek
CG

Rex Hale CG

Shoshone River

74

West Fork

Blackwater Creek

To Blackwater
Fire Memorial

N

0   1   2
Miles

SHEEP MESA

Coxcomb Mountain
11,096'

Blackwater
Natural Bridge

14

90

26

191

25

80

Climbing Sheep Mesa toward Blackwater Natural Bridge.

Now the adventure begins. All of that uphill hiking has simply been preparation for the finale. Standing where the trees end and facing south, you see the vast and open high country and the surrounding cliff faces. The views of the natural bridge come from atop Sheep Mesa. Look at the cliffs to the south and a bit to the east, and you'll see one grassy area leading to the top of the mesa. A sort-of-trail leading to that 1 break in the rock structure is also visible. The climb through that grassy break is steep—not quite fourth-class scrambling, but close enough, and should only be attempted by those with some mountaineering experience. The effort puts you atop a 75-yard wide ridge and offers an incredible view of the large natural bridge and surrounding mountains. Remember that the bridge is at least 1 mile away, even though it looms so large in front of you.

Anyone atop Sheep Mesa is quite vulnerable to adverse weather. And bring water with you to the top.

75 Kitty Creek

General description:	An overnighter into an isolated, high-meadow valley. It gets you up and into the alpine country fast.
Distance:	13 miles round trip.
Difficulty:	Easy to moderate.
Elevation gain:	800 feet.
Key elevation points:	Flora Lake: 8,300 feet.
General location:	45 miles west of Cody, or 9.25 miles east of Yellowstone National Park's east entrance, inside the northwestern fringes of the Washakie Wilderness.
Special attractions:	Moose and other wildlife browsing amidst gorgeous flowers in a very private valley.
Maps:	The Shoshone National Forest north half visitor map; USGS: Eagle Creek, Chimney Rock.
Manager:	Wapiti Ranger District.

Finding the trailhead: U.S. Highway 14/16/20 west of Cody travels approximately 43 miles to where a big sign announces the Buffalo Bill BSA (Boy Scouts of America) Camp. Turn south off of the highway and cross the river. Just beyond the bridge the road forks—the right fork (Forest Road 448) lead south to the trailhead. The last 1.5 miles of this 2.4-mile road won't be very kind to low-clearance vehicles. Near a bulletin board covered with grizzly bear information is the best place to park. The trail begins 0.2 mile further up the road with a ragged sign pointing to a very wide Kitty Creek Trail to the south.

The hike: The Kitty Creek Trail serves as an easier introduction to the amazing northwest corner of the Washakie Wilderness. Note on maps that Kitty Creek lies as a higher and shorter drainage tucked between 2 huge valleys. Eagle Creek to the west and Fishhawk Creek to the east afford much longer and more detailed journeys into this wild Absaroka country. Also note that Kitty Creek is the only drainage of the 3 that doesn't require fording a river at its beginning. Depending on the year and also on immediate weather conditions, the North Fork Shoshone River can be a troublesome crossing.

The first 1.5 miles of this trail climbs steeply up and out of the valley, traversing through a thickly forested hillside. Then it drops back down into the valley, and at about 2 miles the joy of this hike begins. Meadows line the small creek, offering great views of the high mountains in this area. The hiking is slightly uphill and leisurely, fresh water from creeks and springs abounds, and camping sites are a wherever-you-want affair.

At 4.2 miles there is a fork in the trail, the main path being uphill and to the left. A horse packer told me the trail to the right (unlisted on any map) drops into Eagle Creek and makes for rough going. Beyond this fork the trail

Kitty Creek

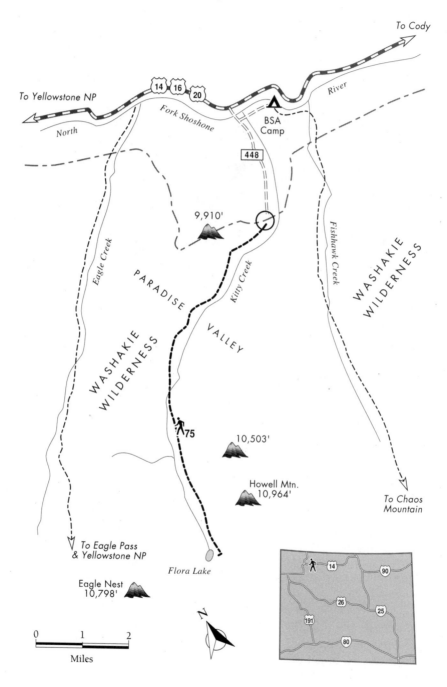

To Cody

To Yellowstone NP

14 16 20

North

Fork Shoshone

River

BSA Camp

448

9,910'

Eagle Creek

PARADISE

Kitty Creek

Fishhawk Creek

WASHAKIE WILDERNESS

VALLEY

WASHAKIE WILDERNESS

75

10,503'

Howell Mtn. 10,964'

To Chaos Mountain

To Eagle Pass & Yellowstone NP

Flora Lake

Eagle Nest 10,798'

N

0   1   2
Miles

14   90

26   25

191   80

Flora Lake at the top of the Kitty Creek drainage.

gets more difficult for a time, but soon returns to easier wandering in even more glorious meadows. Views into the Absaroka Range and the Yellowstone area abound. Did I mention the incredible flowers in these meadows?

The trail fades into bog at 6.5 miles near the top of a pass. Here a tiny pond, Flora Lake, overlooks the Yellowstone/Absaroka boundary. It really feels like the top of the world here, and easy climbs to surrounding ridgetops give you gratifying views of the country around the Thorofare area in Yellowstone.

THE NORTH ABSAROKA WILDERNESS

The 350,488-acre North Absaroka Wilderness, an integral part of the Greater Yellowstone Ecosystem, is situated along the northeastern boundary of Yellowstone National Park. Although the wilderness is touched by over 200 miles of maintained trails, much of the wild country lacks any trail access. The land's character is that of rugged volcanic mountains dissected by numerous creeks, and its vastness is relatively inaccessible. Renowned for its wildlife populations, the wilderness is considered essential habitat for the survival of the grizzly bear. According to the Clarks Fork District of the Shoshone National Forest, hikers tend to leave the North Absaroka Wilderness to horse packers. Quote: "The area is quite rugged and there are numerous stream crossings and almost no lakes. In addition, a limited number of campsites tends to create problems of specific-area overuse."

In 1988 a new thermal feature was added to the Yellowstone area—FIRE! Lightning storms in late June and early July touched off a series of blazes that burned approximately 1.5 million acres of forest land. That equals an area larger than the state of Delaware.

The largest of the 8 major fires in Greater Yellowstone—the Clover-Mist fire—burned huge portions of the North Absaroka Wilderness and the Shoshone National forest. "Black Saturday," or August 20,—when 60-mile-per-hour wind gusts fanned the Clover-Mist and other fires into raging infernos—left massive portions of the wilderness and its surrounding areas blackened. More than a decade later, the land is recovering from this natural (and necessary) cycle of fire. Trails, however, for a long time to come, will be dependent on volunteer (which usually means horsepackers) and Forest Service maintenance crews to keep them open.

A major access trail to the North Absaroka Wilderness follows, as well as 2 nearby trails that range outside of its boundaries. This journey (Hike 76) epitomizes the Clarks Fork District's cautionary statement about hikers in this wilderness.

76 The Crandall Area

General description:	A unique opportunity to experience a diverse, many-day journey into absolute wilderness.
Distance:	22 miles up Closed Creek, one way; 20 miles to Bootjack Gap, one way. Double these distances for round trip.
Difficulty:	Strenuous; experts only.
Elevation gain and loss:	2,850 feet.
Key elevation points:	Trailhead: 6,600 feet; Timber Creek/Closed Creek intersection: 7,400 feet; Timber Creek Pass: 9,450 feet; Bootjack Gap: 9,120 feet.
General location:	21 miles southeast of Cooke City, Montana, in the northern reaches of the North Absaroka Wilderness Area.
Special attractions:	Massive, wild country you can still get lost in, very few people (except during hunting season), and virtually unlimited challenges.
Maps:	Shoshone National Forest's north half visitor map; USGS: Canoe Lake, Hurricane Mesa, Hunter Peak, Geers Point, Stinkingwater Peak, Pollux Peak.
Manager:	Clarks Fork Ranger District.

Finding the trailhead: Travel 14 miles south of Cooke City, Montana, on U.S. Highway 212, to the intersection of Wyoming's Chief Joseph Scenic Highway 296. Turn south here and journey for 7.5 miles to a large sign designating the North Crandall horse and hiking area. If you get to the

The Crandall Area

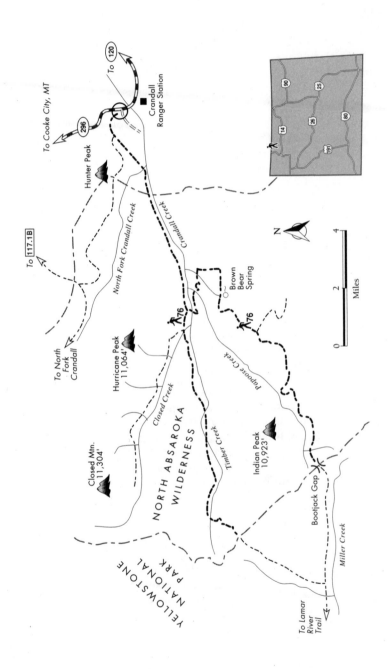

Crandall Ranger Station on the south side of the creek, you've missed the road. About 0.2 mile west on this graveled road places you by a sign marking the Crandall Trailhead. The nearby horsepacking facilities—chutes and corrals and feeding bunks—indicate what variety of backcountry user most frequents this area.

The hike: AUTHOR'S NOTE: Such unrestricted country forms a necessary constituent of Wyoming wilderness, and thus is included in this book. But BE AWARE: Both the author of this hike description and I feel compelled to express many reservations about this area. In her words: "I have mixed feelings about including the Crandall area in a hiking book. Safety is the main reason. I honestly would not enjoy backpacking in Crandall. The area is vast, the drainages are huge, and a challenge to cross on horseback, let alone on human legs. And the bears are thick. Local stories prove that human/bear encounters are too frequent. Current regulations for protection, combined with the handling of problem bears (Crandall is where Yellowstone's problem bears have been taken) have created an aggressive population, particularly in Closed Creek." This trail is the second "absolute wilderness" hike presented in this book (the other is Hike 62).

North of the large horse facilities, the signed trail jaunts to the north for a short distance, then cuts west along a private property's fence line. About 1 mile of hiking puts you at a hard-to-distinguish, unsigned trail junction, with the north and upward route leading to the North Crandall drainage and the westward and downhill path moving into the main Crandall area of this hike description. After 1.3 miles total, you leave the private property behind and face your first creek crossing. The North Fork of Crandall Creek can be belly-deep for horses in July, very swift, and 30 to 50 feet wide. (Author's note: In late August it was a knee-deep (for humans) wade.) Ignore the unsigned leftward trail across the creek which will lead you into a hopeless tangle of downed timber. Instead, take a lesser trail to the right which steeply contours a side hill, placing you above Crandall Creek, and eventually travels from fairly open hillsides into thicker timber.

About 3 miles of hill and ridge hiking place you at an intersection. Take the right fork, which drops down a number of steep switchbacks to Timber Creek. Hiking another 3 miles and across several small creeks puts you at the Timber Creek/Closed Creek Trail intersection. Timber Creek forms a long and thickly timbered, somewhat gradual (except near the Yellowstone Park boundary) journey to the national park border. This trail does continue into the park and eventually empties into the Miller Creek drainage. The Closed Creek Trail again contours along side hills and crosses several rock slides and old avalanche scars. A few meadowed places afford camping, but much of the hike is through thick and dark timber, with lots of bear sign. This trail ends 22 miles from the trailhead at a hunting camp in a meadow. It does not continue into Yellowstone.

Back to that second trail junction. Left or southward the trail continues up a ridgeline toward the Papoose drainage. It's pretty dry hiking for a couple of miles to Brown Bear Spring (which is just a trickle). This little-used trail continues for 11 more miles, eventually dropping into the Papoose Creek drainage before climbing to Bootjack Gap, another way into the Miller Creek area of Yellowstone.

A lot of this Crandall Creek country was toasted in the 1988 fires, and downed timber is a constant. Like other trails in Wyoming, awesome views and panoramic scenery are available, but only at intervals, with long stretches of timbered hiking in between. Again, it's country designed for the experienced wilderness lover—and the cautious, safety-oriented one.

—Debbie Martin

77 Clarks Fork of the Yellowstone River

General description:	A long (4 or more days), rugged, and scenic backpack along the northern fringes of a major mountain river.
Distance:	17.5 miles, one way to shuttle.
Difficulty:	Strenuous.
Elevation gain and loss:	1,520 feet.
Key elevation points:	Clarks Fork River: 6,400 feet.
General location:	55 miles northwest of Cody, along the southern boundary of the Beartooth Mountains.
Special attractions:	Some of the wildest, most spectacular country imaginable. Traces the pathway of a designated "wild and scenic" river.
Maps:	Shoshone National Forest north half map; USGS: Muddy Creek, Hunter Peak, Windy Mountain, Dillworth Bench, Bald Peak.
Manager:	Clarks Fork Ranger District.

Finding the trailhead: Clarks Fork Trailhead begins 5 miles south of U.S. Highway 212 on Wyoming 296. Near mile marker 5, on the west side of the road, lies Shoshone National Forest's Hunter Peak Campground. Opposite this is a trailhead sign marking the Clarks Fork, and Forest Road 167 takes you east for 0.3 mile to the trailhead. Another approach, on what must be the most breathtaking highway in America, is to access Wyoming 296 (Chief Joseph Scenic Highway) 16 miles north of Cody and drive the switchbacks nearly 41 miles, again to mile marker 5 and the Hunter Peak Campground and Clarks Fork Trailhead signs.

The hike: The Clarks Fork River is named in honor of Captain William Clark, explorer and co-leader of the Lewis and Clark Expedition in the early 1800s. This wonderful trail explores the wild country around and beside a designated wild and scenic river. The journey here can be as long as you

Clarks Fork of the Yellowstone River

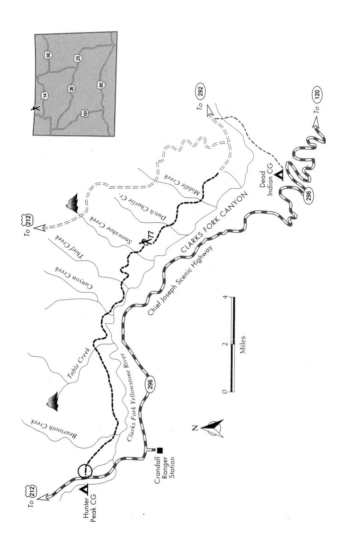

care to make it. A long day or overnight trip will bring you to some incredibly scenic river canyon vistas. Three days of packing will let you stroll beside the timeless flow and see the many changing faces of the pristine river. If you go out for 4 or 5 days, a stomach-grabbing ford of the river (better late in the year, maybe), and a shuttle vehicle at Dead Indian Campground will allow you to follow the entire course of one of the wildest hikes in Wyoming. (I'd suggest hiking Hike 78, the Dead Indian Trail, as a pre-trip day hike to the river for a preview of whether such a proposed ford is possible.)

About 8 miles of hiking are required to reach the river's shores; but what absolute beauty this first stretch offers. The trail is mostly gentle, following a benchland above the river. Many creeks tumble down from the Beartooths, providing good water near the many fine camping spots.

At 3.5 miles the trail climbs steeply north for 0.5 mile to place you on a higher bench where hawks fly overhead and the views expand. After 5.5 miles, the dark, ominous, and towering cliffs of the Clarks Fork Canyon come into view. Although the trail avoids these walls, take a short cross-country journey south through the meadows to view this awesome, gaping hole of a river canyon. The trail fades for a bit in a vast meadow setting at 6 miles. The trick here is to stay high and a bit to the north. Rock cairns dot the meadow and will lead you east to the forest where the trail reappears.

Table Creek, at 6.5 miles, can be a difficult wade in high water, and after this crossing the trail makes a sharp descent to the canyon floor. Tall forests now hide the mighty cliffs, and walking is leisurely along the flat river bottom. One mile later, Canyon Creek forms a big wade, and 1 mile beyond that, the trail decides that 2 miles of river bottom is all you get to experience. Near Thief Creek it leaves the river's shores and steeply ascends the mountainside. About 1 mile of uphill huffing brings you to another bench, and the next 8 miles of hiking are a somewhat rough up-and-down, in-and-out traverse until you intersect with the Morrison Jeep Road.

This is wild and free country. You can hike as far as you desire and then return to the Clarks Fork Trailhead, or, by parking another vehicle either on the Morrison Jeep Road or on Wyoming 292 (which begins approximately 9 miles from the trail/jeep road intersection), you can engage on a one-way expedition through the country.

You should be aware that very few hikers know about or use this trail, but lots of horse packers do. It is a designated grizzly bear use area and has food storage requirements similar to those in Yellowstone Park. Sadly, except right along the river shores, it is a trail open to ATVs. I only met a few, and they did not infringe on the wild and awesomely beautiful aura of this landscape. Also, you will most likely meet some of the many cattle in the area. Even so, this trip remains one of the best true wilderness adventures that Wyoming offers outside of officially classified wilderness.

78 Dead Indian Trail

General description:	A gently descending (except for the last mile) day hike along part of the Nez Perce National Historic Trail.
Distance:	10 miles round trip.
Difficulty:	Moderate.
Elevation gain and loss:	720 feet.
Key elevation points:	Observation bench: 5,920 feet; river bottom: 5,480 feet.
General location:	38 miles northwest of Cody, or about 40 miles southeast of Cooke City, Montana, near the southern fringes of the Beartooth Mountains.
Special attractions:	Peaceful river settings beneath towering granite cliffs. There are many historically significant sites in this area.
Maps:	The visitor map from the Shoshone National Forest north half; USGS: Dillworth Bench, Bald Peak, Dead Indian Meadows.
Fees:	Dead River Campground is run by a concessionaire; campground fees are $7 per night.
Manager:	Clarks Fork Ranger District.

Finding the trailhead: From Cody, drive north on Wyoming 120 for 17 miles, and here turn west onto Wyoming 296. Older maps will show this masterpiece road as being gravel over the Dead Indian Pass area, but the Wyoming Highway Department recently completed paving its entire length. Go 21 miles west on this highway and you'll be at the Dead Indian Campground. Backtrack eastward for 0.3 mile to an unmarked, one-lane road jotting to the north and follow its ruts for 0.4 mile to the signed trailhead.

The hike: This very scenic hike can, via a river crossing, tie into the Clark Fork Trail (Hike 77).

Four states, 13 national forests, 3 national parks, 8 Bureau of Land Management districts, and endless private land encompass the 1,170-mile Nez Perce National Historic Trail—the "Trail of Tears" which chronicles Western American history at its saddest. This little 5-mile section of that trail, depending on your state of mind, may reverberate with the images of fleeing women, children, and older tribespeople. Considering that this rugged country was about 800 miles into their flight only increases the sense of awe created by the story of this trail. The abundance of the term "Dead Indian" in the surrounding geographic labels (creek, hill, pass, peak, summit, and gulch) doesn't seem to be historically connected to the Nez Perce's flight.

The first 2 miles of this more open trail are an easy descent toward the Clarks Fork Canyon. At exactly 2 miles a level platform of rock offers an observation point that anyone who aches inside for scenes of wild beauty

Dead Indian Trail

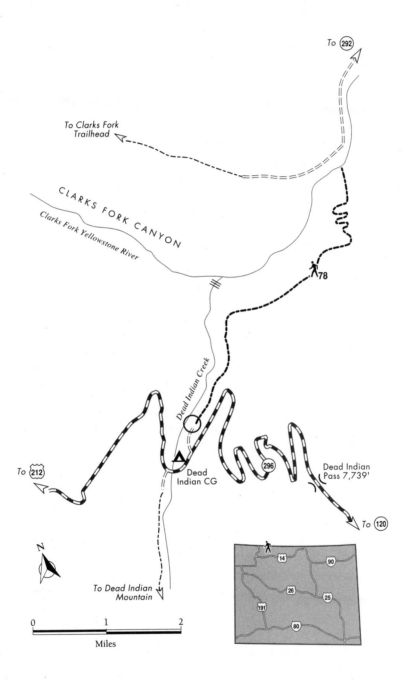

To (292)

To Clarks Fork
Trailhead

CLARKS FORK CANYON

Clarks Fork Yellowstone River

78

Dead Indian Creek

296

Dead Indian
Pass 7,739'

To (212)

Dead
Indian CG

To (120)

N

To Dead Indian
Mountain

14
90
26
25
191
80

0   1   2
Miles

The view into Clarks Fork Canyon from the Dead Indian Trail.

should experience. Wild whitewater from the Clark Fork of the Yellowstone River roars 1,000 feet below sheer granite cliffs, while Dead Indian Creek sprays over the rock face and forms a feathering waterfall that dumps into the turmoil below. All around, the high peaks of the Absarokas tower into the faultless Wyoming sky.

The next 2 miles turn eastward and continue on a fairly easy descent through more wooded country toward the canyon. The sign at the trailhead noted it was 4 miles to the river. It's actually 4 miles to the final mile before the river. This last mile is pretty notable, because here is where all the elevation loss occurs, in a slip-and-slide descent on ball-bearing-sized scree. If you're carrying a backpack, a stout walking stick will help immensely.

Lounging on the large land bars that surround the calm (at this point, anyway) river, one can become immersed in the totally new perspective here: i.e., the contrast of looking up from the bottom of the cliffs, rather than down from the top as was the case just a few miles back. Across the river you can see where the Clarks Fork Trail (Hike 77) descends from its upland bench. Unless it is a really low runoff year, I doubt many hikers are going to wade those deep and cold waters. These bars would be a gentle place to spend a night, playing and fishing along the banks of the river.

Just west from Dead Indian Campground, and across Dead Indian Creek, another short dirt road jogs southward to a continuation of the Dead Indian Trail. This section of trail leads you into some lightly traveled corners of the North Absaroka Wilderness.

THE BEARTOOTH MOUNTAINS

North and slightly east of the North Absaroka Wilderness, bordering and mostly extending into Montana, lie the Beartooth Mountains. These rugged and high mountains are a combination of 75 million-year-old sea bed, 20 million-year-old volcanic lava ash and dust, ancient granite, and glacial sculpting. It's all beautiful. U.S. Highway 212 dips into this high Wyoming lake country of the Beartooth Mountains and travels over Beartooth Pass on its way north to Red Lodge, Montana. The 10,947-foot pass looks out upon the Beartooth Plateau, the highest contiguous stretch of land in North America. This breathtaking area is filled with peaks, huge granite boulder formations, an endless array of alpine lakes, and phenomenal wildflowers. Animal life (including grizzly bears) is abundant, and the area is rich in Native American history.

79 Granite Lake

General description:	A rugged, longer-than-it-looks day hike or overnighter to an absolutely gorgeous, rock-encompassed lake.
Distance:	7.4 miles round trip.
Difficulty:	Moderate to strenuous.
Elevation gain and loss:	600 feet.
Key elevation points:	Granite Lake Pass: 8,820 feet; Granite Lake: 8,750.
General location:	18 miles east of Cooke City, Montana and 20 miles southwest of Red Lodge, Montana, on the very southern boundary of the Absaroka-Beartooth Wilderness Area.
Special attractions:	Awesome lake setting with miles of shore fishing, and great granite faces surround the lake.
Maps:	Shoshone National Forest north half visitor map; USGS: Muddy Creek, Castle Mountain.
Manager:	Clarks Fork Ranger District.

Finding the trailhead: Scenic U.S. Highway 212 curves into the northern part of Wyoming east of Yellowstone National Park from both Cooke City, Montana and Red Lodge, Montana. If coming east from Cooke City, follow this highway about 18.3 miles east to a sign that marks the Muddy Creek Road (Forest Road 136) jogging north. If coming west from Red Lodge, it's 45.5 miles to the same junction. There is a parking area just north of the

View of the southern Beartooths from the rocky shores of Granite Lake.

Granite Lake

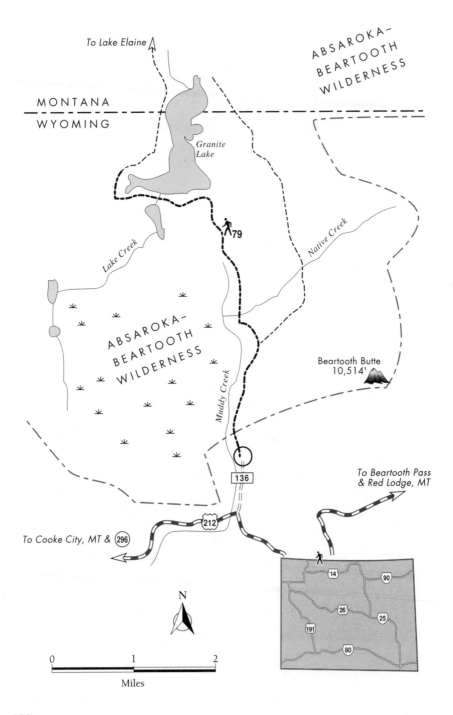

To Lake Elaine

ABSAROKA–
BEARTOOTH
WILDERNESS

MONTANA

WYOMING

Granite
Lake

79

Lake Creek

Native Creek

ABSAROKA–
BEARTOOTH
WILDERNESS

Beartooth Butte
10,514'

Muddy Creek

136

To Beartooth Pass
& Red Lodge, MT

To Cooke City, MT & 296

212

14

90

26

25

191

80

N

0   1   2

Miles

highway, and low-clearance vehicles should park here. Otherwise, a one-lane rock-and-pothole path ends 1.5 miles northward at the trailhead.

The hike: Note: This country is part of the mostly Montana Absaroka-Beartooth Wilderness (some maps designate it as part of the North Absaroka Wilderness) that dips into Wyoming. This hike is designated by Forest Service signs as a loop trail, and overnight camping around the lake makes this hike a great overnighter.

As noted in the other hikes in this book that wander into the Beartooths, don't forget your mosquito repellent. And on this particular trip, wear good waterproof boots, as a fair portion of the trail crosses some mighty boggy land before it climbs to the lake.

The first 1.7 miles of this level but rocky trail skirt the eastern edges of some large meadows. Great opportunities exist, especially around sunrise, to see some big game in these pastures. Halfway across the second big meadow a sign notes that to the right (east) the Upper Granite Loop Trail begins. (There is no visible sign of a trail heading to the east until you've gone a short distance uphill to the edge of the forest.) Continue north on the main Granite Lake Trail at this point, into the forest and across a creek.

The next 0.5 mile of trail offers a choice between a boggy walk along the east edge of the meadow or a very rugged up-and-down traverse along a granite boulder mountainside. The latter trail is blazed for that half mile, but not with official Forest Service blazes. Then the two trails rejoin for a steep uphill climb before again leveling out. Now the granite cliffs that have been on the fringes of the scenery close in on the trail.

At 3.5 miles the trail again becomes a steep climb to a small pass that affords the first views of the distant Beartooth Mountains to the north. A 0.2 mile descent places you by the southern shores of impressive Granite Lake. There's lots of nice camping here and more to come as the trail continues along the lake's western shores. It soon leads northward into the Montana portion of this spectacular wilderness. I can't verify the "loop" designation for this trail. I did remember my mosquito dope, but a leak in the bottle suddenly turned this journey into a "flee-from-a-zillion-impending-proboscises" trip. Granite Lake in itself, though, was worth the journey.

The spectacular alpine highlands of the Beartooths lie a bit to the east (Hikes 80 and 81). Consequently, fewer persons travel the lower elevation trail.

80 Beartooth High Lakes Wilderness Study Area

General Description:	A good day hike or overnighter that begins and returns to Beartooth Lake.
Distance:	Up to 8 miles round trip.
Difficulty:	Easy to moderate.
Elevation gain and loss:	1,980 feet.
Key elevation points:	Beartooth Lake Trailhead: 9,020 feet; Island Lake Trailhead: 10,950 feet; Claw Lake: 11,150 feet; Beauty Lake: 11,000 feet.
General location:	74 miles northeast of Cody, 37.5 miles southwest of Red Lodge, Montana, and 27 miles east of Cooke City, Montana, in the southern Beartooth Mountains.
Special attractions:	Easy trail hiking with gentle grades, beautiful lakes, and high alpine openness filled with wildflowers.
Maps:	Shoshone National Forest north half map; USGS: Beartooth Butte, Silver Run Peak.
Manager:	Clarks Fork Ranger District.
Fees:	Hikers parking at Island Lake can leave their vehicle at the boat launch for $3.

Finding the trailhead: Begin at Beartooth Lake Campground, located approximately 12 miles west of Beartooth Pass along U.S. Highway 212. Parking is provided at a well-marked trailhead.

The hike: Apply liberal amounts of mosquito repellent and bring along an old pair of sneakers for this trip through the boggy inlet area along the east side of Beartooth Lake. About 200 yards beyond the information sign, you will wade across Little Beartooth Creek and begin a gentle arc to the left around the lake. The next 0.5 mile is wet and willowy, crossing Crane Creek and Beartooth Creek along the way. At the north end of the lake, continue bearing left as you approach the lower slopes of Beartooth Butte. Here the trail begins a gentle grade upward to the right (north) along Beartooth Creek through a 2-mile-long open meadow filled with wildflowers. If you brought your wildflower identification book, you may identify 30 to 40 different species in this area. The trail flanks the terraced east slope of Beartooth Butte, 10,514 feet high, looming above and to the left.

Near the ridgetop, watch for a sign indicating the Island Lake Trail to the right. This is the Beartooth High Lakes Trail (formerly called the Upper Highline Trail). The path is indistinct for a few hundred yards, so watch for cairns marking the route. The trail picks its way across the headwaters of Beartooth Creek through subalpine fir, whitebark pine, and massive boulder formations. After a pleasant walk through this parklike area, the summit is reached, and you look down over a beautiful horseshoe-shaped

Beartooth High Lakes Wilderness Study Area

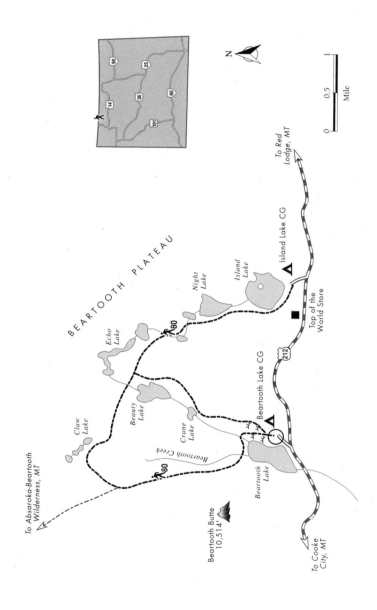

Beauty Lake with Beartooth Butte on right horizon. JERRY SWAFFORD PHOTO

lake nestled in an open alpine basin. This is the first in a chain of 5 lakes that lie along a lush open valley that descends to the right (east). To the north are some of the higher mountains in Montana, with Lonesome Mountain rising in the northeast. The trail runs southeast along this little valley.

Camping sites along these 5 alpine lakes are limitless. Since this is outside the designated wilderness, you are not required to camp 200 feet from lakes and streams, but it is still a good idea.

An ideal plan would be to stay here 1 or 2 nights and explore the area in all directions. The terrain is gentle and open, so cross-country wandering is in order. A topo map is advised.

Proceeding east, the trail stays along the south side until it crosses the inlet of Claw Lake, the lowermost in the lake chain. From here it travels along the north side of the lake for another 0.75 mile, then descends down steep switchbacks toward Beauty Lake. Another 0.25 mile and the trail drops off another steep ridge to the inlet stream of Beauty Lake. Along the southeast edge of this lake sits the trail sign and trail back toward Beartooth Lake. If you are returning to Beartooth Lake, take the trail south along the east side of Beauty Lake. From here it is a pleasant downhill meander for 2 miles to the trail intersection that leads back to the parking area.

If you are continuing to Island Lake, approximately 3 miles ahead, stay on the High Lakes Trail you have been traveling. Climb the 200-foot grade out of Beauty Lake and proceed toward Flake Lake. The trail passes between 2 unnamed ponds. Watch for the waterfall on the far side of the lake.

After leaving this meadow, the trail drops over another steep area toward

Night Lake. Night Lake flows into Island Lake, and the trail continues along the western shore. This area is well traveled by day hikers and anglers. Continue south until the outlet stream of Island Lake is encountered. This crossing is tricky in early season, so find a stout stick for balance. The trail now cuts to the left around the bottom of the lake toward the campground and parking area.

By highway, Island Lake Campground is 3.2 miles from Beartooth Campground, so you will have to beg, borrow, or buy transportation back to your vehicle. Be of good cheer however, for the Top of the World Store is 1.2 miles west on U.S. Highway 212, if you find yourself walking and in need of junk food and pop.

Remember, this country is designated grizzly bear land, and food storage regulations are in effect.

—Jerry and Maryette Swafford

81 Beartooth Loop National Recreation Trail

General description:	A two-day trip along a high alpine ridge, through deep canyon meadows, and along several lakes.
Distance:	12.5 miles round trip.
Difficulty:	Moderate.
Elevation gain and loss:	1,350 feet.
Key elevation points:	U.S. Highway 212 trailhead: 10,500 feet; Camp Sawtooth: 9,150 feet; Stockade Lake: 9,500 feet.
General location:	74 miles northeast of Cody, 28 miles southwest of Red Lodge, Montana, and 41 miles east of Cooke City, Montana, in the southern Beartooth Mountains.
Special attractions:	High alpine fields, forest meadows, 40 to 50 species of wildflowers, pristine lakes, and good fishing.
Maps:	Shoshone National Forest north half map; USGS: Deep Lake.
Manager:	Clarks Fork Ranger District.

Finding the trailhead: From Island Lake Campground (Hike 80), drive 9.5 miles east along U.S. Highway 212 to the Gardner Lake Overlook, which lies in a saddle atop Beartooth Pass. Watch for the rest area and drive exactly 2 miles farther northeast. This trailhead is also 28 miles from Red Lodge, Montana.

The hike: There is a large signboard marking the trailhead, and the trail takes off down to the left of the sign. The ending pickup point is on U.S. Highway 212 at the upper end of Long Lake, 3 miles east of Island Lake, where a sign marks the end of the Beartooth Loop Trail (Hike 80).

Atop Beartooth Pass looking north.   JERRY SWAFFORD PHOTO

The trail descends along the open alpine hillside toward the east side of Gardner Lake. After passing this small and open lake, you must cross its outlet stream on rocks. The trail now bears to the right of the valley and approaches the north end of Tibbs Butte. At 0.75 mile you'll encounter some trail intersection signs, pointing left toward Camp Sawtooth and right toward Losekamp Lake. If your only transportation is at the Gardner Lake Trailhead, you will return to this point from Losekamp Lake and retrace your steps back to the parking area.

Camp Sawtooth Trail goes down into the green, tree-scattered valley and crosses the stream a couple of times before the canyon begins to narrow. This is Little Rock Creek Canyon. The trail crosses the stream again and skirts the left side of this pretty little valley for another mile. After another mile an unsigned intersection greets you: to the left or eastward a lightly used trail heads to Deep Lake, while the national recreation trail continues to the right or southwest.

One more time the trail encounters Little Rock Creek, which is now somewhat wider and deeper but can still be crossed without getting the feet wet. Then a short upward grade to the right or west forces the trail away from the creek. The trail tops a small rise and then begins its descent through pine and fir forest, finally dropping steeply into a large and open meadow replete with flowers. The trail crosses this boggy and wet meadow toward the west (right) and re-enters the pine forest. About 100 yards into the trees, a sign indicates Camp Sawtooth to the left and the Dollar Lake Trailhead ahead. Camp Sawtooth, less than 0.5 mile to the south, is a parklike area

Beartooth Loop National Recreation Trail

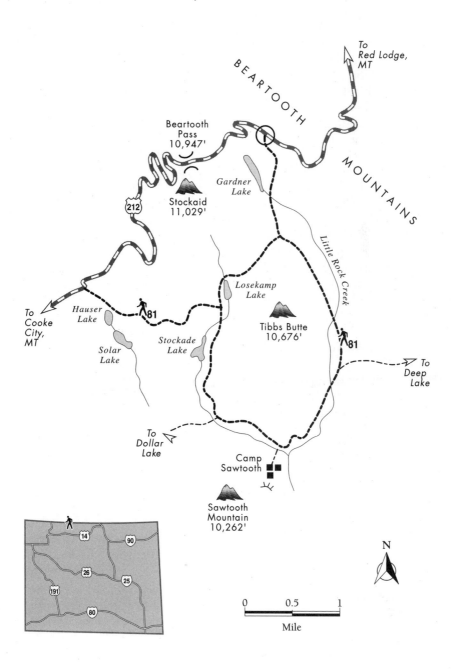

To Red Lodge, MT

BEARTOOTH

MOUNTAINS

Beartooth
Pass
10,947'

Gardner
Lake

Stockaid
11,029'

212

Little Rock Creek

Losekamp
Lake

Hauser
Lake

81

Tibbs Butte
10,676'

81

To
Cooke
City,
MT

Solar
Lake

Stockade
Lake

To
Deep
Lake

To
Dollar
Lake

Camp
Sawtooth

Sawtooth
Mountain
10,262'

14

90

26

25

191

80

N

0   0.5   1
Mile

that has been used as a destination campsite by hunters and campers for at least 50 years. It's a pleasant and clean place to stay. As with all boggy meadow areas, however, mosquitoes are abundant.

Continuing the main loop toward Dollar Lake, the trail meanders through shaded and open forests for another 1.25 miles, paralleling long and open meadows. Here a Forest Service sign points to Stockade Lake Trail angling to the right. Stockade Lake is 1.75 miles and Losekamp Lake is 2 miles farther along this trail. For the next 1 mile the trail climbs gradually through open forest. Tibbs Butte can be seen beyond the ridge to the east. Stockade Lake is an enchanting area with plentiful campsites and waters that teem with trout: a choice place to spend a day or two.

Losekamp Lake is 0.75 mile to the north. Near the lower end of this lake is the trail fork that cuts back southwest toward Hauser Lake. If you plan to return to Gardner Lake Trailhead, you need to take the northeast trail over the north slope of Tibbs Butte (called Tibbs Pass, elevation 10,060 feet). The return to the Gardner Lake Trail is slightly over 1.5 miles and climbs steeply.

If exiting via Hauser Lake to U.S. Highway 212, turn left at the Losekamp Lake junction and proceed southwest. This well-used trail cuts around the bottom of a cliff, along a meadow and then into the trees. After 0.5 mile a sign lets you know that Hauser Lake Trailhead is 3 miles farther. Climb upward to the ridge crest and into subalpine meadows. Here the country is rolling and easy, filled with scattered trees, open grass/flower fields, massive boulders and small lakes. The Absaroka Mountains can be seen to the west, Sawtooth Mountain is south, and the steep cliffs to the southeast mark Deep Lake.

From lovely Hauser Lake, the trail ascends along the right side of a small draw to a ridge. Follow the cairns across the open ridge to U.S. Highway 212 and to the sign marking the Beartooth Loop National Recreation Trail.

—Jerry and Maryette Swafford

THE JEDEDIAH SMITH WILDERNESS

It may be less renowned than bordering Grand Teton National Park, but the western slope of the Teton Range is certainly no less dramatic or awe-inspiring. Densely carpeted forests and lush meadows blanket the mountains' lower slopes, mainly due to the 50-plus inches of yearly rainfall that moisten this country, making it the wettest spot in Wyoming. High, glaciated basins and their accompanying lakes afford splendid hiking opportunities.

Jedediah Smith was a fur trapper and contemporary of Jim Bridger and Tom Fitzpatrick, two other mountain men who are immortalized by Wyoming wilderness place-names. This 116,535-acre, officially designated wilderness area protects the western side of the Teton Range.

Access to the Jedediah Smith Wilderness is possible either by a long hike from Grand Teton National Park over the passes that top the range, or by driving the rowdy road into very western Wyoming from eastern Idaho. Although the following trails describe accesses from Idaho and round trips that return to the original trailheads, excellent options exist for one party to park in Idaho or western Wyoming and a second party to leave a car at a Grand Teton National Park trailhead. Both parties could hike so as to cross paths on a spectacular mountain pass and then continue, each to the other's vehicle. Permits are required to hike and camp in Grand Teton National Park even when entering from the west. These permits are available from both the park and from the Teton Basin Ranger District in Driggs. (See the Grand Teton National Park section for complete permit details.) Earthwalk Press's Grand Teton National Park recreation map offers a wonderful topographic and trail overview of the Jedediah Smith Wilderness and of the following hikes.

82 Alaska Basin

General description:	A semi-rugged, 3- to 4-day trip into paramount glacial basin country.
Distance:	14 miles round trip.
Difficulty:	Moderate to strenuous.
Elevation gain and loss:	2,630 feet.
Key elevation points:	Trailhead: 7,150 feet; Devil's Stair Trail intersection: 7,750 feet; Sunset Lake: 9,780 feet; Hurricane Pass: 10,480 feet; Mount Meek Pass: 10,300 feet.
General location:	11 miles west of Driggs, Idaho, in the southern portion of the Jedediah Smith Wilderness.
Special attractions:	Unparalleled views of the back sides of the Tetons, glorious lakes, challenging and vast alpine country.
Maps:	Targhee National Forest Island Park, Ashton, Teton Basin and Palisades Districts visitor map; USGS: Granite Basin, Mount Bannon, Grand Teton.
Fees:	Teton Basin Ranger District campground fees range from $6 to $8 per night.
Manager:	Teton Basin Ranger District.

Finding the trailhead: Idaho 33 takes you into the small and busy town of Driggs. Near the southern end of town, with the Key Bank on one street corner, Little Avenue jogs westward toward Alta, Wyoming. This soon becomes the Targhee Road, and you want to follow its pavement toward the Grand Targhee Resort for 4 miles into Wyoming and another 2.25 miles to the Alta cemetery. Here, to the right or south, a graveled and signed road (Forest Road 009) leads to the Teton Campground. Follow this road as far as it goes (5.1 miles), past the first parking lot and to the South Teton Creek Trailhead.

The hike: This is a very heavily used area, and hikers are encouraged to acquire a free Winegar Hole and Jedediah Smith Wilderness Area map from the Teton Basin Ranger District which details use regulations. (For example, no fires are allowed in Alaska Basin.) In this particular case, I must confess to being strongly attracted to an area, even though the wilderness ranger advised avoiding it, due to its heavy use.

It's good that this is such a well-used trail: the meadows lining the first 2.5 miles of gentle uphill are so lush with chest-to-head-high plant foliage that the path would soon be swallowed without a fair amount of foot traffic. Continue up the gentler South Teton Trail, instead of opting for Devil's Stairs at this first intersection, and the trail will gain a lot of elevation—but it is so skillfully switchbacked that the hike never seems too difficult. Another 2.5 miles finds the trail weaving through these amazing and huge benches and platforms of polished granite lying flat on the ground. Another 2 miles and a few steeper switchbacks place you in the beginnings of the Alaska Basin.

Alaska Basin

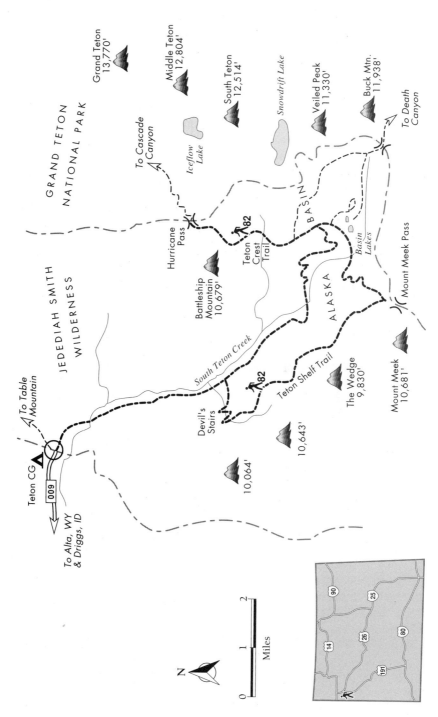

Grand Teton 13,770'

Middle Teton 12,804'

South Teton 12,514'

Snowdrift Lake

Veiled Peak 11,330'

Buck Mtn. 11,938'

To Death Canyon

GRAND TETON NATIONAL PARK

To Cascade Canyon

Iceflow Lake

Hurricane Pass

82

Teton Crest Trail

Battleship Mountain 10,679'

BASIN

Mount Meek Pass

JEDEDIAH SMITH WILDERNESS

South Teton Creek

ALASKA

Basin Lakes

82

Teton Shelf Trail

The Wedge 9,830'

Mount Meek 10,681'

Devil's Stairs

10,643'

10,064'

To Table Mountain

Teton CG

009

To Alta, WY & Driggs, ID

N

Miles

0   1   2

90

25

26

14

80

191

The trees have thinned out to subalpine firs, and the rich multicolored flowers here grow but a few inches high.

I list this as a 3-day backpack but recommend allowing more time. There is so much to see and so many different directions to wander in this area. I highly advise hiking the trail to Hurricane Pass. Sunset Lake, west and below this mountainous area, offers ideal camping spots, and the 2 miles of fairly steep hiking to the top of the 10,480-foot pass affords you every view imaginable. The backsides of the 3 mighty Teton Peaks tower into the sky and over the rocky canyons below.

A great loop back to the parking lot is possible by following the Teton Crest Trail around the head of South Teton Canyon and then turning onto the Teton Shelf Trail and walking north toward Devil's Stairs. This second trail gently slopes downward and along a broad alpine bench for 3.5 miles, tracing a pathway directly beneath a huge and towering wall of stratified cliff.

The Devil's Stairs are not for acrophobia sufferers. The trail is plenty wide but also exposed, and its 1.5 mile distance will work your knees to the maximum.

A few notes of caution: the Alaska Basin area is notorious for its powerful thunderstorms, and there isn't a lot of shelter in the open alpine country. Also, Hurricane Pass didn't acquire its name from gently wafting breezes. Be prepared for extreme weather up there.

The trails are easy to follow, and all trail intersections are well-marked. Camping exists the entire length of the hike. There are a lot of people, but the country is so huge it seems to swallow all of them.

83 Table Mountain

General description:	An exceptional day hike with wonderful views.
Distance:	12 miles round trip.
Difficulty:	Strenuous.
Elevation gain and loss:	3,606 feet.
Key elevation points:	Trailhead: 7,500 feet; Table Mountain: 11,106 feet.
General location:	10 miles east of Driggs, Idaho, in the southern portion of the Jedediah Smith Wilderness.
Special attractions:	A beautiful canyon hike to an upper basin, followed by high alpine ridgetop vistas.
Maps:	Targhee National Forest Island Park, Ashton, Teton Basin and Palisades Districts map; USGS: Granite Basin, Mount Bannon.
Fees:	Teton Canyon Campground is $8 per night.
Manager:	Teton Basin Ranger District.

Finding the trailhead: The North Teton Creek Trailhead may be reached by following the same road directions from Driggs, Idaho, that are listed under Hike 82. The trailhead is located 0.5 mile from the end of Forest Road 009, at the east end of the campground.

The hike: In 1872, photographer William H. Jackson decided he wanted the perfect picture of the Grand Teton summit from the west. He, an assistant, and Molly the mule, loaded with ancient photographic equipment and processing glass photo plates, climbed piles of untrailed rocks for 9 days to reach the summit of Table Mountain. Here Mr. Jackson got his perfect picture.

Bring a jacket or windbreaker and a lunch, and allow 10 to 12 hours for this hike. The first 0.5 mile section of the hike climbs a switchbacked canyonside to join the North Fork of Teton Creek. The trail then levels out and follows the creek through lovely meadows and flower fields within a scattered forest. The Boy Scouts call this first section "Huckleberry Canyon" because of the abundance of huckleberries, but the huge serviceberries are even better. The trail grades gradually upward for another 2 miles before becoming somewhat steep and rough in places. It crosses the creek several times, but good foot bridges make these crossings pleasant.

As it nears the upper end of the canyon, after about 4 miles, the trail crosses the creek for a last time to the right and begins angling up along the south side of the canyon. There is a gentle swing to the right for 0.5 mile (all uphill) into the large and beautiful upper canyon basin. From here the goal, Table Mountain, can be seen looming above and to the east. Continue bearing up to the right and approach the south wall of the basin. Watch for the switchbacks going up the face to the south. Below the switchbacks the trail leaves the last of the water springs, so fill a water jug and drop in an iodine pill.

Table Mountain

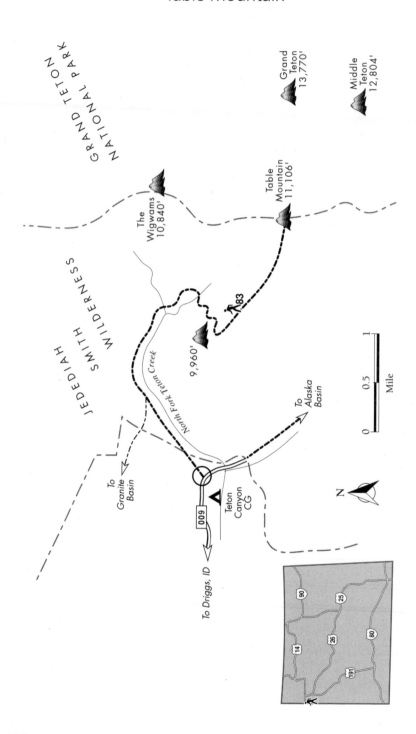

Looking toward Table Mountain from the head of the North Fork Teton Creek Canyon.
JERRY SWAFFORD PHOTO

Now the work begins. The trail climbs out of this beautiful open basin filled with wildflowers to ascend the ridge above. After switchbacking up to the ridge, the world opens in all directions. Table Mountain looks like a mesa stretching to the east, and the top of the Grand Teton stands behind it. The trail skirts the south canyon rim and looks down into a sub-alpine basin to the north. This is a pleasant walk along a high alpine ridge through scattered scrub-whitebark pine.

The final approach to Table Mountain is rocky and steep, with some rock scrambling required to reach the summit. Snowfields are late leaving this area, and there are usually wet areas into August, so watch the footing. As the 11,106-foot summit is reached, you quickly see why you came. The view is simply awesome. Below to the east is a yawning maw: nothing but

2,000 feet of air and a knee-buckling view. The majestic Tetons stand directly in front of you; directly ahead the Grand Teton reaches 13,770 feet into the sky. One does not walk out here at first—one crawls.

This is a heavily hiked trail. The Boy Scouts from Treasure Mountain Scout Camp hike this trail in mid-week, usually on Wednesdays, but the rest of the week is almost as busy. The best time to do this hike is in September.

—Jerry and Maryette Swafford

84 Hominy Peak/Jackass Pass/ South Boone Creek Loop

General description:	A little-known, 2- to 3-day loop that travels along high timbered ridges.
Distance:	18 miles round trip.
Difficulty:	Strenuous.
Elevation gain and loss:	1,460 feet.
Key elevation points:	Jackass Pass: 8,280 feet; Upper South Boone Creek Trail intersection: 8,380 feet.
General location:	25 miles due east of Ashton, Idaho, in the Jedediah Smith Wilderness and the northern portion of Grand Teton National Park.
Special attractions:	Solitude among high virgin-forest ridges, impressive vistas and open mountain meadows.
Maps:	Targhee National Forest Island Park, Ashton, Teton Basin and Palisades Districts map; USGS: Hominy Peak, Survey Peak.
Manager:	Ashton Ranger District.

Finding the trailhead: The road to this hike begins in Ashton, Idaho. Drive east of town on Main Street to the cemetery just beyond the city limits and turn right (south) on Idaho 32. In 1 mile the highway curves to the right. DO NOT follow the curve but continue straight ahead 100 yards to intersect a paved county road, Fremont County 261. A sign here announces Squirrel Meadows due east. Turn left here. The pavement ends at 9.3 miles, Targhee National Forest is entered in 12.1 miles, and dusty Forest Road 264 begins at 23.2 miles. At this point a sign indicates Jackass Meadows is 5 miles south. Turn right onto Forest Road 264 and drive 3.2 miles to the Hominy Creek Trailhead sign (drive past the South Boone Creek Trailhead and campground). A narrow but passable dirt road continues 0.6 mile to the east (left) up a hill and into the forest to the well-signed Hominy Peak Trailhead parking area.

The hike: Begin the trek steadily upward and eastward through the pine forest. The first 3 to 4 miles are a bit of a grind, but then the hardest work is

Overlooking the head of South Boone Creek Canyon. JERRY SWAFFORD PHOTO

over. At 1 mile you will enter the Jedediah Smith Wilderness. At about 2 miles, look to the right for large open meadows in a low saddle. Tiny water channels cut deeply into the meadows and provide the only water on this ridge in late summer. One must listen for the tinkle of the water rivulets in the deep grass.

Then the trail steeply ascends the south slope of Hominy Peak. However, no "peak" can be seen. When the trail levels again after the grade, look for a small sign on the left announcing the presence of Hominy Peak, elevation 8,362 feet. Hominy Peak is a hump in the ridge covered with sagebrush, grass, and flowers. From this altitude, check out the view to the west, across the Snake River plain and toward mountain ranges 100 miles away.

The trail continues east along this high ridge through beautiful meadows and scattered timber. Conant Basin and Hidden Lake, soon visible to the south, are a little over 2 miles away. At 1 mile east of Hominy Peak the trail passes beside more lovely meadows and then begins another steep climb up the final ridge to Jackass Pass. After this climb, the trail tops a timbered ridge and drops into a little open valley where another trail—the Teton Crest Trail—intersects. Signs mark Jackass Pass, elevation 8,280 feet.

At this point the nearest water in late summer is Berry Creek, 2 miles east in Grand Teton National Park. The trail to Berry Creek drops gently through a forested canyon, loops back toward the north, then climbs back out of this drainage to reconnect with the South Boone Creek Trail. This route adds more than 4 miles to the trip.

If you have water and wish to bypass the Berry Creek loop, take the

Hominy Peak/Jackass Pass/South Boone Creek Loop

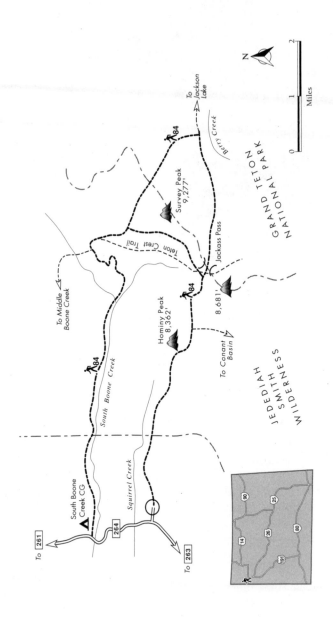

Teton Crest Trail north from Jackass Pass. In about 1 mile the trail circles above the cliffs and rocky bluffs overlooking the South Boone Creek drainage. The view here is expansive. This is a pleasant walk around the canyon's head along the west slopes of Survey Peak. (Survey Peak, like Hominy Peak, is not a "peak" but a grass/flower/tree-covered mountain.)

The trail now wanders west, and after 2.5 miles it begins to descend in a very roundabout way through beautiful high meadows and rolling subalpine fields. The trail intersects South Boone Trail, and a sign notes that it's 6.4 miles back to the Jackass Road. Where the trail snakes back to the south on a large and open meadowed ridge, watch for trail signs indicating a side trail into Middle Boone Creek. Continue bearing left (due south). A few more rolling meanders and the trail drops steeply into South Boone Creek Canyon. This steep, twisting, switchbacking section explains why this route is not recommended for beginners.

South Boone Creek flows through the bottom of a heavily forested canyon, and its cold water is welcome. From here the trail follows the creek west and back to the road, but for no apparent reason the trail designer chose to provide some more climbing while descending the canyon. Uphill grades take the trail hundreds of feet above the creek in places, but it does eventually rejoin the canyon floor and exits at Jackass Road. Here you can drop the packs, soak your feet in the creek, and then amble the 2.2 miles back up the road (south) to your car.

—Jerry and Maryette Swafford

85 Moose Creek and Moose Lake

General description:	A lesser-known, 3-or-more-day backpack into the southern boundaries of the Jedediah Smith Wilderness.
Distance:	20 miles round trip.
Difficulty:	Moderate.
Elevation gain and loss:	2,560 feet.
Key elevation points:	Moose Meadows: 7,650 feet; Moose Lake: 9,360 feet.
General location:	11 miles south of Driggs, Idaho, and 22 miles west of Jackson in the southern end of the Teton Range, near the Idaho/Wyoming border, in northwestern Wyoming.
Special attractions:	Gentle hiking in valley scenery and wildlife galore.
Maps:	Earthwalk Press's Grand Teton National park recreation map; Targhee National Forest's Island Park, Teton Basin and Palisades Ranger Districts forest map; USGS: Victor, Rendezvous Peak.
Manager:	Teton Basin Ranger District.

Finding the trailhead: Travel west from Jackson, over Teton Pass and along Wyoming 22 to the Idaho border, where the highway becomes Idaho 33. At 1.5 miles into Idaho—or 3 miles south of Victor, Idaho—the well-signed Moose Creek Road directs drivers eastward. The paved part of this road lasts for about 1 block; where the road T's, turn left or north for another couple of blocks; here another sign denotes Forest Road 276 and travels east for 2.5 miles to a trailhead parking area with several good campsites in the immediate vicinity.

The hike: Note: This hike offers easy access to the southern reaches of the Teton Range and Grand Teton National Park. The Moose Lake area also serves as a great base camp from which to wander onto other fascinating alpine hikes.

You can't help but notice the large horse outfitter ranches along the road to this trailhead, indicating that a lot of pack trains compete with hikers in this country. On the other hand, as with Alaska Basin (Hike 82), this side of the Tetons receives so much moisture that the horses help to keep the thick undergrowth from overwhelming the trail.

For 0.5 mile the trail gently strolls beneath the lodgepole near Moose Creek. Then it merges with a wide, leisurely roadbed hike for the next 2 miles. Here the path crosses the stream, the horse crossing being to the left and a hiker's bridge to the right. After this crossing, the trail narrows and assumes a more moderate mien, becoming rocky and traversing the contours of the hillsides while providing an overview of the valley bottom. After 3.2 miles some open meadows offer the first good campsites, and

Moose Creek and Moose Lake

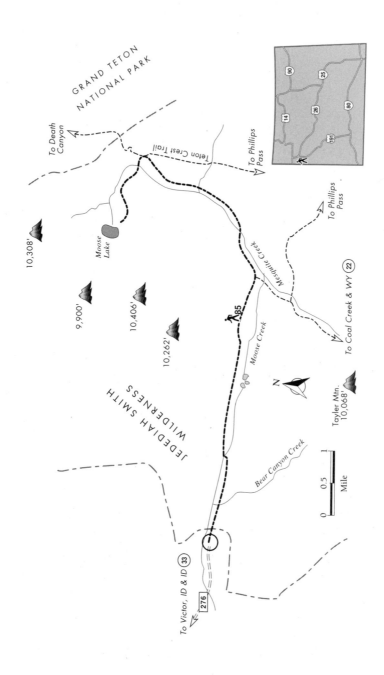

GRAND TETON NATIONAL PARK

To Death Canyon

Teton Crest Trail

To Phillips Pass

10,308'

Moose Lake

Mesquite Creek

To Phillips Pass

9,900'

10,406'

10,262'

85

To Coal Creek & WY 22

Moose Creek

JEDEDIAH SMITH WILDERNESS

N

Tayler Mtn. 10,068'

Bear Canyon Creek

0   0.5   1
Mile

To Victor, ID & ID 33

276

another 0.5 mile takes you to an area where multiple beaver dams block the many braided streams of the creek, affording some willow-hemmed fishing opportunities. (Read the fishing regulations posted on the trailhead information board.)

At 5 miles into the hike you will reach a major intersection with the Mesquite Creek Trail. Just east of this junction you come to massive Moose Meadows. About 3.5 miles later, you will wade a creek and come to an intersection with the Teton Crest Trail. Alpine country predominates more and more as you turn westward and cover the last 1.3 trail miles to scenic Moose Lake perched on a bench below several impressive peaks.

Camping is allowed around the lake (200 or more feet away); fires and stock camping are not. Please use no-impact camping techniques in this fragile country. Rain gear is essential.

86 Phillips Pass

General description:	An awesome day hike into the subalpine and alpine country on the very southern fringe of the Teton Range and the Jedediah Smith Wilderness.
Distance:	8 miles round trip.
Difficulty:	Easy to moderate.
Elevation gain and loss:	2,000 feet.
Key elevation points:	Middle Fork Phillips Creek: 8,220 feet; Ski Lake: 8,600 feet; Phillips Pass: 8,932 feet.
General location:	10 miles west of Jackson, near Teton Pass, in northwestern Wyoming.
Special attractions:	Leisurely hiking amid high mountain splendor, lots of wildflowers, and most of the elevation is gained by car.
Maps:	Earthwalk Press's Grand Teton National Park recreation map; the Bridger-Teton National Forest's Buffalo and Jackson Ranger Districts forest map; Targhee National Forest's Island, Park, Teton Basin and Palisades Ranger Districts forest map (non-topo); USGS: Teton Pass, Jackson, Rendezvous Peak, Teton Village.
Manager:	Jackson Ranger District.

Finding the trailhead: From Jackson drive west 10 miles—or from the crest of Teton Pass drive east and descend for 2 miles (along Wyoming 22 either way)—to a small sign marking the rough-looking Phillips Canyon Road, (30972) which jogs north here. Although the trailhead is 0.5 mile up this four-wheel-drive road, it's best to park near the main highway or in a small parking area across that highway and walk this first stretch. There are no parking spaces anywhere near the trailhead. At 0.5 mile up the road an

Beautiful rolling alpine meadows atop Phillips Pass.

obvious trail lopes uphill and to the left or north. A few hundred yards above this intersection, you'll find the sign noting Ski Lake and Phillips Pass. This trail is open to hikers, horses, and mountain bikes.

The hike: With a backpack and the proper gear, this area can easily serve as a base for further hiking adventures.

Even staid hiking guidebook authors sometimes lose their cool and go bonkers over a special trail. If you're ever near Jackson, especially near the end of July or beginning of August, and you have a sunny day free, take a stroll toward Phillips Pass. This could be one of the most gorgeous trails you'll ever experience.

The first mile is a mellow hike up an east-facing slope to some flower-filled meadows. Truck to the left and around this glen, and a signed intersection offers an easy, 1-mile-long side trip west to Ski Lake. The following mile past this junction and north toward Phillips Pass provides a leisurely stroll through sparsely forested land which supports a profusion of huge lodgepole, fir, spruce, and aspen trees.

Soon the countryside opens to the northwest and offers overviews of Phillips Canyon and the Jackson Hole area. The trail descends for 0.5 mile through a massive spruce forest before crossing the Middle Fork of Phillips Creek and reclaiming the lost elevation as it heads 2 miles uphill to Phillips Pass. Just past this creek crossing a less-traveled trail wanders to the right and down the north side of Phillips Canyon toward the Forest Service boundary and a county road. On the way toward the pass, a couple of side trails jot

Phillips Pass

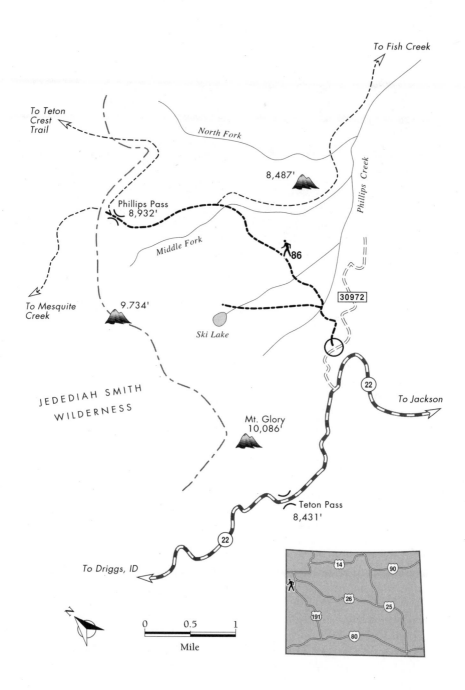

To Fish Creek

To Teton Crest Trail

North Fork

8,487'

Phillips Creek

Phillips Pass 8,932'

Middle Fork

86

30972

To Mesquite Creek

9.734'

Ski Lake

To Jackson

22

JEDEDIAH SMITH WILDERNESS

Mt. Glory 10,086'

Teton Pass 8,431'

22

To Driggs, ID

N

0   0.5   1
Mile

14   90

26   25

191

80

to the left. At these junctures, staying right and uphill keeps you on the proper path.

The flowers, which have been incredibly beautiful the entire trip, now pull out all the stops to paint these last couple of miles into the most colorful landscape you may ever experience. The top of the pass—a perfect lunch spot—is on the southeastern boundary of the Jedediah Smith Wilderness.

It would be easy to camp in some of the tree-sheltered locations below the pass and use this spot as a base for further adventures, such as traveling cross-country along the numerous open ridgetops or heading north onto the Teton Crest Trail. Be sure and carry rain gear. Often the abundant flora is waist-deep and wet.

THE TETON RANGE— GRAND TETON NATIONAL PARK

Perhaps some day a group of ardent and determined climbers will tote enough rocks to the top of the Grand Teton to increase its elevation the 35 feet needed for it to exceed Gannett Peak and become Wyoming's highest mountain. After all, some argue, the Tetons are the most startling, showy, and famous mountains in the state. With no foothills to hinder the spectacular 1.5 miles of vertical towering rocks that rise above the valley floor, why shouldn't the Grand own the state's "number one" classification?

The Precambrian granite core of the Tetons formed from molten rock that was buried at least 4 miles below the earth's surface. This future mountain range mostly escaped the wild faulting and thrusting efforts of the Laramie Revolution that shaped the other ranges surrounding the Jackson Hole area. As Yellowstone volcanoes covered northwest Wyoming with lava and ash, the Tetons remained but a small bubble on the surface of the earth. Then, 10 million years ago, that changed. In a very few years the Tetons climbed to towering heights while the earth's crust in the Jackson Hole area sank. Erosion, plus 3 major Ice Age glacial eras, honed the sharp faces of the range. The result is what older Park Service pamphlets call "the scenic climax of Wyoming."

Grand Teton National Park encompasses most of the eastern side of this mighty range. The western banks of the mountains are occupied by the Jedediah Smith Wilderness. Yellowstone became the world's first national park in 1872 after 2 years of lobbying. In 1950, after some 50 years of political conflict, the Grand Teton National Park was finally enlarged.

An impressive system of more than 200 miles of trails provides access to much of the park. Grand Teton's backcountry rules are distinct from and a bit different than Yellowstone's:

> •Instead of designated camping sites (with a few exceptions), the Teton Park area is divided into camping zones. With a permit, one can stay almost anywhere within a camping zone. These permits have been

non-fee in the past, but park officials are currently debating changing that. Please contact the park for current information (see appendix).

•Grand Teton allows hikers to reserve backcountry camping permits. Up to 30 percent of the available permits may be reserved between January 1 and May 15 of the current year. Write up a final itinerary (including dates, what zones you want to camp in each night, the number of people in your party, a second alternative, and a telephone number) and submit the request in writing to Permits Office, Grand Teton National Park, P.O. Box 170, Moose WY, 83012. Information on the camping zones may also be obtained from this address.

•Other free (again, changes are being proposed) camping permits may be obtained in person at the Moose or Colter Bay visitor centers or the Jenny Lake Ranger Station. The backcountry camping limit is a total of 10 nights park-wide.

•No fires are allowed in the backcountry except at a few designated sites. Camping stoves are usually required.

•Often an ice axe recommendation is in effect in the park until mid-July. Many of the trails begin at more than 6,800 feet and climb from there, so snow is slow to leave the various divides and passes. Check with the rangers for up-to-date information.

•Park entrance fees are the same as those in Yellowstone National Park, and paying for 1 place allows access to the other. A 7-day vehicle pass is $20; a 7-day pass for an individual on foot or bicycle is $10; a Golden Eagle Pass (unlimited access to all National Parks for 1 year) is $50.

87 Hermitage Point Trail

General description:	A leisurely day hike beneath the towering Teton Mountains and by the reflective shores of Jackson Lake.
Distance:	9 miles round trip.
Difficulty:	Easy.
Elevation gain and loss:	Less than 50 feet.
Key elevation points:	Jackson Lake: 6,770 feet.
General location:	Directly south of Colter Bay Village, in the center of Grand Teton National Park.
Special attractions:	Lake-reflected views of the Tetons, lots of wildlife.
Maps:	Earthwalk Press's recreation map of Grand Teton National Park; USGS: Colter Bay, Two Ocean Lake, Jenny Lake.
Fees:	Park entrance fees (see above).
Manager:	Grand Teton National Park.

Finding the trailhead: Colter Bay Village is the main information and lodging center on the shores of huge Jackson Lake. It is well-signed and easy to reach from U.S. Highway 287/89, approximately 13 miles north of Moran Junction. Once there, drive as far west as possible to the visitor center. Here follow the curve of the road south, past the marina, and to the southern end of the parking lot. The Hermitage Point Trailhead sign is quite visible, with the foot trail beginning to the west and a few paces up a gravel maintenance road.

The hike: Here's an easy and special trail that places you directly into that postcard scenery and away from the crowded highway overviews where everyone else stops. You do have to hike 0.5 mile to get beyond the noise of motorboats entering and exiting the marina.

This is an almost 9-mile multi-loop trail that offers views of the northern Tetons dramatically rising above forest and lake waters. Many different loops are possible, so the journey can be as long and varied as you wish. But once you begin, the views are so phenomenal that the next mile is too alluring not to hike. All of the intersections are well marked, but carrying a trail map will give you more perspective on where you are and an idea of what it is you're looking at.

Heron Pond, 1.5 miles from the trail's beginning, captures half the Teton Range in its reflection. If you're lucky, you'll see white pelicans, osprey, kingfishers, and herons all fishing the waters for their supper.

The entire trail is mostly level lodgepole forest hiking. But incredible vistas suddenly pop into view and another half a roll of film disappears. It's easy to return hike along different trail segments. Journey by Swan Lake and view the moose grazing in the water, the endless varieties of waterfowl

Hermitage Point Trail

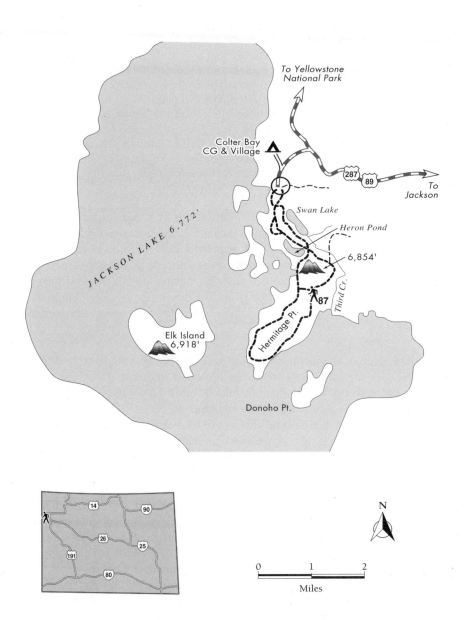

Teton reflections along the Hermitage Point Trail.

and forest birds, and the swan family.

This trail presents many opportunities to contact international hikers and walkers. I met friendly folks from several different countries. Be aware that the only water on this trip is lake water, so carry some of your own.

88 Paintbrush Canyon Trail to Paintbrush Divide

General description:	A steep and rugged journey into the spectacular, rocky innards of the Teton Range.
Distance:	18 miles round trip.
Difficulty:	Strenuous.
Elevation gain and loss:	3,843 feet.
Key elevation points:	Trailhead: 6,877 feet; Holly Lake camping area: 9,600 feet; Paintbrush Divide: 10,720 feet.
General location:	25 miles north of Jackson, in the center of Grand Teton National Park.
Special attractions:	Spectacular Teton cliffs, canyons, mountain peaks, scenery, wildlife, and incomparable beauty.
Maps:	USGS: Grand Teton National Park system map. USGS: Jenny Lake, Mount Moran. The Bridger-Teton National Forest Jackson and Buffalo Districts forest map provide a fair contoured overview of Grand Teton National Park. The best hiking map for the Park and surrounding area is Earthwalk Press's Grand Teton National Park Recreation Map, available at all park gift shops and ranger stations.
Fees:	Park entrance fees.
Manager:	Grand Teton National Park.

Finding the trailhead: At Moose Junction, 15 miles north of Jackson on U.S. Highway 26/89/191, head west toward the park entrance station and the park's headquarters and visitor center. Go 12 miles north along this road to the signed North Jenny Lake Junction. (This same junction is 9.1 miles from the Jackson Lake junction with U.S. Highway 26/89/191, farther north in the park.) Here drive 2.8 miles west and you'll intersect String Lake Road. It's just a 0.5 mile drive along this paved road to the String Lake Picnic Area, whose northern end holds the Leigh Lake Trailhead and beginning of this hike.

The hike: Aptly named String Lake is a wide, calm spot in the creek between Jenny and Leigh Lakes. The trail circumvents its gentle eastern shores for 0.8 mile before crossing a bridge and entering the woodlands to the west. The Paintbrush Trail intersects after 0.7 mile and jogs to the right or north. A fair amount of elevation needs to be gained in the next 2 miles before the trail can enter the mouth of Paintbrush Canyon. Actually, the hardest thing about this section of the trail, at least in late August, is escaping the prolific huckleberry bushes along the way.

As you enter high-walled Paintbrush Canyon, you pass into a wilder kind of country. The creeks go crazy in steep, tumbling cascades; the colorful

Paintbrush Canyon Trail to Paintbrush Divide

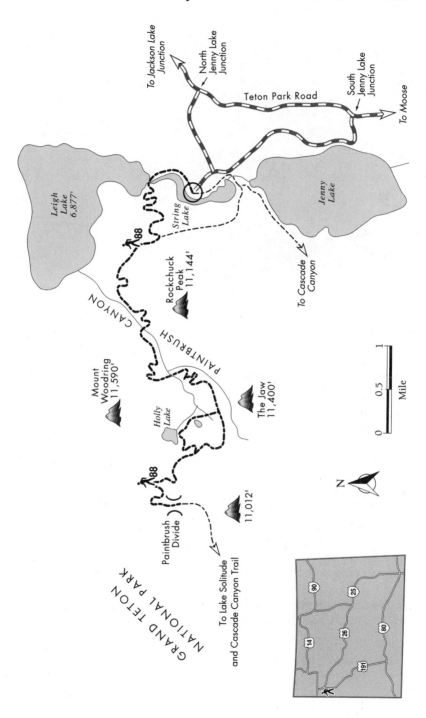

Overlooking Paintbrush Canyon and the Snake River Valley from Paintbrush Divide.

rocks twist up to phenomenal heights; even the forests grow in spastic patterns on the mountainsides.

If you're walking this trail as a day hike, try to get to the top of the switchbacks between 5 and 5.5 miles. Views into the lakelands and high prairies directly below are astounding.

Beyond 6 miles and the Holly Lake Trail intersection, the trail departs from the trees and arcs along the base of a 1,000-foot high crescent of peaks and cliffs. For 2 miles the trail steeply climbs through granite and alpine meadows. The last 0.5 mile leaves all connotations of gentle behind as the trail switchbacks up talus slopes to the barren, windswept, and scenic 10,720-foot high Paintbrush Divide. Paintbrush Divide is one of the areas in the park where an ice axe recommendation is in effect, usually through mid-July. As obvious as this may sound, be sure you know how to use that ice axe. Indeed, even in late August, a fair-sized, steep snowfield may cover the trail and require careful kick-steps to cross.

Paintbrush Canyon hosts 2 camping zones, 1 just above the mouth of the canyon and 1 above Holly Lake. Camping (2 sites) is also available at Holly Lake. A hiker can camp at any of these locations and ascend the divide as a day hike. The Cascade Canyon Trail (Hike 89) can be accessed west and beyond Paintbrush Divide.

89 Cascade Canyon Trail to Lake Solitude

General description:	A long but not too severe hike into the heart of the Tetons.
Distance:	15 to 20 miles round trip.
Difficulty:	Moderate to strenuous.
Elevation gain and loss:	2,250 feet.
Key elevation points:	Inspiration Point: 7,200 feet; South Fork Cascade Creek intersection: 7,840 feet; Lake Solitude: 9,035 feet.
General location:	25 miles north of Jackson, in the center of Grand Teton National Park.
Special attractions:	Steep canyon walls and a cascading creek. More vertical than horizontal country.
Maps:	USGS: Grand Teton National Park system map; USGS: Jenny Lake, Mount Moran. The best hiking map for the park and surrounding areas is Earthwalk Press's Grand Teton National Park Recreation Map, available at all park gift shops and ranger stations.
Manager:	Grand Teton National Park.
Fees:	Park entrance fees; also, the Jenny Lake boat shuttle costs $4.

Finding the trailhead: Approximately 8 miles north of the Moose Entrance Station, or 13 miles south of Jackson Lake Junction, on the Teton Park Road, a South Jenny Lake sign directs you west to a campground and ranger station. Drive to a huge parking lot and follow the signs and the paved paths directing you to the boat dock and the Cascade Canyon Trailhead.

The trail begins as you cross a ramp that spans an arm of the lake's waters by the boat dock. There is a motorboat shuttle that crosses Jenny Lake which eliminates the 2.2 mile walk around the lake's southern shores. Since it knocks more than 4 miles off of the round-trip journey, most hikers opt for this fun ride. The boats arrive and depart at 20-minute intervals, beginning at 8 A.M. Be aware that the last return trip happens at 6 P.M. Miss it, and you'll add a couple of miles to the end of your hike.

The hike: This is the most popular and most hiked trail in Grand Teton National Park. Whether you hike the level terrain around or ride across Jenny Lake, the uphill slopes and the amazing scenery begin immediately beyond the waters' western shores. Above the boat dock at 0.7 mile, a short, well-marked trail places you before Hidden Falls, the powerful cascade of whitewater that the canyon was named for. About 0.5 mile of steep switchbacks places you atop Inspiration Point, another aptly named outcropping that, while sitting beneath pinnacled Teewinot Mountain (12,325

Cascade Canyon Trail to Lake Solitude

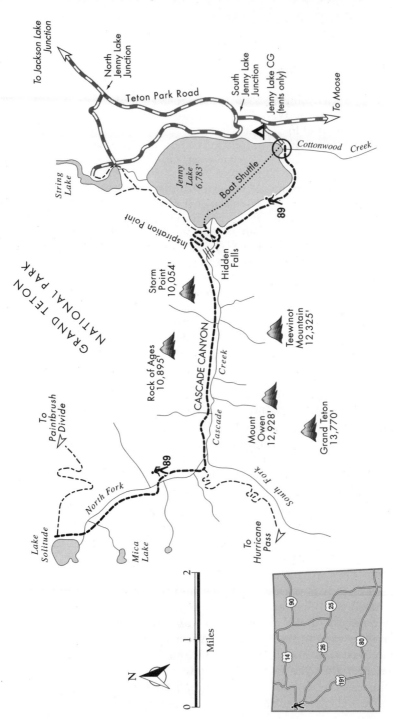

A Cascade Canyon view of the Grand Teton.

feet), overlooks Jenny Lake and the Snake River Valley to the east. It's at this point, and at the canyon mouth 0.7 mile farther, that more than half of most visitors turn around.

The next 3 miles offer what everyone should sometime experience. The trail is gentle and easy to follow, which facilitates your enjoyment of the scenery. The north faces of Teewinot Mountain, Mount Owen (12,928 feet), and the mighty Grand Teton (13,770 feet) form an impressive and nearly continuous southern wall. The northern canyon barriers, including the Rock of Ages, are no slouches either. As the sun moves across the sky, shadows change the stony faces into new forms.

At 3.8 miles above Inspiration Point, Cascade Canyon splits into north and south forks. To the south, 5 miles of climbing places you atop scenic Hurricane Pass (Hike 82). The trip north to Lake Solitude is somewhat shorter and gentler. About 3 miles of scattered subalpine forest and glorious meadow hiking places you beside this quiescent pond beneath a high cirque of rocky mountains. This area (below Lake Solitude) contains the one overnight camping permit zone on this hike.

If you have the time and ambition, try following the trail from Lake Solitude up to Paintbrush Divide (Hike 88). This amazing 3 miles in 3 huge switchbacks provides an easier ascent to the pass than the trail from Paintbrush Canyon. (Easier is a relative concept in this country. This trail still climbs steeply and steadily, and at a high elevation.)

Many people hike the Cascade Canyon and Paintbrush Canyon trails (Hikes 88 and 89) as a loop. Seeing both of these 2 remarkable and completely different canyons sitting side by side will form a remarkable trip. Such a journey is best accomplished by beginning at the String Lake or Leigh Lake Trailheads (see Hike 88) and hiking the northwestern shores of Jenny Lake at the beginning (if up Cascade and down Paintbrush) or at the end (if up Paintbrush and down Cascade). The Park Service quotes this as a 19.2 mile loop hike, but my pedometer and I both think they underrate it by a few miles.

90 Two Ocean Lake

General description:	A flat and scenic day hike in an out-of-the-way corner of Grand Teton National Park.
Distance:	7 miles round trip.
Difficulty:	Easy.
Elevation gain and loss:	Less than 50 feet.
Key elevation points:	Two Ocean Lake: 6,896 feet.
General location:	6 miles north of Moran Junction, in the northeastern corner of Grand Teton National Park.
Special attractions:	A fun place for the family, offering easy trails and swimming opportunities.
Maps:	Earthwalk Press's Grand Teton National Park Recreation map; Bridger-Teton National Forest Buffalo and Jackson Ranger Districts forest map; USGS: Two Ocean Lake.
Fees:	Park entrance fees.
Manager:	Grand Teton National Park.

Finding the trailhead: Moran Junction, where U.S. Highways 26/191 and 287/89 meet, lies 28 miles south of Yellowstone National Park's southern border. Go north from this intersection for 1.5 miles on U.S. Highway 89/287 to a sign indicating the North Pacific Creek Road, which jogs north. Two miles up this paved road another sign points left to a dirt road and Two Ocean Lake. Travel 2.4 miles up this narrow and rough road to a small parking lot. This country is restricted to day use only, with no overnight camping allowed.

The hike: This pleasant trip contains 2 completely different hikes in one 7-mile loop. The trail along the northern stretches of the lake, accessible by dropping down to the outlet creeklet from the northeast corner of the parking lot, offers rock-free and very pretty walking. This 3.5 mile trail to the inlet stream on the west side of Two Ocean Lake travels through aspen groves and open meadows; the scenery is complemented by incredible views of the Tetons towering above the lake waters. I hit the area on the kind of breezy day when no tree on earth chatters as pleasantly as the aspen.

Two Ocean Lake

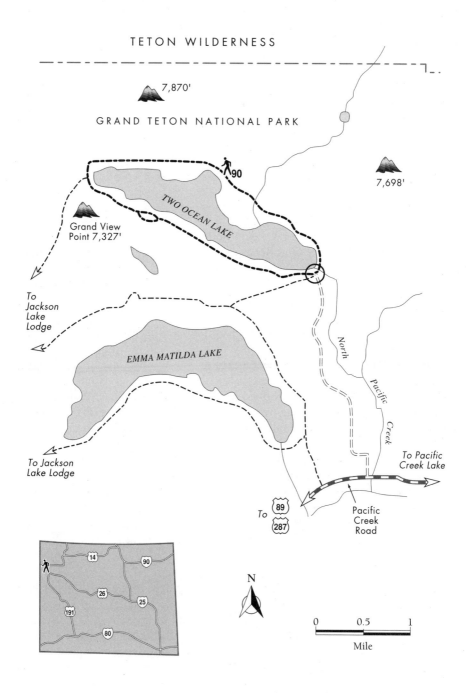

TETON WILDERNESS

7,870'

GRAND TETON NATIONAL PARK

90

7,698'

TWO OCEAN LAKE

Grand View
Point 7,327'

To
Jackson
Lake
Lodge

EMMA MATILDA LAKE

North

Pacific

Creek

To Jackson
Lake Lodge

To Pacific
Creek Lake

To 89
287

Pacific
Creek
Road

14   90

26   25

191

80

N

0   0.5   1

Mile

The second half of the trail—again 3.5 miles—is an enclosed conifer forest hike that eventually returns you to the parking lot. The only potentially confusing spot on this trip is the trail intersection just south of the inlet to the lake. Here a paper sign directs you left and back to the Two Ocean parking lot. Paper signs won't survive long in this country.

Only 2 tiny streams cross the trail on this hike, one 1.5 miles around the north shore trail and one at the far west end of the lake. Both of these contain pretty stale water. If you're up for more flatland day hikes, neighboring Emma Matilda Lake offers a 12-mile loop trip. But Two Ocean Lake boasts the most scenic views.

Yellowstone National Park

Yellowstone is the country's oldest national park. Outside of Alaska, it's also the largest, at nearly 60 miles in both width and length. Its 2.2 million acres is 3 times larger than the state of Rhode Island. Elevations range from 5,000 to 11,000 feet, and numerous complete biospheres intersect to create an ecosystem habitat for an incredible variety of flora and fauna. The steaming geysers and bubbling thermal mud pots, the many lakes and mighty river canyons, the multicolored, extraordinary examples of nature's forces at play almost overwhelm the visitor who attempts to grasp the Yellowstone landscape. One of the earliest explorers of the Yellowstone area, General W.E. Strong, wrote about the area in his diary: "Grand, glorious, and magnificent was the scene as we looked upon it from Washburn's Summit. No pen can write it—no language describe it." Yellowstone takes its name from the Yellowstone River, originally the "Yellow Rock River," named by early French explorers and trappers for the yellow soil and rocks of its canyon.

The park maintains more than 1,000 miles of hiking trails. More variety and beauty await the explorer here than one can possibly imagine. Obviously, *Hiking Wyoming* can serve as but an introduction to this immense area. Falcon Publishing also publishes the latest and most complete Yellowstone hiking guide, *Hiking Yellowstone National Park*, by Bill Schneider. For in-depth explorations of the park, this guide is a great reference. Making an acquaintance with Yellowstone can easily become one of the most rewarding experiences of your life.

The park, certainly one of the most popular places in the world, is visited by millions of people. The rules necessary to protect the land and the experience are much more comprehensive here than in the rest of Wyoming. A brief list of the major regulations associated with hiking the park follows. But be aware that specially designated areas, along with changing conditions and management policies, constantly create exceptions and variations to these rules. Contact a park ranger before you begin a day hike or an overnight trip.

•Permits are required for some day hikes and ALL overnight trips. Also, Yellowstone National Park has a designated backcountry campsite system. Before 1996, everyone had to stand in line at one of several specified ranger stations and hope to acquire a permit to a specific area before someone else did. Now the park uses a computerized reservation system which allows hikers, after April 1 of each given year, to submit by mail or in person (phone reservations are not accepted), their trip and campsite reservation plans. Reservations are on a first-come, first-served basis. You must also pay a non-refundable $15 fee (for each trip) with your reservation, and these reservations must be picked up in person at a ranger station NO MORE than 48 hours in advance of the first day of your trip and no LATER than 10 A.M. of the first day of your trip, or the permit is canceled. Because these rules are so complicated, Yellowstone has published a "Backcountry Trip Planner" which explains the permit process. You can obtain one by calling or writing:

> Backcountry Office
> P.O. Box 168
> Yellowstone National Park, WY 82109
> 307-344-2160 or 307-344-2163

•Open fires are permitted only in established fire rings and only then at certain designated backcountry sites.

•Firearms (including bows and arrows) and pets are prohibited in the backcountry.

•You must suspend food at least 10 feet above the ground and at least 4 feet horizontally from a post or tree. All designated camping sites are SUPPOSED to have food suspension poles, but be ready to improvise.

•The feeding, touching, teasing, frightening, or intentional disturbing of wildlife may win you an appearance before a U.S. magistrate. So might destroying or removing any plant, rock, animal, mineral, cultural, or archaeological resource of the park. This includes throwing or rolling rocks into the geologic thermal features.

•No motorized vehicles or bicycles are allowed in undeveloped areas or on any backcountry trail.

•Unlike many national parks, Yellowstone does require a valid park fishing permit. State licenses and regulations do not apply here. The permit can be acquired from all ranger stations. Children 11 years old or younger do not need permits.

•The park also requires you to follow all of the common-sense rules of no-impact camping espoused in the ethics chapter of this book. All human waste must be disposed of at least 100 feet away from any water source, campsite, or trail (go farther than that, please).

Entrance fees have risen considerably, but the bright side of that is that the money now goes to the park itself rather than the general treasury.

Currently, and subject to change, fees are:

$20 per vehicle for a 7 day pass.

$10 per bicyclist or pedestrian for a 7 day pass.

$50 for a Golden Eagle Passport.

$12 to $14 per night for campground camping.

These entrance fees cover both Yellowstone National Park and Grand Teton National Park.

In 1988, a new dimension was added to Yellowstone's already enchanting nature. More than 800,000 acres of the park were torched by fire. Many of the trails now take you into examples of canopy and mixed burns or into a recovering, scorched landscape. The long-range impact of the fire has created new habitat diversity, and Yellowstone is rejuvenating itself nicely because of this.

---

91 Agate Creek Trail

General description:	A long day hike, mostly atop an open alpine ridge in beautiful and uncluttered country.
Distance:	15 miles round trip.
Difficulty:	Moderate to strenuous.
Elevation gain and loss:	2,220 feet.
General location:	2 miles east of Tower Junction, on the Northeast Entrance Road in Yellowstone National Park.
Special attractions:	Abundant wildlife and glorious views. Probably one of the least known and least traveled trails in the park.
Maps:	Earthwalk Press's Hiking Map and Guide to Yellowstone (the best);. USGS: Tower Junction; there is also a USGS Yellowstone 1:250,000 vicinity map.
Fees:	Park entrance fees, camping permit fees (see above).
Manager:	Yellowstone National Park Headquarters.

Finding the trailhead: East of Tower Junction 2.1 miles, or about 27 miles west of the northeast entrance on the Northeast Entrance Road, there is a wide spot in the road where an interpretive sign explains glaciers and glacial moraines. Across the road to the south is a simple sign reading "Trail Head," with an arrow pointing south. This is actually the west trailhead of the long and scenic Specimen Ridge Trail. The trail to Agate Creek starts here and cuts north from this trail.

The hike: The north-central portion of Yellowstone doesn't house the thermal springs, mud pots and fabled geyser features for which the park is renowned. Its countenance is rather that of high and open country, an easier land that was created by glacial moraines. Its meadows and valleys are home

Agate Creek Trail

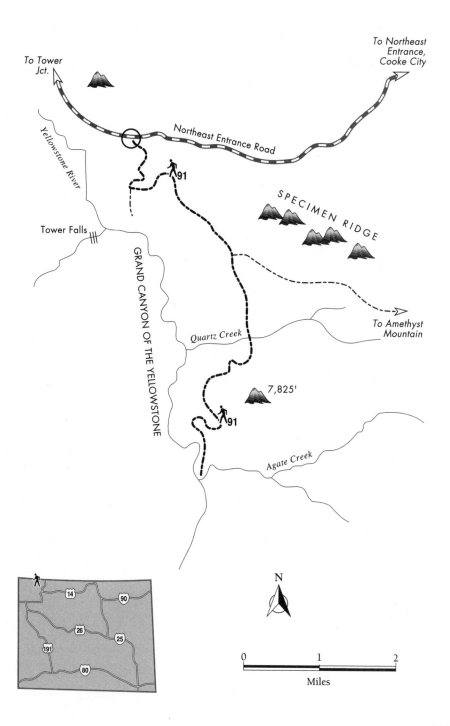

To Northeast Entrance, Cooke City

To Tower Jct.

Yellowstone River

Northeast Entrance Road

SPECIMEN RIDGE

Tower Falls

GRAND CANYON OF THE YELLOWSTONE

Quartz Creek

To Amethyst Mountain

7,825'

91

91

Agate Creek

N

0   1   2

Miles

14

90

26

25

191

80

to many of the wonderful varieties of wildlife that inhabit the park. And this section of Yellowstone seems the least traveled and least crowded.

Agate Creek Trail almost has to be hiked as a day hike. Its final destination, where pretty Agate Creek merges with the Yellowstone River, borders a special bear management area that is closed to humans from March 10 through November 10. One backcountry campsite does exist near the river bottom, but that site is closed Memorial Day through mid-July, AND whenever bear activity is probable. This makes for a 15-mile round trip, but the country is enchanting every step of the way.

A few tenths of a mile along the Specimen Ridge Trail places you at the "official" trailhead and registration box. The first mile of this trail slopes moderately upward, through open meadows and sections of forest to a ridgetop that affords an ineffable view of the Grand Canyon of the Yellowstone River. It's a fun place to be, high and alone on a magnificent overview while across the river you can see hundreds of tourists bumping into each other as they congregate at a roadside scenic pullout. After a steep climb of 0.5 mile to the east, the trail tops out on Specimen Ridge. Here begins an incredible walking experience. The alpine tundra country is so vast, so open, you feel you're at the center of this endless expanse of huge mountainous space. Panoramas of distant peaks accompany every step.

After another mile there is a signed intersection; follow the arrow pointing right or south to Agate Creek. The next 2.5 miles is high country walking at its (speaking literally) level best. After crossing the only water on this ridge, Quartz Creek, I encountered a herd of 250 elk cows and calves, and could only revel in their cries and wanderings. Past Quartz Creek the trail does fade in and out, but it's easy to guess the route. It continues to provide views of the Grand Canyon of the Yellowstone River, and occasional orange markers trace its route.

The final 2 miles of the trail drop steeply to the shores of the Yellowstone River. It's a real sliding, boot-jammer of a descent that ends where a gravel bar intrudes into the river, forming a nice place to enjoy lunch. Fires have done a number on portions of this area, and the hiker can view all kinds of burn patterns. On the hike back, you get to see all the scenery that was behind you as you hiked in.

Watch for bears and elk on this trail, especially as you approach the Yellowstone River. Potential weather changes should be kept in mind because most of the distance is open and exposed. There are so many elk in the country that they tend to create their own trails. Look for the orange trail markers noting the park trail.

92 Blacktail Creek Trail

General description:	A popular day hike or easy overnighter providing access to several other one-way hikes and loops.
Distance:	8 miles round trip.
Difficulty:	Easy to moderate.
Elevation gain and loss:	1,160 feet.
Key elevation points:	Blacktail Creek Falls: 6,560 feet; Yellowstone River: 5,600 feet.
General location:	6 miles east of Mammoth Springs in the north-central sector of Yellowstone National Park.
Special attractions:	Easy access to the Black Canyon of the Yellowstone River, and one of the lowest-elevation hikes in the park, offering a unique flora setting.
Maps:	Earthwalk Press's Yellowstone Hiking Map and guide; USGS: Blacktail Deer Creek.
Fees:	Park entrance fee; camping permit fees.
Manager:	Yellowstone National Park Headquarters.

Finding the trailhead: The trailhead is located 11.9 miles west of Tower Junction, or 6.1 miles east of Mammoth Springs, on the northernmost sector of the Grand Loop Road.

The hike: A pet ploy of mine is to become friendly with people who have extensive knowledge of an area and ask them to direct me to their favorite hikes. This interesting day hike is ranger recommended because it traverses some of the lowest elevations in Yellowstone Park. Early season access and completely different plant ecosystems are two of the special features of this hike.

The trail is well traveled and seems unimpressive for the first 1.5 miles. Rolling hills topped by bald-looking shortgrass prairies rule the landscape. But then conifers began sneaking into the scenery, and after 2 miles the trail drops into the Blacktail Creek drainage. Here the open forest settings become undeniably fascinating. Here also the creek sinks deeper and deeper into the earth, creating an impressive valley which turns into a formidable chasm. And all of this is but a prelude to the mighty Black Canyon of the Yellowstone River.

The last mile of the trail drops steeply into a mountainous gorge of dark-colored volcanic rock cliffs. (Impressive also is the steel suspension bridge that crosses the mighty river.) North of this bridge 0.2 mile, the Blacktail Creek Trail intersects the Yellowstone River Trail. You've actually crossed into Montana here, and if it's the right time of year, the surrounding bench is flagrant with the blossoms of Montana's state flower, the bitterroot. The journey from trailhead to trail intersection is but 4 miles, but the scenery undergoes endless transformations along the way.

Blacktail Creek Trail

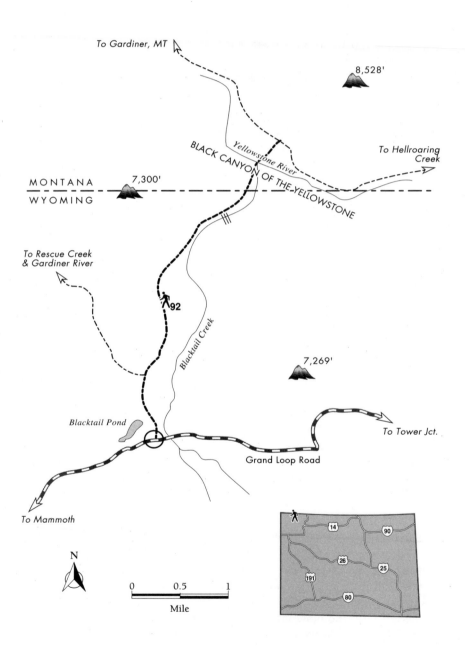

To Gardiner, MT

8,528'

To Hellroaring
Creek

Yellowstone River

BLACK CANYON OF THE YELLOWSTONE

MONTANA
7,300'

WYOMING

To Rescue Creek
& Gardiner River

92

Blacktail Creek

7,269'

Blacktail Pond

To Tower Jct.

Grand Loop Road

To Mammoth

N

0   0.5   1

Mile

14

90

26

25

191

80

One joy of this particular trail is the access it gives a person to so many other hiking opportunities. Several backcountry campsites exist along the route and near the Yellowstone River. One can set up camp here and day hike beneath the towering cliff walls of the canyon, both up and down the river. Other options include a couple of one-way hikes: a 12.6 mile hike west along the river to Gardiner, Montana, and an 11.3 mile hike east to Hellroaring Creek and the many trails that slice through that country. The only warning I heard here was that this lower elevation country can cook during the heat of the summer.

93 Bighorn Pass

General description:	A 2-or-more-day journey into the wild, high peak beauty of the Gallatin Range.
Distance:	20 miles round trip.
Difficulty:	Moderate to strenuous.
Elevation gain and loss:	2,000 feet.
Key elevation points:	Bighorn Pass: 9,110 feet.
General location:	72 miles south of Bozeman, Montana, and 20 miles north of West Yellowstone, Montana, in the very northwest corner of the Wyoming part of Yellowstone National Park.
Special attractions:	Open and vast country, fantastic stream fishing (permit required), large herds of elk and bison.
Maps:	Earthwalk's Yellowstone National Park hiking map; USGS: Joseph Peak, Quadrant Mountain.
Fees:	Park entrance fee; camping permit fees.
Manager:	Yellowstone National Park Headquarters.

Finding the trailhead: U.S. Highway 191 south from Bozeman, Montana, enters Yellowstone National Park at the Northwest Park Entrance. From here travel south for approximately 12 more miles. If coming from West Yellowstone, Montana, drive north on this same highway for approximately 20 miles. At this point a small "Bighorn Pass" trailhead sign directs you east along a one-lane dirt road for 0.3 mile. Here the road ends in a small and open parking area, the trailhead.

The hike: Note: The lower 5 miles of this trail traverses amazingly flat and open country, making for a great day hike; however, this trail can be connected with the Fawn Pass Trail to the north to become a multi-day loop hike.

This wild Gallatin River headwater country offers a huge overview of Yellowstone's grandeur. Part of this quality derives from the enormous variety of wildlife that call this section of the park home. In the fall, dozens of bugling elk may keep you awake all night. This entire area, including

Bighorn Pass

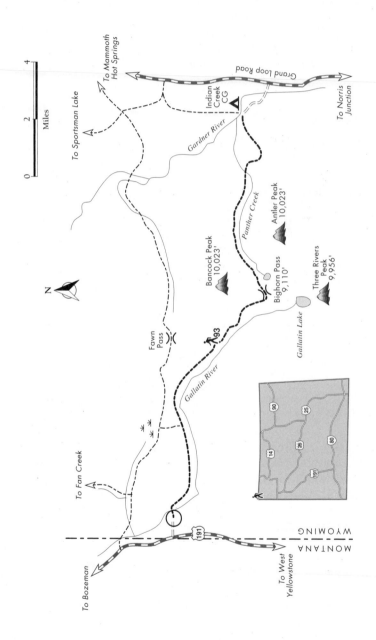

Bighorn Pass Trail, is classified as "Critical Grizzly Bear Cub Production Habitat." A special permit is required to hike the trail, but it's a self-registration permit and available at the trailhead. Hiking off the trail in special bear management areas is prohibited.

Only 0.3 mile up this broad valley a couple of tenuous foot bridges await you. These bridges are on unstable ground and vulnerable to both high waters and to bison using them as scratching posts. They may or may not be available when you visit, so a pair of tennies and a walking stick may be needed to facilitate the wading.

Walk this exceptionally flat trail for 4.1 miles through a vast and broad valley of mixed grass and sage and you will arrive at the Fawn Pass Trail cutoff intersection. I must admit that the "stay on the trail" regulations are easy to break when one encounters bison sleeping on the trail (a good reason NOT to be hiking this country after dark). Just above this point sits the first overnight camping site, a good base from which to begin an ascent of the pass the next day.

Hike 2 more miles through meadows until the trail grows rocky and becomes a forest hike for 2 more miles. Up this trail a total of 8 miles now, you break out of the trees, and the rest of the way to the pass is a steep (but not too steep) hike to the divide and its amazing views down both east- and west-facing valleys. Just before the final 2-mile ascent, the trail skirts the creek, offering one last chance for a drink. For these last couple of climbing miles, enjoy the expanding scenery accompanying the increasing elevation. East from the pass, the trail gently descends another 7.5 miles to Indian Creek campground and the Grand Loop Road.

This country's vastness allows you to see where you are heading for a long time, and the area is replete in big game and other wildlife. A near 50-mile loop is possible by combining this trail and the Fawn Pass/Creek Trail to the north (when tied together by the Howard Eaton Trail near Indian Creek Campground).

94 Fairy Falls/Imperial Geyser/ Queens Laundry

General description:	Two short, flat, half-day hikes into the steaming heart of Yellowstone's geothermal activity area.
Distance:	3.6 to 6 miles round trip.
Difficulty:	Easy.
Elevation gain and loss:	Less than 250 feet.
Key elevation points:	Maximum elevation: 7,500 feet.
General location:	6 and 8 miles south of Madison Junction (which is 15 miles east of West Yellowstone, Montana), in the west-central part of Yellowstone National Park.
Special attractions:	Intense geothermal activity of all kinds, large herds of wildlife, attractive and impressive waterfalls.
Maps:	USGS: Lower Geyser Basin, Buffalo Meadows; Earthwalk Press's Yellowstone National Park hiking map. (Note: the trail loop connections are a bit different than what these maps portray.)
Fees:	Park entrance fee.
Manager:	Yellowstone National Park Headquarters.

Finding the trailhead: From West Yellowstone, Montana, and the park's west entrance, it is approximately 15 miles to Madison Junction. Driving south from here along the Grand Loop Road (or north on this highway 11 miles from the Old Faithful complex) leads you to a well-marked paved road—Fountain Flat Drive—jogging off to the southwest. Go south about 1.7 miles on this paved road; this places you on a highway bridge that crosses the Firehole River. The Queens Laundry Trailhead sits just south of this bridge, on the west side of the road. South 0.3 mile from this bridge the pavement yields to gravel, and another 0.4 mile south it passes a small parking area with a large sign noting the Fairy Falls and Imperial Geyser Trailhead.

The hikes: Note: These 2 hikes could be combined to create a longer day hike loop.

Fairy Falls and Imperial Geyser: Check out some of the geographic names in this area: Firehole River Geyser Basin, Hot Lake; and not too far to the south resides that paragon of geysers, Old Faithful. These trails provide quick and easy access to the epitome of Yellowstone's geothermic activity and splendor.

This has to be the flattest, widest trail in the world. In the vast grassy meadows surrounding the first 2.5 miles of this path, one can view the steam and vapor trailing out of potholes and small geysers in the distance. This is especially true on crisp autumn early mornings. Large herds of elk, bison and flocks of geese frequent this area. The forest begins at this 2.5

Elk and geothermal activity can be viewed on the trail leading to Imperial Geyser.

mile distance; this area was particularly hard hit in the 1988 fires, but regeneration is evident everywhere in the form of new grasses, fireweed, and emerging lodgepole trees.

After those 2.5 miles you encounter a trail intersection noting that Fairy Falls is 0.4 miles to the left, or west. For the past 0.5 mile this beautiful, fluttering 100-foot sheet of liquid cascading over dark volcanic rock has been visible. Now the sound of the waterfall combines with the visual to create a motion-filled drama in the midst of a totally burned-out mountainside.

From this same intersection, 0.3 mile to the north, will be found a moonscape of steamy, bubbling caldrons. The sounds of hot water boiling from deep under the ground supplement the bizarre red, pink, and gray colors of the hot-water algae living within. Imperial Geyser never did erupt for me, but a short hike downstream to roiling Spray Geyser and some patient waiting eventually let me view hot frothing steam and spray blasting 12 feet into the air.

BE AWARE of slippery rocks and scalding water in this area.

Queens Laundry: This easy-to-follow hiking trail cuts along the forest edge overlooking massive and open Sentinel Meadows. Ancient steam vents, mineralized into huge conical mounds of powdery rock, dot the boggy landscape, adding eerie undertones to the scene. Though the trail stays in the forest, the fire-burned trees do not impede the spectacular overviews. Lots of big game live and play in these meadow areas.

Fairy Falls/Imperial Geyser/Queens Laundry

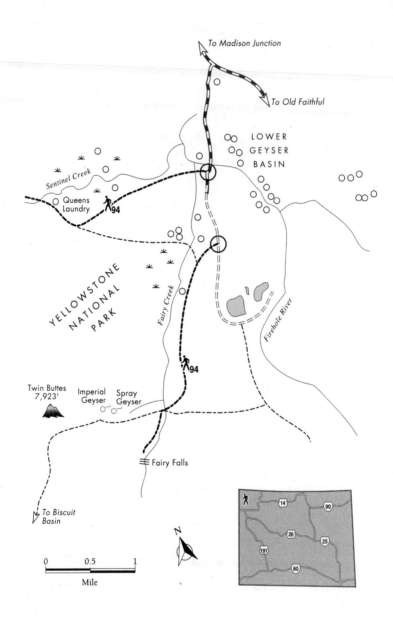

To Madison Junction

To Old Faithful

LOWER GEYSER BASIN

Sentinel Creek

Queens Laundry

🚶94

YELLOWSTONE NATIONAL PARK

Fairy Creek

Firehole River

🚶94

Twin Buttes 7,923'

Imperial Geyser

Spray Geyser

Fairy Falls

To Biscuit Basin

N

0   0.5   1

Mile

14   90

26   25

191

80

Only 1.3 miles along this occasionally hilly path, a re-routing sends the trail down toward the meadow. Here you are walking toward a massive, steamy cauldron which is in fact the Queens Laundry. The new trail skirts the meadow border for a short distance, then comes to an (at the time I was there) unsigned intersection. Head west (right) to reach Queens Laundry, where these unfathomable, huge earth-pots of dark blue, bubbling, boiling water allow for quite a journey of the imagination: "Whatever is down there?" "How deep are these holes in the earth?" If only I could follow them into their underground crevices and caverns." (With water temperatures near 200 degrees F, don't step past imagination or too close to the edge.)

Heading south (left) from the above trail intersection allows you to connect with the Fairy Falls/Imperial Geyser Trail in 1.1 miles. The actual trail layout is slightly different than the topo maps portray.

Again and always, use extreme caution near these geothermic formations. Crusty, mineral-deposited rock shelves often do NOT provide a solid rim on which to stand beside boiling water.

95 Bechler Meadows

General description:	A day hike into the exceptionally unusual, lesser-known southwest corner of Yellowstone.
Distance:	11 miles round trip.
Difficulty:	Easy to moderate.
Elevation gain and loss:	Less than 100 feet.
Key elevation points:	Trailhead: 6,400 feet.
General location:	24 miles east of Ashton, Idaho, in the southwest sector of Yellowstone National Park.
Special attractions:	Many square miles of hiking through grassy and absolutely flat meadows. Long distant views and wildlife abound.
Maps:	Earthwalk Press's Hiking Map and Guide to Yellowstone; USGS: Bechler Falls, Cave Falls. Also the USGS Yellowstone National Park 1:125,000 vicinity map.
Manager:	Yellowstone National Park Headquarters.
Fees:	Possible camping permit fee.

Finding the trailhead: From the small farming community of Ashton, Idaho, journey east on Idaho 47 for 6 miles to a highway sign pointing the way toward Cave Falls and Yellowstone National Park. Traveling 6 miles along this road brings you to the pavement's end and the beginning of Forest Road 582. This well-maintained gravel road travels 11.1 miles east before it is intersected by a well-signed road running north and to the Bechler Ranger Station. This more primitive outpost was originally an army post where soldiers were stationed to protect the Yellowstone area, before the National

Bechler Meadows

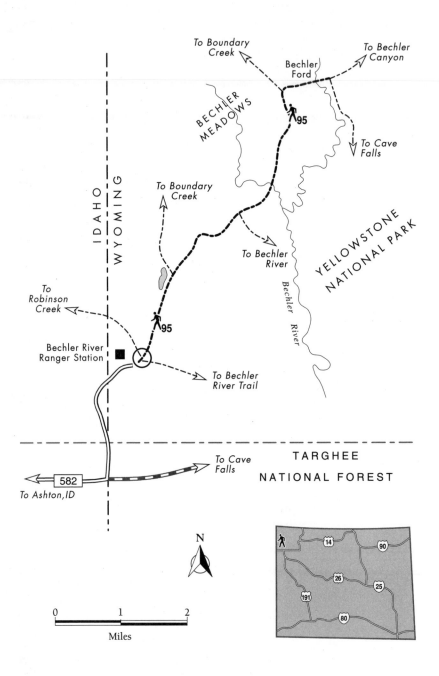

To Boundary Creek

To Bechler Canyon

Bechler Ford

BECHLER MEADOWS

95

To Cave Falls

To Boundary Creek

IDAHO

WYOMING

To Bechler River

YELLOWSTONE NATIONAL PARK

Bechler River

To Robinson Creek

95

Bechler River Ranger Station

To Bechler River Trail

TARGHEE

To Cave Falls

NATIONAL FOREST

582

To Ashton, ID

N

14

90

26

25

191

80

0   1   2

Miles

Vast sea of grass in Bechler Meadows.

Park Service was created in 1916. The trailhead begins northeast of the station's few buildings.

The hike: When the startling call of trumpeter swans greeted the rosy dawn, I had a feeling this day's hike was going to be unique. G. B. Bechler (pronounced bek-ler), when he mapped this southwest corner of Yellowstone National Park in 1872, must have had the same premonition.

The Bechler area is unique in that it's forested land where you can hike for miles and miles and never gain or lose more than 20 feet in elevation. The first 3.5 miles of the trail wanders through a grassy lodgepole woodland that never varies in elevation. One of the few areas unscathed by the 1988 fires, the Bechler area forest sports trees in all stages of development.

Then the forest ends, and for the next 2 miles you walk through fascinating, undisturbed grassland meadows. Eons ago this area was a vast lake that became silted and allowed a grassy biosphere to claim it. If a pack train happens by, you can actually feel the hollow earth undulate from the party's weight and motion. Low, forested hills surround this seemingly endless savannah. Long-range views of the Tetons augment the picture. Swampy areas exist throughout the route, but the Park Service has spanned them all with bridges.

At 5.5 miles the trail fords the Bechler River. The first week in August this crossing formed a most refreshing, mid-thigh-deep wade across a sandy and gravelly bottom. A single-person suspension bridge provides a secondary route across the river. In a short distance from this crossing, the Bechler

Meadows Trail ends at an intersection with the Bechler River Trail. From here you can return via the same route, you can wander further up Bechler Canyon and view its many waterfalls, or you can make a loop circle back to the Bechler Ranger Station via the Bechler River Trail (both described in Hike 96).

There is no camping at the Bechler Ranger Station. If you arrive at night, you'll need to camp on the surrounding Targhee National Forest lands or at Cave Falls campground. Also, 0.1 mile beyond the trailhead is the first of many well-signed trail intersections—the Bechler River Cutoff Trail. To journey to the meadows, be sure and go left or north at this point. A wide variety of loop trips are possible in this area.

96 Bechler River Trail and Bechler Canyon

General description:	A 3- to 5-day backpack trip into an incomparable river canyon.
Distance:	40 miles round trip.
Difficulty:	Moderate.
Elevation gain and loss:	1,300 feet.
Key elevation points:	Trailhead: 6,250 feet; Ranger Lake: 6,960 feet; Colonnade Falls: 6,800 feet; Three River Junction: 7,550 feet.
General location:	27 miles east of Ashton, Idaho, in the southwest sector of Yellowstone National Park.
Special attractions:	The Bechler River in all its moods and aspects.
Maps:	Earthwalk Press's Hiking Map and Guide to Yellowstone; USGS: Warm River, Grass Lake, Old Faithful, Buffalo Lake; also the USGS Yellowstone National Park 1:125,000 vicinity map.
Fees:	Possible camping permit fee.
Manager:	Yellowstone National Park Headquarters.

Finding the trailhead: If you haven't already acquired a backcountry camping permit by mail, you'll need to go to the Bechler Ranger Station and get one. Follow the trailhead directions for Hike 95 to the Bechler Ranger Station. Then return to Forest Road 582 and continue east for 3.1 miles on what will suddenly become a paved road. Just beyond spectacular Cave Falls (on the Falls River) the road ends at the Bechler River Trailhead. It may be advisable to park at the Bechler River Ranger Station and hike the Bechler River Cutoff Trail or the South Boundary Trail over to the Bechler River Trail. The ranger station provides more safety from car break-ins, and current trail information is more readily available.

Bechler River Trail and Bechler Canyon

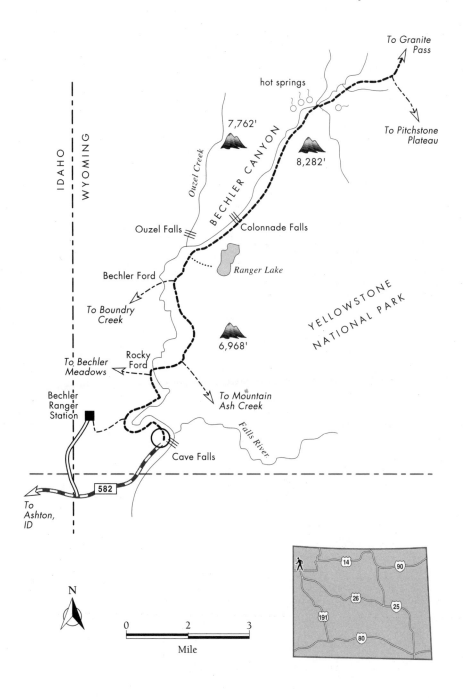

To Granite Pass

hot springs

To Pitchstone Plateau

7,762'

BECHLER CANYON

8,282'

Ouzel Creek

IDAHO

WYOMING

Ouzel Falls

Colonnade Falls

Bechler Ford

Ranger Lake

To Boundry Creek

YELLOWSTONE NATIONAL PARK

6,968'

Rocky Ford

To Bechler Meadows

To Mountain Ash Creek

Bechler Ranger Station

Falls River

Cave Falls

582

To Ashton, ID

N

0   2   3
Mile

14   90
26   25
191   80

The hike: For the first 0.4 mile the trail follows the Falls River, beside a series of impressive and thundering cascades. Then the Bechler River Trail takes its own path, and for the next almost 20 miles you and the ever-changing Bechler River are going to make many acquaintances.

The first 2 miles of level forested hiking reveal a river rushing in delicate rapids over a rocky-bottomed floor. The next 2 miles of level forested walking show you the quiet, noiseless, and completely smooth face of the winding waters. Here, at Rocky Ford, you get to negotiate a 35-yard wade in the crystal-clear river. In August the waters were never over my knees (although it can rise to mid-thigh depths during some years), but a walking stick was a necessity because the flat-but-rocky river bottom was moss-covered and a bit slippery. The next 3 miles of hilly and forested walking will place you near the Bechler Ford and at the intersection of the Bechler Meadows Trail (Hike 95). Another 1.5 miles of varied country puts you in the mouth of Bechler River Canyon and into yet another phase of the many-faceted river.

This rocky and forested canyon allows the river a mostly gentle and peaceful passage. But every few miles a series of impressive waterfalls appear to torture the smooth waters. Just beyond the beginning of the canyon, to the right and 0.5 mile southeast (watch your map), sits Ranger Lake, a large lake surrounded by forest. There's no official trail to this lake, but apparently some pretty good fishing can be found in these waters. Up the canyon 2.5 miles, Colonnade Falls offers you a short side trip to an incredible double falls. Another 5 miles of easy and sometimes rocky hiking brings you to an equally beautiful falls, Ragged Falls, and the end (beginning, actually) of Bechler Canyon. Designated campsites dot the canyon, as do hot springs, thermal areas, waterfalls and soul-warming scenery. In the canyon the trail twice fords the river, the first wade being somewhat deep and swift.

This trail actually continues all the way to the Old Faithful area, making it an excellent two-vehicle or drop-off hike. If you do return to the Bechler River Trailhead, hike the Bechler Meadows Trail (Hike 95) to the Bechler River Cutoff for a unique loop experience.

Fishing in the Bechler area is catch-and-release only.

97 Beula Lake

General description:	A short day hike to a serene lake amid dense lodgepole forested hills.
Distance:	7 miles round trip.
Difficulty:	Easy.
Elevation gain and loss:	377 feet.
Key elevation points:	Beula Lake: 7,377 feet.
General location:	15 miles west of the south entrance to Yellowstone National Park, along the very southern border of the park.
Special attractions:	Quiet, solitude, fair fishing, and a unique mountain-lake microenvironment.
Maps:	Earthwalk Press's Yellowstone map and guide; the Bridger-Teton National Forest Buffalo and Jackson Ranger Districts visitor map; USGS: Grassy Lake Reservoir.
Manager:	Yellowstone National Park Headquarters.
Fees:	Possible camping permit fee.

Finding the trailhead: Approximately 2 miles south of Yellowstone National Park's south entrance station, along U.S. Highway 287/89, the paved and signed Grassy Lake Road jogs to the west. This is also signed as the road to the Flagg Ranch Campground (not the Flagg Ranch Village, which is 0.5 mile farther south on the main highway). Follow this wide road west 0.5 mile to a T, here turning right or west toward Ashton, Idaho. The road is paved for a couple of miles as it crosses the Snake River, and then it becomes a narrow gravel lane. The last 4 miles of this 10-mile passage are some of the roughest two-wheel-drive road in Wyoming. Not quite 0.3 mile after you exit the John D. Rockefeller Jr. Memorial Parkway and enter the Targhee National Forest, at the uppermost end of Grassy Lake Reservoir, you will reach a signless parking area to the north that accommodates about 3 vehicles and forms the Beula Lake Trailhead. This rugged Grassy Lake Road also serves as access to hiking trails in the very northern fringes of Grand Teton National Park.

The hike: You don't meet many of them these days, but Beulas were quite prevalent among Wyoming pioneering women. Several land features in the state have been given the name "Beula," all of them named after settlers' wives.

Up the trail 0.1 mile, a registration sign will let you know you are indeed on the Beula Lake Trail. This mellow and peaceful hiking trail is an ideal, easy trek for families or for people who simply want to wander leisurely through the woodlands with no real exertion. The first 0.2 mile forces you to climb a slope, but the rest of the trail's 3 miles affords a gently rolling and amiable walk. As with most trails in Yellowstone, this path offers lessons in

Beula Lake

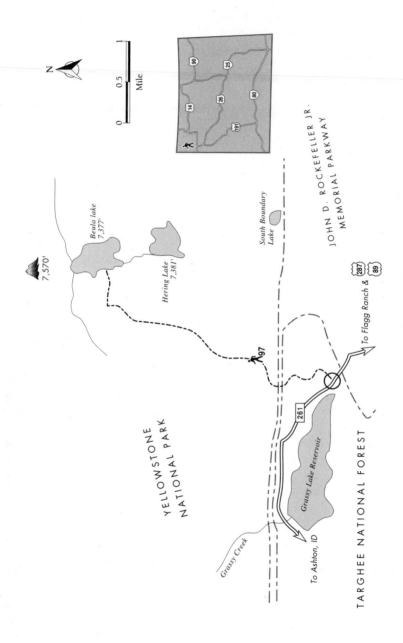

Beula Lake.

forest fire ecology. In fact, for a fair distance the trail itself serves as the barrier between a mixed burn setting and a spared forest.

The lake is surprisingly large and creates a unique watery oasis in a sea of dense lodgepole. Designated campsites dot the lake's western shore. It's a typical downed lodgepole forest walking adventure to circumvent the lake's shores. To make a complete circle around the waters, you'll also have to wade a few swamps. Birds and waterfowl, frogs and dragonflies are the denizens of Beula Lake. The atmosphere surrounding the lake's setting is one of almost overwhelming serenity.

Overnight camping does require a permit from the Park Service. Also, catch-and-release fishing is the rule. The lake, shallow and surrounded by brackish wetland, furnishes the only liquid in the area, so be prepared to boil or filter drinking water.

General description:	A long, somewhat level (after the first 0.5 mile) and gentle hike into a vast, high elevation grassland plateau.
Distance:	16 miles round trip.
Difficulty:	Moderate.
Elevation gain and loss:	965 feet.
Key elevation points:	Phantom Fumarole: 8,500 feet; high point on Pitchstone Plateau: 8,977 feet.
General location:	30 miles north of Moran Junction, in the southwestern sector of Yellowstone National Park.
Special attractions:	A unique journey into some severe forest burn remnants. Beautiful, open land and large, encompassing meadows.
Maps:	Earthwalk Press's Hiking map and guide; USGS: Lewis Canyon, Lewis Falls, Grassy Lake Reservoir, Shoshone Geyser Basin. Also USGS Yellowstone 1:125,000 vicinity map.
Fees:	Park entrance fee and camping permit fees.
Manager:	Yellowstone National Park Headquarters.

Finding the trailhead: On the South Entrance Road of Yellowstone, about 14 miles south of West Thumb Junction or 8 miles north of the South Entrance, a "Trailhead" sign points to the west where a tiny, widened spot in the road, one able to accommodate 3 cars, forms the parking lot for this access to Pitchstone Plateau. This isn't one of the park's most popular or heavily traveled trails.

The hike: The word "plateau" means a level, table-like surface of high elevation. The French linguist who invented this word must have somehow visited the Pitchstone Plateau in Yellowstone, because it is the epitome of a plateau. Also noteworthy is the word "pitchstone," meaning "glassy igneous rock resembling hardened pitch." The lava flows in this area represent the most recent volcanic action in the park, and the rocks scattered over the plateau's surface are indeed black and shiny.

The trail diagonals up the eastern slopes of the plateau side for about 0.5 mile in a steep beginning. Then the land flattens out and the rest of the 8 or so miles to the heart of the plateau vary little in elevation. The first 3.5 miles of this hike wander through some incredibly intense burn remnants of the 1988 forest fires. When I first hiked here in 1991, it was as if some kind of alien death ray had zapped the miles of flat landscape into blackened nonbeing. Even now, as the land slowly rejuvenates, there are still zones where nothing lives. Almost no wildlife shows itself, and no noise exists but an occasional tree falling in the distance. Even the breezes sound awkward because they're wafting through charred posts instead of pine boughs. The

Pitchstone Plateau

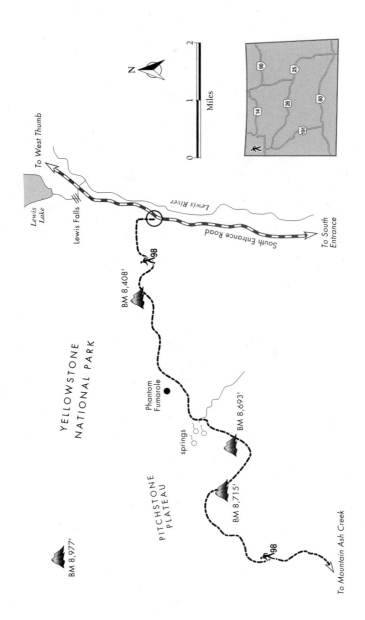

Moose are a fairly common sight in the Yellowstone backcountry. CHRIS CAUBLE PHOTO

beginning of this hike will either enthrall you or give you the heebie-jeebies.

After 3.5 miles, the lodgepole and spruce forests begin to show more beetle kill than fire kill. Meadows, some quite large in size, are interspersed between the forests. After 4.5 miles you encounter what's called the Phantom Fumarole, a colorful and active, bubbling mudpot of gasses and hot water. It may be called "Phantom" because whiffs of its spent-fireworks scent have been noticeable for the last mile while no indication of their source is discernible. CAUTION: Don't approach this thermal wonder. The surrounding ground is a catacomb of vents and recent volcanic activity. If the earth collapsed and you fell into any of these holes, you'd become the Cooked Phantom of the Fumarole.

At 5.5 miles huge, plateau meadows begin to appear. The first meadow contains the only water on this trip, a stream emanating from several welcome springs. The 2 designated campsites happen to be here as well. If you have a permit to camp in this area, it makes a great base from which to explore.

The next couple of miles weave through the various meadows and forests leading to the endless plateau. Once here, the trail often ceases to exist as a path; follow the series of rock cairns stacked at various intervals through the short-grass fields. BE ADVISED: It is imperative that you always be able to return to the last cairn you passed. Leaving the trail is ill-advised. Tempting as it might be to explore the massive plateau area, if you couldn't relocate the trail cairns, 8 miles of burnt-lodgepole hell-hiking would be the only way out. If you can't find the next cairn on this trail, look around, but

don't lose sight of the last cairn. You do not want to have to find your way
back to the trailhead through this timbered and burned country without the
benefit of a trail.

Pitchstone Plateau's vastness was the culmination of my journey. A point-
to-point, 20-mile trail option continues southward, intersecting the Mountain Ash Trail, which eventually intersects the Grassy Lake Road south of
the Park (Hike 97).

99 Heart Lake

General description:	A long day hike or 2-to 3-day trip to a large and beautiful mountain lake.
Distance:	16 miles round trip.
Difficulty:	Moderate.
Elevation gain and loss:	1,025 feet.
Key elevation points:	Heart Lake: 7,450 feet.
General location:	South of Yellowstone Lake and west of Lewis Lake, in the south-central section of Yellowstone National Park.
Special attractions:	The lake supports loons, otters and bald eagles, and occasional elk and bear wander the surrounding countryside. Thermal pools and geyser basins add wonderful dimensions to the trip.
Maps:	Earthwalk Press's Hiking map and guide; USGS: Mount Sheridan, Heart Lake. USGS quads Snake Hot Springs and Mount Hancock are optional for some of the loop trips available in the Heart Lake area.
Fees:	Park entrance fees; camping permit fees.
Manager:	Yellowstone National Park Headquarters.

Finding the trailhead: The well-signed Heart Lake Trailhead and parking
area sits 0.5 mile north of the northern shores of Lewis Lake. Travel approximately 15 miles north of the South Entrance or approximately 9 miles
south of West Thumb, both on the South Entrance Road.

The hike: An old, pre-1870 Wyoming hunter and trapper, Chat (sometimes
called Hart) Hunney, had this large Yellowstone lake named after him. Mapping the country soon revealed that the lake carries a sort of heart shape,
and the spelling of Chat's name was altered to accommodate the new information. My history source doesn't say whether Mr. Hunney was pleased,
displeased, or dead when this happened.

The Heart Lake Trail is a well-used, wide, and well-maintained trail with
a gradual uphill beginning. After 2 miles of easy climbing, the hiker can see
the lake in a broad valley below. The trail then gradually descends into
Witch Creek, which begins as a few steam vents on the hillside of Factory

Heart Lake

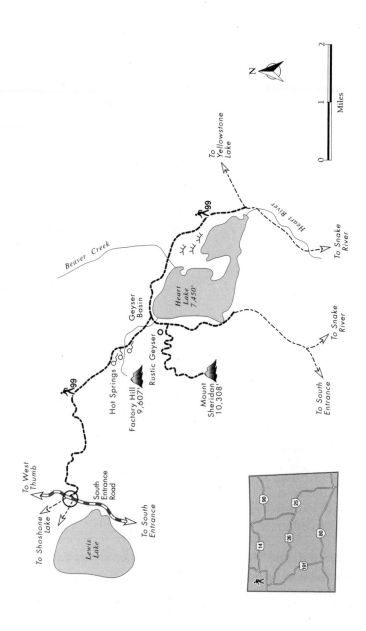

Recent fire ecology is now part of many Yellowstone trails.

Hill (named because the venting steam looks like a factory's emissions). Soon it becomes a small hot-water creek flowing into the lake. The trail roughly follows the creek down through a beautiful meadow and comes out at the Mauger Ranger Station (usually manned) at lakeside.

Rustic Geyser Basin lies across Witch Creek to the south, on the way to the designated campsites for the area along the west side of the lake. Caution is urged here and at the Geyser Basin Area, as the earth's crust is thin and the water is hot—up to 190 degrees F. The hottest pools are a beautiful, deep blue, and the patient hiker will see Rustic Geyser spout off at irregular intervals.

The Heart Lake Trail did not escape the fires of 1988. In fact, this area was heavily burned, especially on the rise between the trailhead and the lake. Be aware of the potential of falling trees in the years to come. Heart

Lake itself is simply massive; its surface is more than 2,000 acres, and its waters run 180 feet deep.

Mount Sheridan (10,308 feet) rises above the western end of the lake and offers grand vistas for those willing to follow its steep ridge trail for 3 miles (one way, 2,700-foot elevation gain). This spur trail starts near the first campsite, just south of Rustic Geyser.

The Heart Lake Trail accesses the well-developed and extensive Yellowstone Trail System, and it is possible to continue your hike around the north and east ends of the lake to other campsites. Heart River flows from the south end of the lake, joining the Snake River. Here the adventurous hiker can turn southwest or downstream and hike all the way to the South Entrance Ranger Station, or one can jog upstream or southeast and hike to the Snake River headwaters, out of the park and into the bordering Teton Wilderness. Actually, there are several hundred miles of trail options in this country. Consult your maps, or Falcon Publishing's *Hiking Yellowstone National Park*.

—Mike Gossi

100 Avalanche Peak

General description:	A half-day or longer, exceptionally steep hike offering 360-degree vistas of the entire Yellowstone and northern Absaroka region.
Distance:	5 miles round trip.
Difficulty:	Moderate to strenuous.
Elevation gain and loss:	2,086 feet.
General location:	8 miles west of the East Entrance Station in eastern Yellowstone National Park.
Special attractions:	A trail that is one of the best-kept secrets in Yellowstone. The views over Yellowstone Lake and into neighboring states are astounding.
Maps:	Earthwalk Press's Yellowstone Hiking map and guide; USGS: Sylvan Lake. Also, USGS Yellowstone 1:125,000 vicinity map.
Fees:	Park entrance fees.
Manager:	Yellowstone National Park Headquarters.

Finding the trailhead: West of the Park's East Entrance Station 8 miles, or 1 mile west of Sylvan Pass, a small picnic area opens up the western shores of tiny Eleanor Lake. The unsigned Avalanche Peak Trail begins directly north and across the highway from this picnic ground. A trailhead register and information sign is found a few hundred feet up the trail.

The hike: East-central Yellowstone Park is a special parcel of land. For one thing, it's one of the few areas in the park that escaped the massive fires of

Avalanche Peak

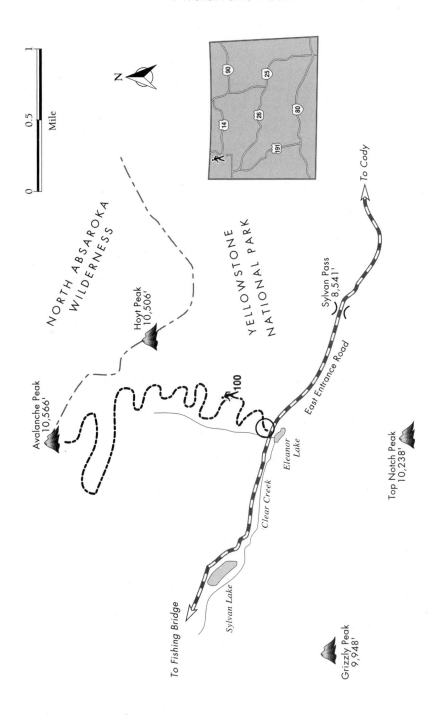

N

North Absaroka Wilderness

Yellowstone National Park

Avalanche Peak
10,566'

Hoyt Peak
10,506'

△100

Eleanor
Lake

Clear Creek

East Entrance Road

Sylvan Pass
8,541'

To Cody

Top Notch Peak
10,238'

Sylvan Lake

To Fishing Bridge

Grizzly Peak
9,948'

0   0.5   1
Mile

90   25
14   26   80
191

1988. The landscape remains green, fresh, and invigorating. Secondly, the park's eastern border meets the western edges of the mighty Absaroka Range. Huge lava flows, some several thousand feet thick, created the region. Severe winter conditions have turned that rock into cracked and broken rubble piles, and these stark landscapes form many of the slopes of the surrounding peaks.

Be prepared. In 2.5 miles you are going to ascend more than 2,000 feet of elevation. The trail begins with steep uphill climbs and continues to climb steeply for its entire length.

At 0.6 mile there is a tricky area that looks like a trail intersection. Don't follow the path heading directly up the drainage. The Park Service is trying to phase out this overly steep and erodible section of old trail. From the stream, turn east (or right) and trace the trail traversing the slope for 0.25 mile into an avalanche chute, then continue the climb. So rapidly does this switchbacking trail ascend the mountain that you'll pass through variegated forests, lodgepole stands, spruce woods, and fascinating limber pine forests in a single mile's distance. At 1.2 miles the trail tops out on a ridge, the forests end, and you'll be standing beneath a vast and beautiful bowl beneath a crumbly, rubble-strewn, towering mountain. The chutes on Avalanche Peak's flanks show you how this peak got its name.

Above-timberline hiking now predominates. Your gaze will soar over Yellowstone Lake, across to the Tetons to the south, and toward the ranges looming to the west in Idaho. The last 0.3 mile—a high ridgetop walk to the summit—is the easiest part of the hike. Now you stand amid 360 degrees of every mountainous view imaginable. Yet at the same time, it's just as captivating to observe the tiny alpine plant species—so delicate, yet so hardy.

This is not a recommended trail for those folks doing their first hike of the year. Some endurance is necessary. The landscape is steep and rocky, and tennis shoes aren't appropriate. During an average summer there are snowdrifts along the trail into July. The downhill return trek has the potential to demonstrate an old mountaineering platitude: "Rolling rocks under Vibram soles are no fun." Leaving early in the morning helps one avoid afternoon thunderstorms and other weather considerations. Carry water and a snack to the top.

APPENDIX I

FEDERAL, STATE, AND LOCAL LAND ACCESS REGULATIONS

One of the trickiest and stickiest aspects of traveling Wyoming is dealing with the reality of public and private land access. The state is both blessed and cursed with an absolute hodgepodge of intertwined federal, state, and private lands. Sometimes every other section is owned by a different agency or private party, and thus a different set of rules can apply every mile. Understanding a modicum of the state's land laws at least allows you to know what choices are available. This is the West, and sentiments, legal and otherwise, tend to favor private landowners over public access needs.

•First, Wyoming law states that it is the public's obligation to know the ownership classification of the land traveled. This includes knowing, topographically and geographically, the boundaries of private, state and federal land. Put in simple terms, the statement "I didn't know it was private land" will not hold up when you're in court facing trespassing charges.

•You do have the right to access public lands (i.e., federal and most state-owned lands) only when a public road or right-of-way provides an access to that land. Here's a sticky part. If a piece of public land is surrounded by private land, and no easement for public access exists across that private land, you have no right to cross those private lands, even for the purpose of reaching said public land, unless you first obtain permission from the landowner. The landowner is under no obligation to grant such permission. And here's another tricky part. The law states that all public lands intersected by a public road may be used by the general public free of charge; but sometimes distinguishing public roads is a real chore. State and county roads are fairly recognizable in that regard. But Forest Service and, more often, Bureau of Land Managment roads, especially if the signs proclaiming the road's status have been removed, may be indistinguishable from private roads. As noted above, it's up to you to know which is which.

Actually, the reality of traveling Wyoming isn't as harsh as the above legal description makes it sound. Most private lands are quite well posted as such, and most public access roads are also well marked. In addition, the BLM has the state divided into 56, 1:100,000 named topographic quadrants and has compiled a surface management map of each section that details every square inch of land ownership. Ordering information may be obtained from any of the BLM offices listed in the Appendix or from the Wyoming State BLM office at 5353 Yellowstone Road, P.O. Box 1828, Cheyenne, WY, 82009, 307-775-6256.

Another mitigating factor is that most of Wyoming's private land owners are wonderful people who are not averse to allowing access across their lands. If you can locate the owner, and if you can convey the impression that you won't harass livestock or leave gates open or wreck private structures, most will gladly let you explore or cross their territory.

A special land classification applies to the Wind River Indian Reservation. This includes the de facto wilderness of the Wind River Roadless Area. Much of the land here is exceptionally unique and wild, but to hike on the reservation requires a tribal permit and may require a hired guide as well. Contact the Wind River Indian Reservation, Shoshoni and Arapaho Fish and Game Department, P.O. Box 217, Fort Washakie, WY, 82514, 307-332-7207, for further information.

WYOMING CULTURAL NORMS

In Wyoming, you can count on sharing a number of your hikes with cows, pack horses, and off-road vehicles (ORVs).

Cattle gave the state its beginnings. Cattle form a Wyoming way of life more deeply rooted than any other calling. Grazing is allowed in wilderness areas. It always has been. Remember, cows (and cowboys) won't bother you if you don't bother them. The exception to watch for, as with any animal, is placing yourself between a mother cow and her baby calf. Thorough water purification—everywhere but especially in cattle-grazing country—is not a game you want to play halfheartedly.

Rumor—at least in Wyoming—has it that God first created the mountains. Then He created cattle. Then He created horses to herd the cattle and more horses to pack people and gear over those mountains. Horsepackers and outfitters are another grand and embedded Wyoming tradition. Long before hikers discovered they had legs, horses were carrying people and loads into Wyoming's wilderness areas. They're good people, horsepackers. A lot more trail maintenance happens thanks to horsepackers than anyone could ever document. And they are good animals, horses. Be a good and courteous hiker by stepping off the trail (a fair distance away on the downhill side) as they pass. And don't make any sudden noises or spooky movements. At the same time, don't "hide" from the horses; make your presence known, or they might spook if they suddenly discover you.

The final reality I know God didn't create, but He's stuck with it and so are we. Machines permeate almost every aspect of our lives, and roads take us almost everywhere. Why anyone would want to inject more machines into the last sanctuaries of quiet is beyond comprehension, but ORVs, especially motorcycles and those cursed four-wheel all-terrain-vehicles (ATVs), are now a legal part of much of the mountain trail experience outside classified wilderness. The unfortunate truth is that more people—in fact, a majority of people—are claiming their right to earn the scenery via machine. Administrating offices can then only do as the public directs. And so, several of the trails in this guide (outside of classified wilderness) are open to motorized use. But the areas are too beautiful not to enjoy hiking them just because some other folks motor over them. The machines pass in a few minutes and the quiet returns. The people riding them are more often than not friendly. You can minimize contact by hiking ATV-open areas on week-days, before Memorial Day, and after Labor Day.

An adjacent though far less intrusive reality comes with the increase of mountain biking as a means of traveling hiking trails. Meeting or passing each other on one-person-width paths is an easy negotiation when everyone travels at a walking pace. Add a 10-mile-per-hour blur of wheels and metal coming around a blind corner to the scene and things can get complicated. Add again a pack string to this situation, and it becomes dangerous. The hiker is the one who can most easily step out of the way and let everyone else pass.

MAPS AND TRAILS

I planned many of the hikes in this book at home by scanning topographic and Forest Service maps of areas. That often proved to be a most inaccurate means of preparation, especially outside of national parks and classified wilderness areas. The experience of hiking revealed the USGS topographic maps to be unfailingly accurate in one aspect alone: topography. Many of these maps were compiled in the 1960s and 1970s. Many more roads have been cut into the land since then; many trails have been logged, rerouted, or erased by forest fires or lack of maintenance since then. The Forest Service maps tell much the same story. Although usually more up-to-date than the topos, endless inaccuracies and changes leave the trip itself as the final guide, and the map as an aid and beginning. It is probably best to have a couple of different maps to use as reference, and even better is to check with the nearest administering agency before starting out.

The other trail writers and I searched for a taste of Wyoming's unknown and unusual hiking to include in this book. Off-the-beaten-track in many cases means just that: the track is no longer beaten. Land agencies, the Forest Service, and especially the BLM never have afforded recreation top budgeting and manpower priority, and it's even more true today. Trail maintenance and signing can fall years behind, and if it's a hot fire year, they can be forgotten altogether. Also—and this was mentioned at the book's beginning but is such a Wyoming reality it bears repeating—realize that cattle and horses tend to create their own trails. I can hike an area and write about its trail system one year; then a herd of 300 cattle or sheep can wander through next spring, and when you explore the area that summer, it's a world with trails contrary to everything I've stated. Pack trains often create trails that look better than the official one. Hunters often blaze trees to help them find their game when they return. Add a rarely traveled trail in an unknown range to this picture, and you inherit the exciting pastime of route-finding on your hike.

A few of this book's hikes have trail portions that require a keen eye and trail sense to follow. I've tried to mention the tricky spots in the hike descriptions, but be aware that 30 years of hiking these kinds of trails puts me at a real advantage. If you lose a trail, go back to the path's last known location and just stop. Look for cairns, which are rock piles of various sizes that mark trails. Look for blaze marks on the trees. The official Forest Service trail blaze is a smaller square atop a larger perpendicular rectangle etched into the bark of a tree. Many times I've located a faint trail by looking for horses' hoofprints on the ground, and often a trail's path can be found by looking for old maintenance-cut trees lying on the ground. If they disappear, most trails do so in meadows, so scan the distant land for a sign of the path's exit. And finally, use your maps. If they say the trail continues up a ridge or beside a stream, it usually does, and by journeying in the general direction indicated, you can relocate the trail.

Hiking Wyoming is actually the most up-to-date guide available.

HUNTING AND FISHING

If hiking is your love, and hunting isn't, you may be wisest not to plan your hiking trips to Wyoming during hunting season. Unfortunately, that also happens to be a fine season for hiking. The dates vary every year, but from the beginning of September until about mid-November those hills and woods and prairies can sometimes become insanely crowded with hunters. Most hunters are courteous and safe sportsmen, but while a wilderness ranger, I heard a lot of shots taken in absolute darkness and picked up a lot of discarded booze bottles from abandoned hunting camps. At the very least, during hunting season, wear lots of orange and don't tie a pair of antlers found on the ground to your pack.

Good fishing and Wyoming are synonymous. The lakes and streams are productive, fun, and rewarding for any angler. And they are regulated. Wyoming has recently simplified its fishing license categories into two sections: residents pay a $15 yearly license fee or a $3-per-day fee; nonresidents can pay either $65 for a yearly license or a $6-per-day fishing fee. There are also a lot of area-specific regulations, and a booklet explaining them can be acquired by writing or calling the Wyoming Game and Fish Department, Information Section, 5400 Bishop Blvd, Cheyenne, WY, 82002. Call 307-777-4600 for general information or 307-777-4597 for license information.

I really suggest getting a license if you fish. The game and fish personnel manage to be ubiquitous without being numerous. As a wilderness ranger, I saw those red-shirted officers pop up in the darndest places to ask surprised packers for their fishing or hunting licenses.

Yellowstone National Park has separate fishing regulations and requires a special permit. It's available at any ranger station.

APPENDIX II

MAP ORIENTATION, BY MIKE GOSSI

Maps are little more than rough and expensive toilet paper unless you know how to use them. Fortunately, map orientation is easy with a good compass and a couple of rules:

- •Rule one: Never assume.
- •Rule two: Carry a GOOD compass.

On the bottom of every USGS topographic map rest a pair of lines showing the magnetic declination. One line notes Grid North. This line, if extended, goes all the way to the official North Pole and Santa's house. The other line shows where the colored end of your compass needle will point and is called Magnetic North. These two norths are not the same and will vary, depending on where you and your compass are located.

If you have a round compass that looks like a watch face with little N, S, E, and W markings and little or nothing else on it, go buy another compass. Good compasses, with swiveling 360 degrees of numbered markings, short rulers and direction lines, and optional sighting/signal mirrors, are much cheaper than search parties.

To orient yourself and your map, first turn the movable degree scale on your compass so that north or 0 degrees aligns with the arrow on your compass body. Laying your map flat and level and with the straight side of your compass body along the map edge, turn the map so that the red end of your compass needle points at the number of degrees your map says the declination (Magnetic North) is. Your map is now aligned with the world, or oriented.

TO DETERMINE YOUR POSITION:

Your position is always in reference to everything else. Leaving your map oriented with the world, sight a prominent landmark (such as a peak, lake, or large drainage—make sure it is one you are absolutely certain is the same as one on the map) alongside the edge of your compass body. While sighting the landmark, note the degree numbers the compass needle is pointing to. Now put the compass on the map with the edge of the compass body on the sighted topographical feature and with the needle pointing at the noted degree number. Draw a line along the compass's edge. Your position is on that line. To determine precisely where on that line you reside, make a second and different topographical feature sighting and draw another line; X marks your spot.

First orient the map and prove or find your position. Now lay the edge of your compass body along the line of your intended course. So that it will not be necessary to pull out the map every time you wish to check your bearing, align the N with the centering arrow on your compass body to your intended course direction and note the degree number the red end of your needle is pointing to. This simple procedure will allow you to check your bearing at any point along the way by making sure the compass's red needle end is still aligned along the degrees noted. Then your intended course will be in the N direction. With careful and frequent checks, it is possible to navigate cross-country, even in blizzard white-out conditions.

Please, please, and please practice and become proficient at these map and compass techniques before you wander into the field—which is to say, before they are needed. Enjoy, and good luck.

Author's note: Since both the above treatise author and myself have never navigated by satellite technology (the Global Positioning System, or GPS), we don't feel qualified to discuss it.

APPENDIX III

SOME FINAL NOTES

The boundaries of wild Wyoming shrank by a large amount between the time I was a wilderness ranger and when I wrote the first edition of this hiking guide. In that time span, a lot of wilderness became overcrowded and permitized; a lot of roadless areas no longer hold that sacred and needed classification; a lot of wildlife habitat disappeared for good. In the 8 years between that first edition and this one, the degradation of the word "wild" has intensified even more. To the above add that several inviolate streams are now quite violated, that air quality has degraded substantially in many places, and that too many sections of private land within public land have been posted and are either cutting off public access to many beautiful areas or dividing those areas into look-alike ranchette subdivisions.

The ever-growing list of environmental attacks hitting wild Wyoming goes on and on and on. But fly over the boundary between Yellowstone National Park and neighboring Targhee National Forest, or over the boundary between the North Absaroka Wilderness and the Shoshone National Forest in the Clarks Fork area, and witness first-hand how vast the tide of development is. The cut-up landscape that looks like a sheep-shear gave it a butch haircut is huge; the protected sanctuaries grow smaller and more crowded every year. Wyoming's legislature is notoriously anti-anything having to do with preservation, and extractive industries don't even hesitate when proposing a mega-development in the middle of a sacrosanct area (the infamous Yellowstone area gold mine is a good example).

Without offering a long listing of the many axes chopping away at natural and beautiful Wyoming, and also without my ticking off a long list of organizations trying to parry the blows, I simply and strongly urge you to get involved in protecting the special land you have just hiked. Most libraries have a Conservation Directory available that lists the many ecologically oriented groups working for the world in general and Wyoming in particular. Many major national conservation groups sport a Wyoming chapter, and grassroots efforts exist most everywhere in the state. Become informed about what is happening and in some way become involved. Please.

Finally, I'd love to know your comments on *Hiking Wyoming*. One doesn't just hike Wyoming trails and country. The state is so full of verve and life and adventure and laughter and spirit that a portion of these qualities has to seep into both the person hiking and hopefully the guidebook writing. It's my hope that you not only gained valuable information from this book, but also enjoyed the learning. Also, in the heat of organizing a hundred hikes and completing their many aspects by a deadline, if I said something was "east" when I should have said "west," and didn't catch that or any other mistake in the rewrites and revisions that followed, do let me know so that it can be corrected for future editions.

The hardest thing about writing a book like this is knowing that you will be drawing even more folks to the isolated, special, and/or secret spots you treasure. Perhaps one of the greatest joys in writing such a book comes from the same knowledge. Until shown otherwise, I get to assume that those venturing into my beloved Wyoming as a result of acquiring this book are the ones who will care for the land in turn; who perhaps need what peace or beauty or glory a particular area has to offer; who will enjoy the treasure they are beholding.

I can be reached by mail through: Hiking Guidebook Editor, Falcon Publishing, P.O. Box 1718, Helena, MT, 59624.

APPENDIX IV: Land Managers

NATIONAL PARK SERVICE

Superintendent
Devils Tower National Monument
P.O. Box 10
Devils Tower, WY 82714
phone (307) 467-5283
fax 307-467-5350

Bighorn Canyon National
Recreation Area
20 Highway 14A East
Lovell, WY 82431
(307) 548-2251
(The folks working the information
desks may not be hikers. Ask to
speak to somebody who is.)

Fossil Butte National Monument
P.O. Box 592
Kemmerer, WY 83101
(307) 877-4455

Grand Teton National Park
P.O. Drawer 170
Moose, WY 83012
(307) 739-3309

Yellowstone National Park Headquarters
P.O. Box 168
Yellowstone National Park, WY
82190
(307) 344-7381

BUREAU OF LAND MANAGEMENT

Platte River Resource Area
815 Connie Street
P.O. Box 2420
Mills, WY 82644
(307) 261-7500

Worland Resource Office
P.O. Box 119
Worland, WY 82401
(307) 347-5100

Buffalo Resource Office
1425 Fort Street
Buffalo, WY 82834
(307) 684-1100

Rawlins Resource Area
1300 North Third Street
Rawlins, WY 82301-0670
(307) 328-4200

Lander Resource Area
P.O. Box 589
Lander, WY 82520
(307) 332-8400

Cody Resource Area
P.O. Box 518
1002 Blackburn St.
Cody, WY 82414
(307) 587-2216

USDA FOREST SERVICE

Bearlodge Ranger District
P.O. Box 680
Highway 14 West
Sundance, WY 82729
(307) 283-1361

Douglas Ranger District
2250 East Richards Street
Douglas, WY 82633-8922
(307) 358-4690

Medicine Bow National Forest
Laramie Ranger District
2468 Jackson Street
Laramie, WY 82070-6535
(307) 745-8971 or (307) 745-2300

Medicine Bow National Forest
Brush Creek/Hayden Ranger District
204 West Ninth Street
Encampment, WY 82325
(307) 327-5481

Medicine Bow National Forest
Brush Creek/Hayden Ranger District
South Highway 130
Saratoga, WY 82331
(307) 326-5258

Tensleep Ranger District
2009 Bighorn Avenue
Worland, WY 82401
(307) 347-8291

Bighorn National Forest
Tongue Ranger District
1969 South Sheridan
Sheridan, WY 82801
(307) 672-0751

Bighorn National Forest
Buffalo Ranger District
1425 Fort Street
Buffalo, WY 82834
(307) 684-1100

Medicine Wheel Ranger District
604 East Main
P.O. Box 367
Lovell, WY 82431
(307) 548-6541

Washakie Ranger District
333 East Main
Lander, WY 82520
(307) 332-5460

Kemmerer Ranger District
308 Highway 189 North
P.O. Box 31
Kemmerer, WY 83101
(307) 877-4451

Greys River Ranger District
125 Washington
P.O. Box 339
Afton, WY 83110
(307) 886-3166

Big Piney District
Highway 189
P.O. Box 218
Big Piney, WY 83113
(307) 276-3375

Jackson Ranger District
25 Rosencranz Lane
P.O. Box 1689
Jackson, WY 83001
(307) 739-5400

Buffalo Ranger District
Blackrock Ranger Station
P.O. Box 278
Moran, WY 83103
(307) 543-2386

Greybull Ranger District
2044 State Street
P.O. Box 158
Meeteetse, WY 82433
(307) 578-1297

Wapiti Ranger District
203A Yellowstone Avenue
Cody, WY 82414
(307) 527-6921

Clarks Fork Ranger District
1002 Road 11
Powell, WY 82435
(307) 754-7207

Teton Basin Ranger District
P.O. Box 777
Driggs, ID 83422
(208) 354-2431

Ashton Ranger District
P.O. Box 858
Ashton, ID 83420
(208) 652-7442

Wind River Ranger District
1403 West Ramshorn
P.O. Box 186
Dubois, WY 82513
(307) 455-2466

Pinedale Ranger District
29 East Fremont Lake Road
P.O. Box 220
Pinedale, WY 82941
(307) 367-4326

STATE OF WYOMING

Superintendent
Keyhole State Park
353 McKean Road
Moorcroft, WY 82721
(307) 756-9667 or 756-3596

Superintendent
Guernsey State Park
Guernsey, WY 82214
(307) 836-2334

Superintendent
Glendo State Park
P.O, Box 388
Glendo, WY 82213
(307) 735-4433

Park Superintendent
Bear River State Park
601 Bear River Drive
Evanston, WY 82930
(307) 789-6547

Sinks Canyon State Park
3079 Sinks Canyon Road, Route 63
Lander, WY 82520
(307) 332-6333

South Pass City State Historical Site
125 South Pass Main
South Pass City, WY 82520
(307) 332-3684

Index

Numbers in bold type refer to photographs.
Numbers in italic type refer to maps.

V

Valley View Trails 17
Vedauwoo 41-43, *42*, **43**
Venus Creek 226
Venus Creek Fork 228
Vista Pass 145
Volksmarch Trail 36, 81, 111, 113, 118-119

W

Wagner Pass 154, 156
Warbonnet Peak 33
Warren Peak 27
Warren Peak Lookout Road 22
Washakie Range 199-207
Washakie Wilderness 213-238
Way Trail, The 154-156, *155*
Welty's General Store 214
West Tensleep Lake Trailhead 92, 94, 96
West Thumb Junction 312, 315
Western Wind Rivers 129-148
Wheatland 35, 38
Whiskey Mountain Trail 123
Wiggins Canyon 217
Wiggins Fork 214, 217-220, *218*, 228
Wiggins, Jack 217
Wildcat Peak 200-202, *201*
Williamson Corrals 126
Willow Creek 119-120
Willow Lake 99-101, **99**, *100*
Wilson Bar Mine 120
Wind River foothills 113
Wind River Indian Reservation 110, 228, 322
Wind River Peak 116, 134
Wind River Peaks 145
Wind River Range 82, 110-120, 122-123, 125,
    129-130, 133, 135-136, 145-146, 154, 173
Wind River Roadless Area 322
Wind Rivers 4, 114
Wind Rivers (North) 122-128
Winegar Hole 262
Witch Creek 315
Witherspoon Pass 150
Wolf Mountain 186, 196-198, *197*, **198**
Woodrow Wilson peak 128
Worland 85, 91, 96
Wyoming 296 (Chief Joseph Scenic Highway)
    244
Wyoming Boulevard 68
Wyoming Game and Fish Department 122, 324
Wyoming Range 162, 165-166, 171, 173, 181
Wyoming Range National Recreation Trail 165,
    170

Y

Yellowstone Lake 315, 318, 320
Yellowstone National Park 11, 199, 203, 214,
    229, **234**, 238, 240-244, 246, 251, 277-278,
    288, 290-320
Yellowstone River Trail 208, 211, 213, 244-247,
    245M, 249-250, 294-295, 297

get FALCON GUIDED

Hiking Guides

Hiking Alaska
Hiking Alberta
Hiking Arizona
Hiking Arizona's Cactus Country
Hiking the Beartooths
Hiking Big Bend National Park
Hiking Bob Marshall Country
Hiking California
Hiking California's Desert Parks
Hiking Carlsbad Caverns
   and Guadalupe Mtns. National Parks
Hiking Colorado
Hiking the Columbia River Gorge
Hiking Florida
Hiking Georgia
Hiking Glacier & Waterton Lakes National Parks
Hiking Grand Canyon National Park
Hiking Glen Canyon
Hiking Great Basin National Park
Hiking Hot Springs
   in the Pacific Northwest
Hiking Idaho
Hiking Maine
Hiking Michigan
Hiking Minnesota
Hiking Montana
Hiker's Guide to Nevada
Hiking New Hampshire
Hiking New Mexico
Hiking New York
Hiking North Cascades
Hiking North Carolina

Hiking Northern Arizona
Hiking Olympic National Park
Hiking Oregon
Hiking Oregon's Eagle Cap Wilderness
Hiking Oregon's Three Sisters Country
Hiking Shenandoah
Hiking Pennsylvania
Hiking South Carolina
Hiking South Dakota's Black Hills Country
Hiking Southern New England
Hiking Tennessee
Hiking Texas
Hiking Utah
Hiking Utah's Summits
Hiking Vermont
Hiking Virginia
Hiking Washington
Hiking Wisconsin
Hiking Wyoming
Hiking Wyoming's Wind River Range
Hiking Yellowstone National Park
Hiking Zion & Bryce Canyon National Parks
The Trail Guide to Bob Marshall Country

Best Easy Day Hikes

Beartooths
Canyonlands & Arches
Best Hikes on the Continental Divide
Glacier & Wateron Lakes
Glen Canyon
North Cascades
Olympics
Shenandoah
Yellowstone

■ *To order any of these books, check with your local bookseller
or call The Globe Pequot Press® at **1-800-243-0495**.
Visit us on the world wide web at:*
www.FalconGuide.com

FALCON®

American Hiking Society (AHS)

is the only national nonprofit organization dedicated to establishing, protecting, and maintaining America's foot trails—the same trails that are detailed in this book and around the country.

As a trail user, your support of AHS is important to ensure trails are forever protected and continually maintained.

Join American Hiking Society today and you will learn about trails to hike, their history, their importance, and how you can help protect them. American Hiking Society is:

A strong voice. With increasing threats to our treasured open space and wilderness, American Hiking Society exists to actively represent hikers' interests to safeguard these areas. To protect the hiking experience, AHS affects federal legislation, shapes public lands policy, collaborates with grassroots trail organizations, and partners with federal land managers. As a member of AHS, feel assured that while you are hiking, AHS is going *the extra mile* for you.

A helping hand. With more than 200,000 miles of trails in America, AHS steps in with needed maintenance for trail managers and hiking clubs. Through our Volunteer Vacations program, we provide more than 24,000 hours of trail work annually to help preserve some of the most scenic places in America. As an AHS Member, you can take advantage of this opportunity to give back to the trails that you use and love.

A critical resource. Each year, crucial trail funding continually falls behind trail maintenance demands. Your favorite trail will **not** be next, thanks to American Hiking Society! Our National Trails Fund annually awards financial grants to local and regional hiking clubs for land acquisition, volunteer recruitment, and trail maintenance. As you support AHS, you share in the satisfaction of helping grassroots trails clubs nationwide.

Join TODAY!

American Hiking Society

1422 Fenwick Lane · Silver Spring, MD 20910 · (301) 565–6704
www.AmericanHiking.org · info@AmericanHiking.org